The Nun S Story

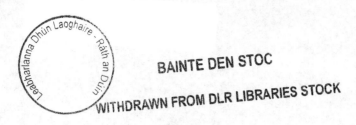

The Nun's Story

For
CHARLOTTE S. MACK
with love and admiration

Twenty-third Printing

ATLANTIC–LITTLE, BROWN BOOKS
ARE PUBLISHED BY
LITTLE, BROWN AND COMPANY
IN ASSOCIATION WITH
THE ATLANTIC MONTHLY PRESS

Published simultaneously in Canada
by Little, Brown & Company (Canada) Limited

PRINTED IN THE UNITED STATES OF AMERICA

The Nun's Story

by KATHRYN HULME

An Atlantic Monthly Press Book
Little, Brown and Company
Boston . Toronto

The Nun's Story

Books by Kathryn Hulme

ARAB INTERLUDE

DESERT NIGHT

WE LIVED AS CHILDREN

THE WILD PLACE
(Atlantic Nonfiction Prize Award, 1953)

THE NUN'S STORY

I

THE short black cape hooked at the neck and dropped without flare to the middle of the forearms. It was odd to be thinking about Lourdes as she put it on, as though that recent experience had had something decisive to do with her choosing the religious life.

She bent her elbows and brought her hands together beneath the cape. It was a practice garment of sorts, to be replaced by the nun's robe after the six months' postulancy, after her hands would have learned to stay still and out of sight except when needed for nursing or for prayer.

Forty other young women, mainly Belgian like herself, with a few English and Irish girls, stood with Gabrielle Van der Mal in the anteroom to the cloister, putting on similar capes but taking more time about it, especially some red-knuckled girls from the farms who seemed to be searching through the folds of their capes for sleeves.

Lourdes, she thought, I'm not that impressionable. But quite suddenly she was riding again in the hospital train that made the annual pilgrimage, the only lay student nurse from the training school chosen by Sister William to help escort the convoy of bedridden patients from Belgium. The faith of the prostrate pilgrims that they would survive the journey, and, moreover, return from there cured, frightened her. Her

3

pulse-readings, her diagnostic eyes, even her nostrils that knew the smell of death told her that some could not possibly live until Lourdes and she ran to Sister William crying, Fevers, blood-spitting, cancers advanced to screaming stage and not a sound out of any of them except crazy hopes; I've got three in the car who should be receiving last rites this very instant, Sister. And Sister William had stopped her with a look. No one will die en route, my child, they never do, she said. I've taught you many things, Gabrielle, but what you are soon to see is beyond my competence to describe or prepare you for. Now say a *Pater* for having called faith a crazy hope and go back to your duties.

Lourdes was a bonfire in her memory. It was made up of thousands of candles and burning cries and a week of rising suns over an esplanade where stretcher cases lay side by side, end to end, waiting for a priest to come with a monstrance that gathered sun to its gold and blazed in the sign of the cross above the stretchers. With each individual benediction a new voice, hoarse, hysterical, screaming or murmuring, joined the storm of sound which carried the glittering processional forward like a wave that never crested or broke until the last twisted body had been blessed. *O Jesus, Son of David, cure me . . .*

And there were cures, she remembered, which she could see in the archives of X-rays that had been made before and after baths in St. Bernadette's water, changes in tissue textures or even occasionally in the bone structures which she could read like print on a page.

On the journey back to Belgium, taking care of the same number of cases she had escorted out, she remembered how she had looked at the faces she bathed, still worn and emaciated with disease. Inexplicably they seemed to have retained

4

some of the glow that had played upon them when the stretchers had been carried into the candlelit Grotto at the foot of the Pyrenees.

Their happiness! she exclaimed to Sister William on her rounds.

Naturally, my child. That is the *real* cure. Not those debatable X-rays I saw you poring over with the doctors who consider only what films show. But this (Sister William inclined her head to the quiet *wagon-lit* as if the name of Jesus had been spoken) this is the visible grace given to all who go with faith.

And then Sister William had given her sleeve a little tug in the discreet manner of the vowed, who, Gabrielle knew (because she had been educated by nuns) must never lay hands one upon the other. Crazy hopes! the little nun whispered as she passed.

The pull at her sleeve had been more unusual than Sister William's teasing words, for it was the attention-drawing language of nun to nun, rather than of nun to lay person. *As if I were one of them!* Gabrielle had thought with surprise.

And now she was one of them, or very soon to be. She looked at her companions in the anteroom. Their introspective faces, flushed and slightly nervous, suggested that they too were going over the steps that had brought them to this prim parlor in a convent in Brussels.

Gabrielle thought of her own steps consecutively. She began with childhood, with the cook, Françoise, who had never cut into bread without first tapping the knife in the sign of the cross over the big round loaf. The child who watched the bread-cutting ritual used to go with the cook to first Mass every day, not because she understood then anything of its significance, but because there was something wonderful and

5

mysterious about candles and singing before sunlight and the sight of so many grownups doing without breakfast until a small white wafer had been dropped upon their tongues. Then there were the visits she used to make with her doctor father to homes in the provinces as they were in the old days, every one with a big old-fashioned rosary hanging on the wall from two pegs spaced far enough apart to make the crucifix fall heart-shape to a point at the base. You seldom saw such visible piety now. Nor did you see nowadays the great single eye in a triangle which used to be painted over the zinc bars of country cafés where her father refreshed himself after his rounds. She remembered his explaining that the strange compelling design meant that the Eye of God was upon the place and no cursing would be permitted. The old-fashioned religious childhood, she thought. God was like one of the family and this above all is why I am here. I learned to love Him when I was very young. Before Jean . . . long, long before . . .

She pressed her clasped hands against her heart and looked at the austerely beautiful face of Sister Margarita, the Mistress of Postulants. She knew that she must be looking at *une Règle Vivante*, a Living Rule, of whom it was said that if the Holy Rule of the Order were ever destroyed or lost from the printed record, it could be recaptured in entirety by studying such a perfect nun.

Sister Margarita's immense coif starched stiff as a shell and curving shell-like about the ageless Flemish face turned, almost imperceptibly, as the Mistress examined her new postulants to make sure that each had her black veil pinned over the hair and her cape hooked properly. Then she spoke in a voice exactly pitched to reach to the edge of the caped crowd and not a breath beyond.

"Now we will go to the chapel for a little colloquy with God." She turned and opened, as though it were a soundless panel of felt, a heavy oak door, and Gabrielle saw how one hand dropped over the ring of keys hanging from her leather belt so they would not clink together as she moved.

"You will follow me in pairs," said Sister Margarita. "We walk with eyes lowered and hands out of sight." She glided through the doorway and down a vaulted corridor toward bracketed candles with motionless flames.

Gabrielle took a last look at the smaller door to the visitors' parlor, where good-bys to the families had just been said. Her father would still be standing there, his square surgeon's hands stroking his spade beard as he acknowledged the salutations of those who recognized the foremost chest surgeon and heart specialist of Belgium, pretending a pride like the others for having given his only daughter to God.

She could feel on the skin of her forehead the cross he had traced there with his spatulate thumb when he had said farewell. She could still taste the plump fine oysters from Zeeland that he had ordered for her last meal in the world, the dry sparkle of the vintage Rudesheimer which had cost him the fees of at least five visits to patients, and the ice cream richly sauced with crushed glazed chestnuts which she loved. Because he opposed her entering the convent, he had called for all the tempting things of life to speak to her where he had failed, unaware that what he was really putting into her like a probing pain was her last view of him tucking his napkin into the wing collar under his beard, smelling the wine cork before allowing the waiter to pour a drop and drinking the juice from the big rough oyster shells with gusty gourmet pleasure. And, over the coffee, the last sight of his round-bowled meerschaum golden-brown with age and fondling, and of his

7

blue eyes looking at her through the smoke while he talked as to a colleague of his medical problems. He never once mentioned the convent or gave her a chance to tell him that it was not Lourdes or schoolgirl admiration for any nun which had brought her here, not heartbreak because of his refusal to let her marry Jean (because his mother had died in an insane asylum, and her doctor father could not put upon her the risk of reproducing madness), but the pressing sum of them all. . . . "And maybe, even, *cher Papa*," she whispered to the closed door as she passed it, "maybe even a calling to the vocation because of the way you brought us up."

She stared at the ankles of the girl ahead of her, obviously one who had just stepped out of sabots into her first shoes — her sister now, one of that mixed multitude of unknown women who would be the only family she would ever have again. Why had her devout father opposed her entry?

The peasant ankles stirred, the brogues shuffled forward. Gabrielle followed, walking erect with folded arms and hidden hands as she had learned to walk when scrubbed and sterile during the surgery-room stage of her nursing training. She turned the corner and saw in one upward disobedient glance the whole chapel and the sisterhood that must replace in her heart all the lively affections she had ever known. It was a family of statues at which she stared.

Some two hundred sisters were already on their knees in soldierly rows down the long nave. The professed nuns in black veils knelt in the double row of carved stalls along either wall and the novices in white veils in three straight rows down the central aisle that ended at the altar. The folds of their choir capes fell around them on the floor and covered their turned-back feet. Viewed from the visitors' gallery, where the Mistress led the postulants, it was a faceless community of draped and motionless torsos lined up and spaced evenly one from the other as though set down by a precision instrument.

Jean seemed to slip in beside her as she tried to pray, taking the place of the caped figure kneeling at her right. His hushed voice was without bitterness now as he reminded her of the many things she had given up, besides himself. She pressed her palms more tightly against her eyes to darken the bright scenes his words evoked — of high windy ledges in the Ardennes where they used to rest after climbs, of bicycle paths through Flanders leading always toward the sea, of hidden hollows among the dunes into which they often dropped breathless after racing each other . . .

I'm going to miss your wide wide world, Blessed Lord, she whispered tremulously, possibly even more than the man who opened it up for me. I must not have loved him enough to fly in the face of Papa's disapproval. I must have loved Papa more . . . or was it simply that old-fashioned obedience to a parent's wishes which gave me strength to resist? Obedience . . . it's a key word in this sanctified place, so they tell us. Am I just one small step along the obscure way to You for having been able to obey Papa instead of my heart? Obey . . . it has *audire* in its root. *Audire* . . . to hear, to give ear to. But I seemed to hear nothing, Blessed Lord, during all those weeks of tormenting indecision except Jean's voice calling challenges . . .

She heard nothing now except her own inner voice and the quickened breathing of her caped companion, who was looking through her locked fingers at the rows of nuns below.

For the first five days they were kept apart from the community of nuns in a special wing that had its own dormitory,

9

study hall and refectory. But they could feel nevertheless its vast and disciplined presence as they prepared for their entrance into it, learning the signs that took the place of speech and the ways to open doors without rasp of hinge or lock, accustoming their eyes to look downward and their hearts to lift up to the ultimate goal of being in constant conversation with God.

It was, Gabrielle thought, like being in quarantine before a border crossing into a country of silence. They practiced the gestures of life in that country and learned its laws in daily readings from the Holy Rule. The Rule was a Baedeker to the cloistered life. It mapped monuments and battle-grounds and described the customs of poverty, chastity and obedience in minute detail. You even learned that the long serge skirt must be lifted from the rear when going down-stairs, to prevent its wasteful wearing on stones.

The new frontier extended beyond sight and imagination into the unexplored terrain of interior, as well as exterior, silence. Gabrielle felt it pressing inward to include within its metes and bounds that central place where many voices talked back to her in undiminishing echoes from her past.

"Interior silence," said Sister Margarita, "is one of the bases of the monastic life, one of the powers of God." The Mistress's singular low voice gave Gabrielle the impression that she was lip-reading. It took all her will not to turn her head to see if her companions had heard anything.

Interior silence, she repeated silently. That would be her Waterloo. How without brain surgery could you quell the rabble of memories? Even as she asked herself the question, she heard her psychology professor saying quite clearly across a space of years, "No one, not even a saint, can say an *Ave* straight through without some association creeping in; this is a known thing." He had on the table before him a plaster of Paris model of a human brain which came apart. He lifted off the parietal lobe and used it to gesture with as he repeated, "Not even *one Ave* . . ." and she saw the bright red and blue tracery of its painted veins and arteries superimposed, momentarily, on Sister Margarita's scapular.

It was more awesome to look at the silent world of the sisterhood than to receive instruction about it. Each morning when the postulants filed into the chapel for Mass, the nuns were already in place, looking as if they had not moved since the first day.

Gabrielle could not imagine how they could stay so still, especially the novices kneeling down the central aisle with nothing but air to support them. No spine sagged, no muscle moved to disturb a marble fold. She knew there were old and young ones in that community — nervous novices fighting for the perfection of immobility, rheumatic nuns perhaps soon to celebrate their golden jubilees in the religious life, nursing sisters from the convent hospital who might have sat up all night in vigil over a patient, and some quite possibly who had spent the night on their knees in penance or prayer. But no signs of age, infirmity or weariness could be detected.

Later on, when she was one of them and had learned that the older nuns always put their best foot forward when new postulants were present, living up to their discipline with almost superhuman courage and endurance to set a good example, she would still carry intact the reverent wonder of her first impressions.

As she peered at them through her fingers, she would think of the one strand that tied her already to the statuesque scene. This was the number assigned to her the day she was registered — 1072, the number of a dead nun. The filament of number 1072 stretched far beyond the kneeling figures, beyond the sanctified grounds of the mother house, beyond the borders of Belgium and the shores of Europe. It described an arc over the curve of earth like an imaginary line of longitude and ended in a thatched hut in the Katanga district of the Belgian Congo. There, barely two months before, a missionary sister had been stabbed to death by a black man gone berserk.

In one of the recreation periods when speech was permitted, she had learned about the previous holder of her number. The Mistress of Postulants, walking with her tongue-tied flock, had asked some of them what their numbers were, and to Gabrielle had said:

"You are blessed, Sister. You have the number of Sister Marie-Polycarpe." With a restrained and holy pride she had told the story.

It was strange how alive the numbers were. Not one had been allowed to lapse since the Order was established at the end of the eighteenth century. How many postulants had passed through this mother house could never be guessed because there was no way of knowing how many times any number had been assigned for the lifetime of a nun. In some vellum-bound ledger in the Superior General's office, Gabrielle supposed there was a continuing record kept. A head-count as they called it in the world. She thought of it as a leaf-count on a sturdy old vine that replenished itself from within and never put forth a new shoot until every stem below was tipped with life.

Each time she looked at the sisterhood, she saw something new and unexpected. She could hardly believe that she had lived with nuns through all her boarding-school days, had had adolescent crushes occasionally and, in her nursing training, had copied their calm in surgery when something went wrong and everyone else lost his head.

You could grow up with nuns and never really see their secret and singular way of being. She could not believe her eyes when the Mistress of Postulants showed how the Little Office was held by every nun and had been held so since the beginning of their cloistered time. Why had she not observed this before, she who loved to look at hands?

Sister Margarita held her breviary in the curved palm of her right hand with the thumb just touching the leather edge of the back cover. With the marker, she opened to the Office of the day and brought her left thumb, with a bit of paper beneath it, over the pages of the left side to hold them open.

"This bit of paper under the one finger that touches the pages," she said, "preserves them from stain. We each make our own little thumb pad. Mine, you see" — she held up the paper disk — "has a holy picture pasted upon it because I was not dowered for art and could not paint it prettily in water color as many sisters do."

The Little Office, she explained, was read seven times daily at the appointed hours by every sister wherever she might be. Staring at the hands holding the book just so, Gabrielle could not recall having seen before what she was shown now — an edge of paper beneath a thumb, a touch so light and careful that the pressed page seemed to be open for the first time.

"Our work," said Sister Margarita, "does not always permit us to go to chapel for devotions. Sometimes we must read them in kitchens, hospitals, schoolrooms, laundries — on trains or steamships if we are traveling. Wherever we are we follow the hours of the mother house. Thus, the care to keep our Little Office pure of soil. It must last a long time."

She lifted her thumb and let the bit of paper slip back be-

13

tween the pages as the book fell shut in her hand. She glanced at it without possessiveness or pride as she added, "This one was given to me when I made my first vows. It will be replaced next year on my silver jubilee."

The Living Rule rose up from her chair in a single movement of strength that flowed straight from her knees. She motioned the transfixed postulants to their feet and waited until the shuffling subsided. Her hands slipped beneath the scapular as she started to speak.

"Now, my sisters, you will go to the chapel for your last prayers before you enter our blessed community." She smiled and nodded. "Tomorrow is the day. You will pray for the help you need, each one speaking to God in her own way. As when you were children in the world and wanted something very badly, ask Him now to give you the things of the spirit. Ask Him in silence for strength in the practice of silence. Remember . . . interior silence is the very marrow of perfection as told in our Holy Rule."

My Waterloo, Gabrielle said again to herself. But I'll smother every voice that talks back to destroy my inner quiet. I don't know how I'll do this but I will. All for Jesus . . .

All for Jesus, Sister William had said in the ward, pulling on the rubber gloves. Say it, my dear students, every time you are called upon for what seems an impossible task. Then you can do anything with serenity. It is a talisman phrase that takes away the disagreeable inherent in many nursing duties. Say it for the bedpans you carry, for the old incontinents you bathe, for those sputum cups of the tubercular. *Tout pour Jésus*, she said briskly as she bent to change a dressing foul with corruption. Gabrielle, Jeannine, Charlotte . . . come closer and watch how I do this. You see how easy? All for Jesus . . . this is no beggar's body picked up in the Rue des

14

Radis. This is the Body of Christ and this suppurating sore is one of His Wounds . . .

All for Jesus. They used the talisman when they met each other in hospital corridors carrying bedpans and kidney basins, elevating their reeking receptacles and murmuring *All for Jesus!* as they passed. Yet, although they said it sometimes with the hysterical irreverence of youth, it did really work. As it had worked presumably for the courageous spirit of Sister William, who, until she had come from her ancestral château to the paupers' ward of the convent hospital, had not known the difference between a urinal and a flower vase and had remarked, as she arranged roses in the tubular glass container, This vase is quite original in form, is it not?

Gabrielle smiled as she advanced in the procession of postulants, unaware that her interior silence was nonexistent. She went on thinking about Sister William. The sturdy little nun stood forth like a signpost sure and readable in that *terra incognita* of the community she was to enter. It was like having something vital from her personal past waiting for her in the cloister, something she would not be required to uproot and cast out from memory any more than she would be expected to shake from her hands the nursing knowledge Sister William had trained into them. She held imaginary dialogues with her teacher as she paced slowly. "Associations, Sister . . . now just exactly *what* do you do to subdue them . . ."

She could not know then that it would be three years before she was allowed to address anything other than strictly duty words to Sister William, that although the familiar figure would often be within range of her longing eyes, the traditonal separation of the perpetually vowed from postulants and novices would stand between them like a block of clear ice through which Sister William herself would permit nothing more to pass than her silhouette and an occasional clinical glance.

In the chapel Gabrielle prayed God to forgive her for taking comfort from the thought that someone else who knew her well, besides Himself, would be there next day to welcome her into the community.

I I

HER entrance into the community was a break with the past as clean as amputation. The first day was the only one she could recollect in entirety afterwards. All the others telescoped into one six-months-long sunrise-to-dark struggle to synthesize in her mind the mass of minutiae on which convent conduct was based and to teach her body to behave accordingly.

The day began with a sound she never had expected to hear inside this house of silence — an electric alarm that shrilled simultaneously in every corridor of the big dormitories where two hundred nuns slept in semipartitioned cells. The bell tore her from sleep with shock. She sprang from her straw sack as if the current of electricity had passed through it and had stood her up in the four-thirty dark like a stiff electrocuted thing that would fall the moment the vibrations ceased.

Instantly, lights were flashed on above the honeycombs of cells and she saw through the gap of her curtain the silhouette of a nightgowned nun on the gray curtain opposite flung bolt upright from sleep like herself. From a distance the voice of the senior nun called out "Praised be Jesus Christ!" so promptly after the alarm and the lights that you could believe all three were connected to the same switch.

The sound of two hundred bodies dropping to their knees was the clue to what to do next. A few sighs could be heard as the knees went down on the oak floor. Then another voice began the Hail Marys.

Gabrielle tried to think the prayers until her voice would come back but she could think only of the way she would be awakened for the rest of her life. She looked down years of dark dawns and knew that her nerves would never learn to accept without a quiver the shattering discipline of that electric bell.

Even before she had taken a step inside the community, she had experienced more discipline than she had ever dreamed existed. The wooden planks under her straw sack had disciplined her bones all night and the straw sack itself, stuffed tight and economically with old pulverized straw, had been as a bed of sand that gave the muscles no ease. The sheets of unbleached serge were the harsh equivalent of a hair shirt, and the morning bell had stripped away the luxury of a slow natural awakening.

She listened incredulously to the *Aves* rising up from all the cells except hers. There was a clear note of gladness in the salutation to the Virgin, a sort of breathlessness when the nuns chanted ". . . full of grace . . ." as for a grace discovered that morning for the first time by all two hundred of them.

How could they pray so perfectly after being shocked from sleep? How could they sound so happy after a night on those sacks of straw?

She followed the sounds again, stood up and stripped her bed. She folded the covers as the Mistress of Postulants had demonstrated, in three exact folds each, then hung them over the chair, careful to see that no edge touched the floor — an

18

imperfection that would be. It calmed her to have things to do with her hands.

Then she heard the sisters dressing — starchy rustles from the nuns who were putting on the stiff white guimpes, clinks of keys as leather belts were buckled on and the click of wooden beads as rosaries were lifted from tables and hung from belts. She made an effort to ignore these involuntary private sounds as, during the night, she had tried to ignore the snores and muted cries of nightmares. Sisters already dressed were gliding past her gray curtain, reminding her that if she were late for chapel she would have to do that appalling penance of prostrating herself on the floor behind the *prie-dieu* of the Mother General.

Meditations, Prime and Tierce. The admittance ceremony, then Mass. She rehearsed her debut. Breakfast afterwards in the huge refectory, where she must remember the repertory of exact small gestures which the Mistress had run through just once — the upraised hand with waggling index to ask for water, the cutting motion of the back of one hand against the palm of the other to tell the server that bread was wanted, the down-hooked middle and index fingers to say, Fork please, the two humble taps on the breast to say, Excuse me. There were scores of such things to keep in mind. You would have to live, she thought, at the maximum effort of awareness every waking moment until repetition would perfect the pantomime.

She pinned her veil over her hair and felt the edges to make sure it was not askew. It was strange to be in a world without mirrors, stranger still to think of the many women around her who had not seen themselves for years, save in the photographs they were permitted to have taken for their families at times of vesture, vowing and jubilees.

19

She pulled her curtain and stepped out into the corridor. Most of the sisters in her wing were already gone. The thin cotton hangings that gave them the only privacy they had, the half-privacy of being heard but not seen, were left drawn back from their cells. It was difficult to lower your eyes as you hurried past their bleakness and quite impossible to realize that women with such varied tastes and backgrounds inhabited those similar cells without leaving in any one of them some trace of the individuality.

Every member of the community including the Superior General was housed here regardless of age, rank or function. Choir nuns, artists, doctors of medicine and the humanities, cooks, laundresses, shoemaker nuns and the peasant sisters who worked the truck gardens lived in those boxlike cells, each one identical in form and content, in arrangement of bed, table and chair and thrice-folded coverlets over each chair. Incredibly, every nun had her cell changed each year to prevent her becoming attached to its location.

In the main corridor that led to the chapel, Gabrielle stepped quickly into the file of nuns and novices walking along close to the walls. Her heart missed a beat. She had almost forgotten that practice of humility which, when she had heard about it from the Mistress of Postulants, had impressed her. Like the matter of the protected finger on the breviary page, the humble effacing of self along the edges of any wide thoroughfare was something she had lived with but never seen in training days in the convent hospital. She understood now that this habit of the nuns was what gave the great white hallways their look of peace and quiet even as here in the mother house there was the sense of very few people about.

A line of sisters moved flat as shadows along the opposite wall. A timid postulant, caped and short-skirted like herself, walked between two nuns and was reduced by their handsome regalia to a stunted shape that was all legs and anxiety. That's how I look, Gabrielle thought. A wave of self-pity swept over her as she entered the chapel.

She genuflected to the altar, then turned halfway around to make to the Superior General the reverence she had practiced in the dark of her cell. It had seemed easy then, all alone, but now in the august presence of the one who must be recognized as the Christ in the community, she felt like a goosegirl bowing before a queen. Her body broke like a stick at the waist and her arms fell straight down with her bow, then crossed so her flattened palms covered her shaky knees. She blushed for her awkwardness and backed away.

The lanes of kneeling nuns, which had had limits when she had first looked down them from the guest section, were now an endless maze, frightening to pick your way through, with swirls of skirts covering the floor and very little space left for laggards to walk in. When she reached her place far down in front, she sank to her knees with the suddenness of complete exhaustion as if she had been years on the way.

The morning prayer lasted fifteen minutes. The two hundred voices were keyed low for it, like the gray light coming through the Gothic windows from a world still fast asleep. Then the postulants were led apart for the meditation. They looked at each other furtively when they were in the study hall. Gabrielle saw one of the Irish girls tying her shoelaces, and another with her veil pinned so low it covered her eyebrows and gave her an aboriginal look.

"Now, my sisters," said Sister Margarita, "we will meditate on a line I shall read from today's Epistle. We will have thirty minutes to take these inspired words into our minds and to think profoundly on what they mean."

She opened her missal and read, *If I speak with the tongues of men, and of angels, and have not charity, I am become as sounding brass, or a tinkling cymbal.*

Gabrielle wondered uncharitably if anyone in the room could meditate on anything else except the straw sacks, the mirrorless dressing and the bow to the Superior General, which were already behind them, and of the hazards which still lay ahead — the admittance ceremony, the refectory and its manual vocabulary and all the other unfamiliar activities of this first day which she could scarcely believe was not yet one hour old.

"And . . . have . . . not . . . charity," said the Mistress, picking up their thoughts and leading them to the crux of the matter. Gabrielle knew the Epistle. She said it silently through to the line that used to make her sad in her youth. *When I was a child, I spoke as a child, I understood as a child, I thought as a child. . . .*

She had never been a child. Her three brothers had been children but she had been the replacement for the mother who had died so early that only she could remember her clearly. And her father, of course, who remembered so clearly and constantly that he could never bring himself to take another wife, although all the uncles and aunts tried to persuade him to do so. *But when I became a man, I put away the things of a child. . . .* Gabrielle put away the things she had never had and tried to think about Charity.

Presently Sister Margarita snapped her metal cricket. One click stood them up, two clicks moved them into processional order. Gabrielle moved to the place that would ever be hers, third in the line of forty postulants. She was third oldest in the group because she had been third to register on that day less than a week ago when the Order had opened its doors to new entrants. From that moment, her chronological age had ceased and the only age she would henceforth have, her age in the religious life, had started.

The two girls ahead of her were only a few minutes older and the thirty-seven behind her were all her juniors, although two or three whose aristocratic faces she had remarked most certainly had been born in the decade before her. It struck her that there was something quite bold and magnificent in the way age was discarded in the religious life. Man's time meant nothing here. Only the time that was given to God, as was every minute of convent time, counted. Nobody else in the whole congregation was your exact age. You stood alone in this separated world that had its own time spiral, a haughty hierarchy that gave you privileges for your seniority but not a single contemporary.

"Now you know your places in chapel, I shall not lead you," said Sister Margarita. "But after Tierce, you will wait." She nodded to the number one postulant. "I shall take you to the chapel hall for the admittance ceremony."

They had practiced for this and knew exactly what they had to do. This would be the first time they would meet the whole community face to face.

"One last reminder," said Sister Margarita. "Remember, in chapel, you are not to join in the psalmodizing. You will follow the Office with your eyes only and keep them on your books. For the first three weeks you will listen. Then, when your ears will have caught the precise tonalities of the Hours, you may sing with your sisters." She started the procession forward with a nod.

The two hundred sisters were exactly as they had been left a half hour before, kneeling, motionless, eyes on the altar. Folded down in the humblest position that the human can assume, they seemed to be shapes of strength that had no like-ness on earth among living things. It was frightening to be among them, like being lost in mountains.

The Superior rapped twice with her gavel to begin the *Deus in Adjutorium*. The clear voice of the Hebdomadary seemed like a cry from Gabrielle's own heart . . . *O God, incline unto my aid.* The response from the other side of the chapel was the answer to that cry and its reinforcement . . . *O Lord, make haste to help me.*

Then the sisters began to sing the first Hour. Eyes on the pages of her Little Office, Gabrielle followed the Latin easily through psalms and canticles. She had never heard anything more beautiful than those two treble choirs passing pure Gregorian back and forth as the first light of day slanted down from chapel windows. Her fingers trembled as they turned the pages. Now and again her eyes went back to lines of special beauty . . . *Emmanuel, He shall eat butter and honey . . . Thou didst descend like rain upon a fleece . . .*

The hundred voices in each opposing choir sang as from a single throat, alternating from side to side without missing a beat, the whole contained within the bounds of just two notes pitched high and piercingly sweet. Plain song was her passion. She had always hoped to go to Solemnes one day to hear the Benedictine monks chant this most ancient music of the Church. But now, she thought, she was hearing it in her own house — perhaps a few octaves higher but with the same pure effect of unison and cadence.

Deo gratias, sang the choir on her side.

Grace is spread abroad on thy lips, replied the other.

Even the glimpse of the Cantatrice walking ceaselessly up and down the aisles of the choir nuns could not dismay her. From the corner of her eye she watched this famed Gregorian scholar pause near a novice to listen to her breath control, or perhaps to some forbidden excess of feeling that escaped from the young throat. The Cantatrice did not look at the novice; she turned her head slightly toward the voice she was inspecting and let her coif capture sound like a shell.

The devotions ended. Waiting in the cloister gardens until the community would be assembled in the chapter hall, Gabrielle listened in vain for sounds of life in the streets beyond the vine-covered walls. It was astonishing how many things nuns had to do before anyone else in the world was awake. She thought of them now gathering for this extra ritual of welcoming postulants, and of the Superior General, whose slightest word, even unspoken wish if a sister could guess it, was law in this house called hers. When she had had her audience with the Reverend Mother Emmanuel to tell the reasons why she wished to enter the convent, she had not had the slightest idea of the mountains that separated her from the stately woman who had sat barely an arm's reach away from her across a desk, watching her waving hands and listening intently to her words. There had been some questions, but she could not now remember the voice. There had been a smile, but she could not now remember the face.

The doors of the chapter hall were opened by two novices. The postulants entered, made their hand-crossing bow to the woman on a thronelike chair under an immense crucifix at the far end of the hall, then prostrated themselves flat on the floor, leaning on their elbows with faces buried in their hands. The glimpse she had had of the gaunt Gothic face of the Superior General recalled the words of the Mistress of Postulants. "The Reverend Mother Emmanuel," Sister Margarita had said, "is neither man nor woman. She is the Christ among us and, as such, she is loved by us." The Christ among us . . . Gabrielle waited for the voice.

"What do you ask, my children?" It was not the voice that had spoken to her that day across a desk. It seemed to come from a great distance now and it sounded lonely.

"To be admitted into the congregation," the postulants said into their hands.

"Arise in the name of God." They arose to their knees.

The Superior General was standing. She was tall and spare. Her plain face had a carved simplicity, like an early Flemish primitive, but when she smiled, there was a sudden beauty cast over the countenance that made you catch your breath.

"Every one of us," said the Reverend Mother, "has prayed that you would have the strength to join us." She nodded right and left to the assembled nuns, who, in turn, nodded as one to the postulants. "Now that you are part of our blessed congregation, do not reject the graces that will come to you, my children. Cooperate with those graces, for you will need all the strength they will bring."

Gabrielle looked at the face of goodness with dark glowing eyes and wondered how she had missed that saintliness the first time. Gently the Reverend Mother warned of the difficulties that lay ahead.

"It is not easy to be a nun," she said. "It is a life of sacrifice and self-abnegation. It is a life against nature."

A life against nature . . . the words startled Gabrielle into remembering her father, who had said exactly the same thing.

"A life against nature," the Superior General repeated without any inflection of emotion. "Poverty, chastity and obedience are extremely difficult." She reminded them that some would have more trouble than others and that never any two would react in the same way. She cited the case of Christ's own disciples, who counted in their much smaller group one who doubted, one who denied thrice and one who betrayed, and suggested that God might possibly have permitted those defections of the disciples to illustrate how difficult was the way to Him.

"But there are always the graces if you will pray for them. Pray that you may all become St. Johns, lovers of Christ." The Superior General paused. Then she began again and gave her exhortation in Flemish.

For the farm girls, Gabrielle thought, and she knew how they must love the Reverend Mother for her robust accent in their native tongue. As she listened to the talk a second time, she studied the woman who, during her religious life, had served as missionary in India, as teacher in Poland, as supervisor in the psychiatric institutions of the Order, including the heartbreak home for uneducable idiot children which broke most nuns after a tour of duty there. She knew the Superior held degrees in philosophy, the humanities, and was a diplomaed nurse besides, and that her memory was said to be phenomenal. Every six years when she visited the missions of the Order all the way from the Great Wall of China to the Himalayas, she could call every nun by name without prompting from the local Mothers Superior. She's not one woman, Gabrielle thought, she's a multitude of women.

The Superior General gave her talk in English, then paused for the third and final time. Her right hand, knife-thin and long, appeared from beneath her scapular. She made the sign of the cross over them, a compact gesture without any energy-wasting sweep, gave them her benediction in Latin and sat down.

She remained seated while the postulants stood up on signal from the Mistress, and recited the *Veni Creator*. Then

27

they bowed and left the hall to return to the chapel for Mass. Not until she was about to enter the chapel did it occur to Gabrielle that she had been too absorbed in the Gothic woman who was henceforth the ruler of her days to have noticed if Sister William had been present for the ceremony.

I I I

THE six months were almost over. Gabrielle discovered one day when she counted her comrades that three were misssing. The rigid surveillance of every minute of the postulants' time had permitted so little impression to be made one upon the other that she had no idea which three of the group had dropped out and returned to the world.

Time in the convent belonged to the bronze bell in the chapel campanile which announced every activity of the close-packed days. This tolling bell, Sister Margarita had explained, was more than a summons to duties and devotions. It was the voice of Christ calling them for His things, which obviously made compliance with it one of the most desirable of their obligations. The Holy Rule moreover underlined this desirability. If, on the instant of the bell's peal, you did not stop mid-air, mid-voice, whatever you were doing or saying, you committed an imperfection against the rule of obedience.

Had that been the stumbling block for her three departed comrades? Gabrielle wondered. Her own frustration smoldered because she could not learn to cut a word in half and swallow the unspoken syllable at the sound of the bell, nor teach her fingers to drop pencil or chalk and leave a letter unfinished — a *y* without its tail, a *t* without its cross.

In the school for deaf-mutes to which she was assigned, she

saw the nuns and their novice helpers do these things without any look of rebellion or any visible desire to complete an unfinished act. She knew, because she struggled to emulate them, that it took the strength of a giant to submit to that paralyzing power of the bell. She knew also that if she could not achieve that command over herself in this simplest of all acts of obedience, she would never come near the final goal of becoming obedient to the will of God for which these seeming idiosyncrasies of conduct were, so to speak, the gymnastic training.

Though the campanile bell was quite light and musical in tone, it carried to the uttermost corners of the mother house enclosure, into hospital wards and linen closets, into schoolrooms and kitchens, and if there were some exceptionally noisy spots like the foundling nursery where you might just possibly miss its first peal and be able, with clear conscience, to complete an act in transit, there was always an older nun around who had the bells in her blood, who would lift her fist and pull twice down on air to pantomime that Christ was calling. Even patients sometimes made this silent signal and once, to Gabrielle's shame and astonishment, a deaf-mute child propelled her hand, holding a glass of milk to his lips, away from him when the bell which he could not hear had sounded.

The grilling routine was the most exasperating and the most compelling challenge she had ever experienced. It demanded an all-or-nothing way of being, a conscious and complete submission of self. There were rewards which came often enough to keep you trudging toward them. There was the renewal force of the daily Mass, whose mysterious beauty could never dim or diminish. There was the singing of the Seven Hours spaced through the day. The most magic moment was the final anthem to the Virgin each night just before the beginning of the grand silence when all the sisters assembled in the chapel and sang the day to its close with the *Salve Regina*.

It began after Lauds and the seven-minute examination of conscience which followed this last devotion of the day. In the brief silence while the community examined its two hundred separate consciences, you sensed the struggle in the bodies kneeling in self-judgment and heard pencils scratch across notebook pages, harsh whispers of sound that said *Mea culpa, mea culpa, I accuse myself*. There was no feeling of a molded community around you then. Each nun seemed momentarily to have escaped from the mold to exist briefly apart from her sisters in the lonely atmospheres of her own conscience. Then five peals of the bell brought them together to perform with a single fervent heart their final act of the day. The *Salve Regina* . . .

One by one the lights in the chapel would be extinguished until there were left only the vigil light at the altar and the shaded lamp that illuminated the statue of the Virgin Mary. When everything else was dark the nuns began to sing. For Gabrielle, this was the moment that made every next day possible. Even after the postulants were permitted to sing with their sisters, she could not trust her voice. The awesome antiphon swelled in the dark and expanded it. It seemed to her then that every convent, monastery and remotest mission on the planet was somehow brought into her own chapel and that the pure voices she heard close to her were but the top level of sound in the cry for mercy that was welling up at that moment to the Mother of God from every place where vowed ones lived behind walls. Their eyes of trust like those of children in the dark, thousands upon thousands of them, seemed to be looking out through her own, fixed on the single lighted figure to which the voices sang *O dulcis Virgo Maria*.

In the dark the sisters filed out of the chapel line by line, the postulants first and the youngest of these at the head, then the novices and finally the professed nuns, with the oldest in the life bringing up the rear — the processional sequence for the total community *en marche*. Shadowed in this traditional formation, Gabrielle saw the outlines of a great family with the youngest out in front under the multiple eyes of the senior sisters and the local Mother Superior of the house (or Reverend Mother Emmanuel herself when her work schedule permitted) there near the door to receive their reverence and to give them her benediction. Her youngest novice stood beside her holding the pot of holy water with which she sprinkled them. You could not see clearly in the gloom the aspergillum that rose and fell rhythmically and occasionally dipped into the pot the novice held, but you felt sometimes on your face a few cool drops falling with the Latin words of blessing that sent you off to bed.

It seemed to Gabrielle during the months of trial that the harder she tried, the more imperfect she became. The notebook in which each morning she recorded her first examination of conscience, as did every other sister in the same bell-bracketed ten minutes wherever she might be, read like a record of rebellion against the Holy Rule. *Ran upstairs. Talked after bell. Let door slam. No spirit of poverty again today in refectory, still longing for plate instead of wooden plank to eat from* . . .

In the study hall once a week the postulants read aloud to Sister Margarita the list of their imperfections. Their voices cracked, their faces perspired and Gabrielle agonized for each one until her turn came. Often she had the impression she was reading the wrong week. Her faults repeated themselves week after week, identical in number and kind.

It might have helped, she thought, had she been able to compare notes with her struggling comrades, but the life gave no opportunity for this. They had all been dispersed from the first day, each to the department for which she had special qualifications, and when the group came together for the daily hour of recreation, all conversation had to be kept to matters of general interest. Since it was a strict rule that the past must never be mentioned, there was very little left to talk about with these comparative strangers except the scenery, which was always the same. Generally, on recreation, the postulants were as uncommunicative as the cocoons hanging in the poplar trees beneath which they strolled and breathed deeply, as the Mistress of Postulants urged.

Gabrielle was aware, however, of growing perceptions which seemed almost extrasensory, since she could not recall exactly when she had first understood this or that hidden aspect of convent life. During her postulancy, a group of novices made their first vows and changed into the habit of the professed. She had never thought of their fierce temptation to see how they looked in the transforming black. Even when, one morning, leaving the dormitory, she paused to allow a former novice to precede her and glanced into the cell from which the flustered new nun had emerged, she made nothing of the black apron she saw hanging behind the pane of the half-open window. But weeks later, when Sister Margarita was talking of the temptations of vanity, to explain why the Rule permitted nuns to shine their shoes only once weekly instead of daily as some might wish to do, Gabrielle knew in a flash that her sisters must sometimes try to steal looks at them-

33

selves in their mirrorless world, though there was no connection then in her mind between this mysterious certainty and the memory of a black apron hung behind a pane of glass to cast a dark reflection.

Each step of preparation for the novitiate was taken, as it were, in the midst of it, for there were novices ever present to study secretly and beyond these were the professed nuns. It was like living in your future before you came to it. You could look at it and think about it endlessly, but you could never speak with it. Yet, somehow, the air was charged with communication.

It was amazing how much seemed to be said when Sister William passed her in a corridor. *Don't struggle so alone, my sister*, said the sharp eyes that barely glanced at her. *Leave a little leeway for the graces. Saints are seldom made and never in a day. You master one imperfection and ten others sprout like dragons' teeth. It's a never-ending affair trying to be a good nun. Endless, endless . . . but never forget our saying, When God orders, He gives . . ."* And she would be gone then and only her serge skirts would have spoken in the discreet rustle of uninterrupted passage.

God gave her the strength to wake up each morning ready to start all over again. As the mysteriously acquired awarenesses extended her understanding of the inner life of nuns, it struck Gabrielle that perhaps each one of them, no matter how old in the religious life, had to begin each day as if it were a first.

The penances confirmed her idea that a life against nature could never become habitual, could never be lived through the reflexes, but had to be fought for constantly. The late arrivals in chapel, who had to prostrate themselves in the center of the nave and stay that way until the Superior signaled her aide to pluck their sleeves and send them to their pews, were as often as not the professed nuns whose imposing number of keys indicated their importance in the community.

The refectory penances were performed in the bright light that slanted down from many windows. Here the late arrival kneeling beside the Superiors' chairs at the head of the U-shaped tables was seen by all. Moreover, when she received permission to be seated, she had the additional mortification of disturbing her sisters on the bench.

It was like having to disrupt an immense *tableau vivant*, archaic in design and significance. It gave Gabrielle a shiver every time she saw it happen, as if already the nun's dread of conspicuousness had entered her spirit. When the late sister's place was midway on the bench, ten sisters had to stand up and file out while she went in to her place. They had first to remove the big napkins which were both serviettes and individual tablecloths. These unbleached squares of sacking were tucked into the starched bibs and were anchored in place on the table by the wood planks that served as plates. A sideways glance down the table gave the impression that all the nuns were connected to it by a continuous membrane of poverty, which was what the coarse napkins really were in both intention and substance. The disturbed nuns disconnected themselves by laying their napkins forward on the table. Then they stood up, bowed to the Superior and filed out. The laggard, passing before them, tapped her breast twice to each — *Excuse me, excuse me* . . . then she crept in between bench and table. No matter how tall, how young or how regally ancient she might be, she always seemed to creep.

Gabrielle prayed she would never come late for meals. Being prostrate in the chapel did not seem half so appalling as having to derange a whole row of your sisters and put them, at a moment when they had half-chewed food in their mouths, to the test of living up to that part of the Holy Rule which said, *The sisters should always have a serene visage and a gracious air.*

Although each step toward the novitiate was described before it was taken, and could be seen around you in practiced pantomime, this did not, however, remove the element of surprise. As the day of vesture approached, there was much discussion of detachment. This was an alpine peak over which the Mistress of Postulants led them so gently in thought that it seemed to Gabrielle she had already gone over that divide. Detachment from family and friends was an accomplished fact. Since her first day, her struggles had been so intense and absorbing, she had written but one letter home. The hopelessness of trying to communicate anything of what she was thinking and feeling made the letter as brief and banal as the spirit messages her brothers used to buy from turbaned seers at county fairs . . . *All goes well.*

Detachment from things would be no more difficult than detachment from family had been, she thought. Sister Margarita explained that the night before vesture they would be expected to make a total severance from all cherished personal possessions, to destroy all letters and photographs, and, into a basket for the poor which would be passed around, to cast any object that might attach them to a memory. She touched the fine gold pencil from Jean which she kept in her skirt pocket. When the time came to drop it into the basket for the poor, she would say *All for Jesus* then, and feel less pain.

Sister Margarita spoke softly when she came to the cutting of the hair which would detach them from worldly appearances. "The hair," she said, "is the chief adornment of women in the world."

36

Gabrielle felt no emotion at the prospect of her head being clipped, although she knew that in the lay world the nun's bare head under bands and bonnet disturbed the imagination almost more than any other aspect of cloistered women. To be shorn of your hair seemed to her not only the most logical of detachments but also the most healthy for those who must henceforth wear a skullcap weighted with coif, starched supports and the final long veil. She had no curiosity about the actual operation for she had already seen it performed one day when she was sent to the laundry.

Postulants from a previous group were seated on wood benches over which presided three nuns with clippers and shears. The heads were already clipped bare as a kneecap and the stone floor adrift with chestnut and blond locks, some of which clung to the shoes of the barber nuns. More interesting than the barbering was the sight of the nuns talking with the postulants — a special permission, she supposed, to ease the nervousness of the shorn ones who had a tendency to giggle when they saw how the others looked.

That glimpse of her future made the final act of detachment seem no more macabre than any of the others. Your photos of Papa and the brothers, your gold pencil, your last gossipy letter from Tante Colette, your hair, she said to herself, and did not realize that there were ramifications of detachment which reached inward beyond the emotions associated with persons and places to the deep instinctive humanity which had been part of you since the day you were born.

The first time she saw a novice faint in the chapel, she broke every rule and stared. No nun or novice so much as glanced at the white form that had keeled over from the knees, though the novice fell sideways into their midst and

37

her Little Office shot from her hands as if thrown. For a few moments while the prayers continued, the surrounding sisters seemed to be monsters of indifference, as removed from the plight of the unconscious one as though she were not sprawled out blenched before them on the carpet. Then Gabrielle saw the nun in charge of the health of the community come down the aisle. The nursing nun plucked the sleeve of the nearest sister, who arose at once and helped carry the collapsed novice back down the aisle, past a hundred heads that never turned, past two hundred eyes that never swerved from the altar.

She trembled as she realized that she had been staring not at heartlessness but at a display of detachment which transcended every discipline she had thus far tried to emulate. How could you train yourself to a detachment so deep-reaching that it cut you off from the very breath and heartbeat of your common humanity? She would never achieve that goal, she told herself with despair, unaware that when she had stifled her nurse's impulse to rush forward and give aid, she had already struggled up the first rise of that alpine climb.

Later on, when she had trained herself to the exquisite charity of not seeming to see a sister in torment, kneeling alone in the chapel and crying quietly into her hands, or one who fasted furtively to starve an ardent nature into obedience, she would know that few of them ever really reached the icy peaks of total detachment but only seemed to have done so, a position, in actual fact, much more perilous to maintain.

There was a week of retreat before vesture and on the last evening they were given their nun's underclothing. Each piece was stitched with the postulant's number in the Order. Gabrielle had the odd feeling, as she tried on the black hand-knitted stockings with drawstrings at their tops and the long-sleeved chemise that came to the knees, that Sister Marie-Polycarpe was watching the 1072 garments fill out with new life. The face of the martyred missionary, familiar through photographs in the convent's magazine, seemed to be tilted toward her, a pale oval reflecting the ghost of a smile. It was like having a mirror in her cell.

She lifted the black serge skirt over her shoulders and watched its fullness drop to the floor as she hooked it about her waist. It was a graceful garment. She walked from wall to wall and back again, watching the heavy hem swinging. Her hands found the pockets and slid into them and now she imagined Sister Marie-Polycarpe shaking her head regretfully as she explored what could be, if permitted, such a wonderful hiding place. The pockets were so large and so cleverly hidden among folds, you could carry more than everything you owned in them and have nothing show in silhouette.

The Mistress of Novices, who was another Living Rule, sterner than Sister Margarita but equally as beautiful, had listed the items a nun could carry in those pockets. If she sequestered any others, her conscience would eventually compel her to report the disobedience. Gabrielle looked at the six allowed items ready on her dressing stand — a wallet of strong black leather in which it was permitted to carry an India-paper edition of the Little Office, the conscience note-book and a few pamphlets; a small circular tin box with hinged lid in which was set a pincushion already studded with white-headed pins for the novice veil; a small rosary in a leather pouch; a penknife; a thimble; and a large cotton bandanna in blue and white — the one bit of color a nun might possess.

When she was vested, she would have one other permitted storage space — beneath her scapular, that outer garment whose origin was lost in antiquity. It was a sleeveless robe made of two panels of wool which dropped from the shoulders to the hemline, back and front, a symbol of the yoke of Christ, so the Mistress had said. The leather belt buckled over it and made a handy pouch where such things as black-bordered letters announcing a death in the family or cards with printed prayers for loved ones might be carried, above the heart. But nothing slipped beneath the scapular must ever be detectable. There could be no telltale bulges.

She took her hands from the pockets and stood still for an instant mentally adding the white gown, scapular, veil and cape to the clothes she had on and gazing inward at the image of herself as her family would see her in the morning, thankful that her congregation did not send its postulants to vesture attired as real brides. She could imagine what her brothers would make of such a show. She saw their merry faces as she removed the practical workaday clothing; then her fingers touched the cap on her clipped head and she shut off her imaginings abruptly. That's what this thing is for, she reminded herself.

The white cotton cap was called a *serre-tête*. It clasped the head closely and had drawstrings in it. "The tighter you draw those strings," the Mistress of Novices had said, "the better will you restrain the imagination. Tie it down well, my sisters. We do not waste God's time with daydreaming. . . ." She loosened the drawstrings, which she had pulled too tight in her eagerness, then knelt beside her straw sack to say her last prayers as a postulant.

40

Sleep always came quickly after days that began in the dark of the dawn, but this night she heard every hour tolled from the cathedral in town. The chimes drifted in through the dormitory windows to mingle with the sighs and rustlings of straw she heard all about her. She reviewed her talk with the Superior General that afternoon when she had confided her secret hope of one day being a missionary sister in the Congo. The Reverend Mother Emmanuel's dark glowing eyes seemed to have pulled it out of her. She had meant to say only that she hoped she might become a good nurse and a good nun willing to go wherever she was sent, and not really caring where that might be as long as there was an abundance of God's work to do. . . . The tolling bells counted midnight.

"We shall see, my child," said the Reverend Mother, smiling as at one who had reached for the moon too soon. "We select only the very strongest sisters for our missions. Your nursing qualifications would seem to make you a likely candidate, but you are still very far from being in the mold. The mold is the armor of our missionaries and this is not forged in a day. It takes patience and the graces from infinite praying to achieve."

We shall see . . . We shall see . . . Three bells chimed like an echo. In less than two hours, Gabrielle thought. She lay in wait for the electric alarm whose shock she had learned to subdue by anticipating it.

Meditations, Prime, Tierce, and Mass, and at seven they were ready for vesture. While the Monsignor from Malines was preaching a sermon to the community of nuns and the close family members in the guest section, the postulants filed into the sacristy, where the remaining clothing for the novice

41

nuns was laid out on two trestles — leather belts, starched guimpes, veils and scapulars segregated into thirty-seven neat piles. Gabrielle saw everything as if she had a thousand eyes looking in all directions at once.

The four highest ranking in the community — the Superior General, the Mother Superior, the Mistress of Novices and the Mistress of Postulants — were waiting like handmaidens to dress them. The farm girls blushed when these important personages dropped the white gowns over the black skirts and fitted the board-stiff guimpes under their chins. The veil and scapular had been blessed and had to be kissed before they were put on, as each morning for the remainder of their religious lives they must kiss these items of the habit. Waiting her turn, Gabrielle looked at the first ones dressed. When the coif was pulled forward around the face, her companions underwent a subtle transformation. Flemish, English and Irish identities disappeared and they began to look alike. Like angels slightly surprised, Gabrielle thought.

She discovered why they looked surprised when the Mistress showed her how to pull the guimpe up and forward from the back, to make a starched frame about her face. Side views were cut off as effectively as though blinders had been saddled to her eyes, which was, she remembered, just what the coif was designed to do. It kept you looking in the only direction you were supposed to look, straight ahead toward God.

But, when she was moving in procession down the chapel aisle, looking toward the altar and the officiating priest, Gabrielle knew as if she had seen through the back of her head that Jean was there in the guest section. The certainty gave her a momentary shock, but only because he had promised never to try to see her again and he was a man of his word.

With her inner eye she saw him in the last row near the door, hunched forward and staring at the white forms going by, unable to tell which one was hers. Then she realized that the free-swinging athletic walk she had stripped away concealed her from his eyes more than the concealing garments she wore.

The Monsignor intoned the *Veni Sponsa Christi*, which brought them forward to the altar one by one to have a circlet of orange blossoms laid atop the veil. She walked with the slow passionless pace which still required all her attention to maintain. The opposing choirs of nuns sang joyously of crowns until eternity and she passed between them as between two protecting walls that closed her off from everything save the carpeted steps of the altar which led her to her crown and to the name by which she would henceforth be known — Sister Luke.

Afterwards, it took a long time to embrace all the sisters of the community. Their cheeks deep within the coif were hard to get at and you had to be careful not to crush the starched guimpes. Even for so light an embrace, she found it unnerving to touch them physically and to feel on her arms the occasional pressure of their hands when they saw she had tears in her eyes. She wanted to tell them that her tears were not for fear or self-pity as with some of the new novices. Or for God-given joy as with others. They are simply tears of relief, she wanted to say, plain practical relief because I've come to the crossroads and crossed.

As she made the ritual rounds and came now and again to a face drawn back like a turtle's into its starchy carapace, it struck her that that was how she would be years hence when she, in her turn, would be receiving the "kiss of peace" from new novices and fighting not to respond emotionally to

43

youthful faces under orange blossoms as they pressed into her sanctum of starch to find her cheeks.

She was trembling when she went into the parlor to greet her second family. Her father came forward like an Edwardian gallant and took her two hands in his. Tante Colette, his spinster sister, stood behind him holding the youngest brother by the hand.

"The family of the doctor!" she said softly to her father, mocking him with his favorite phrase of pride.

"And you?" He concealed his emotion under a professional scrutiny. "You are thinner. You seemed nervous during the ceremony."

"You'll be nervous too, dear brother," said Tante Colette, "when you go to God . . . if you ever do." Her aunt kissed her vigorously and whispered into the coif band over her ear, "Poor Jean, he slipped in and slipped out, as of course you were well aware."

The brothers shook her hand gravely and could think of nothing to say except the youngest, who asked if the orange blossoms were real.

"They're wax," said Tante Colette for her. "Now you boys go over and sample the cakes the good sisters have baked for this occasion."

"She has them tamed already," said her father.

"And you also, my old one." Her aunt nodded briskly at the brother she idolized and said, "You will note, dear Gaby, that he wears his muffler."

Her father seemed to find conversation difficult. He looked too often at his watch as he made small talk. If her aunt had not been present to bridge the silences with gossip, the reunion would have been unbearably stiff. Her aunt asked her sharply if she got enough to eat in this place and then assured her that her father had his round dozen of Zeeland oysters delivered fresh on the half-shell every Friday at exactly a quarter past one.

She was relieved when the visiting hour came to an end. The efforts of her father to appear natural with her were painful and puzzling. Her sister novices seemed to have had similar experiences with their families. They came from the parlor with troubled faces and removed their circlets of orange blossom even before the Sacristaine came around with a basket to collect them. Was it the wreath? she wondered. Could that one symbol borrowed from the world have been the factor that held their families tongue-tied?

She had her answer unexpectedly that same night when she reported for duty in the hospital ward. She had just taken over the desk from a sleepy old nun when all the call-bells started ringing at once. She could not know that the same thing was happening throughout all the hospitals and charity homes of the mother house enclosure, that everywhere the old patients who had been under care for years, and who by now had the life of the convent fixed in the spirit as if they themselves were members of the community, had waited up to see the new novices. She looked with alarm at the blinking red lights and hurried into her ward.

All her patients were sitting up with eyes on the door through which they knew she must come. She started down the rows of beds, rearranging pillows, giving sips of water and easing bandages, pretending not to hear the disobedient whispers that broke the grand silence. . . . *How beautiful you are, Sister!* . . . but hearing them with a sudden lift of heart as she saw the surprise in faded old eyes which had last seen her in the short black dress of the postulant.

As Papa saw me last, she thought, and blessed them silently

45

for telling her, with the surface emotions of the sick, what her father had been too confused to say.

"Ah, Sister, you make a beautiful nun!" they sighed with satisfaction.

I V

IN the first year of the novitiate, struggle seemed to go deeper and ceased to be mainly for physical perfections. It turned into a lonely war against pride and self-will. Since after vesture she never again heard her given name Gabrielle, she often had the illusion that she was contending with a stranger and that the stubborn characteristics she fought belonged to someone else. Only her conscience performed familiarly. It watched her doing something new like a motion-picture camera recording without pity or prejudice the laborious development of someone called Sister Luke.

No novice left the mother house during that formative year. The house was the cradle of the religious life and the community itself was the mold that pressed, restrained and supported the wavering white forms that slowly shaped to strength.

The community, which in postulant days had appeared to Sister Luke as a vast amorphous body with four hundred eyes and ears, revealed its hierarchic outline more clearly now that she had gone up the ladder one step. A new group of postulants, over whom she took precedence in speech, was below her now, and above were the first professed, who had made their first vows as she would make them at the end of the year. The fully professed were, like the local Superior and Mis-

47

tresses, the perfected top-level beings who supervised hospitals, schools and homes for the aged and foundlings, and, outside of duty, spoke with no one except themselves and the Superiors. Above all like a central sun was the revered person of the Reverend Mother Emmanuel, with whom any sister might speak without first asking permission from her immediate supervisor.

Although separated by speech privileges from whole segments of the community, you were nevertheless in it and a part of it all the time. You slept with it, worked with it, ate and prayed with it. There was no escape from it. Where the community was, there was the Christ. Except for some major reason approved by the Superior, you could not absent yourself from community life. You might long to go off in a corner and read or meditate all by yourself, but this could never be. You were learning the hardest lesson of all — to live in harmony with women of all ages and of every kind. Sometimes the realization that she would never be alone again, physically alone in her own separate pool of silence, would dismay Sister Luke more than any other aspect of the life against nature she had chosen. Even more, she thought, than the culpa, which was its weekly trial by fire.

The culpa was the proclaiming before all your sisters of your failures in the Rule — faults that resulted from negligence, forgetfulness or rashness rather than from deliberate intent. And, after you had disclosed all that you could remember, the sisterhood was invited to complete, for charity's sake, the record of failures forgotten. The culpa was obviously, as the Mistress of Novices had explained, a training in charity, forbearance and humility, but to Sister Luke it was a personal trial by fire.

It was held in the chapter hall every day except Sundays and feast days, when most of the sisters were assembled for spiritual reading. Each nun had her day and time assigned and ten or twelve could be heard in any assembly period. The dozen whose turn it was prostrated themselves and waited until the Superior of the house rapped twice with her gavel. Then the oldest in the group rose to one knee and began the travail of telling on herself. *Ma Mère, I say my culpa* . . .

Sister Damiensus accused herself of speaking unnecessarily ten times, of eating a chocolate from a patient's box, of opening a window in the recreation room without first asking if everyone wished more air. Sister Jean de Christ accused herself of the breach of poverty of spilling milk twice in the refectory, of walking with precipitation to avoid being late for devotions, of forgetting to kiss the floor and say three *Glorias* when she let doors slam . . . and all of it sounded like trivia wrought out of senseless scrupulosity until your turn came and until you felt beneath your scapular the white-hot burn of humiliation which told you how much of your pride was still alive within you and how far away was that perfection in humility toward which this weekly ordeal heated, hammered and fashioned you.

At first the culpa made Sister Luke think of guillotine days of the French Revolution. The spectator nuns sat with books of spiritual readings instead of knitting and seemed always to be absorbed in their pages. But their retentive memories could almost be heard clicking like small hidden projectors as they reviewed their versions of the culpa that was being said. Then those who had seen or heard something more would stand up, one, two or three of them, but never more than three. The culpa had rules. Only three times in a single session might a nun be proclaimed by her sisters, and no one younger than she in the religious life was permitted to disclose a forgotten fault.

After several months of the culpa had somewhat accustomed her to its dread but never to its burning humiliation, Sister Luke began to see something heroic in the nuns who proclaimed a sister. They have courage, she thought. They carry it even beyond the point where Christ stopped. They state the failure in detail and name the name, whereas He said only that one shall betray and it is: *One of the twelve, who dippeth with me his hand in the dish.*

The body of the community eventually revealed through the culpa more of its composition. As she heard certain sisters proclaimed repeatedly for the same imperfection in outward conduct, Sister Luke began to see where, in the community life, the muscles, the mind and the emotions lay. The nuns proclaimed most often for impetuous walking were those who had been sports enthusiasts in their former lives. The intellectual nuns lost in the clouds of their private thoughts were those most frequently proclaimed for refectory faults like forgetting to pass things at table and spilling the milk they poured absent-mindedly into coffee mugs. And there was one choir nun with a face like St. Cecilia's who was regularly proclaimed for having been "carried off by a bird song" during a meeting of the teaching staff, or for having broken the grand silence by whispering "Listen!" when tree frogs sang at night.

The bravest of the emotionally vulnerable were the sisters who stood up together in the culpa and proclaimed each other — for having gone out of their way to be near to one another, or perhaps for having talked together in recreation in a way that excluded others. Their tormented but clearly

50

spoken disclosures of a nascent affinity gave it the *coup de grâce* which they themselves might not have been able to do, for the entire community would henceforth see to it that these two would be kept far apart. The pair would be helped to detach themselves from one of those spontaneous personal attachments which often sprang to life in the body of the community as unexpectedly as wildflowers appeared, now and again, in the formal geometric patterns of the cloister gardens.

Sometimes when she knelt after her culpa and listened to the voice of a sister quietly reporting faults she had been unaware of, Sister Luke momentarily lost her identity as companion nurse sharing night duty with that sister. The familiar voice would suddenly become that of a stranger, leaving her with the impression that she was listening to the voice of the community grieving as a single body over its imperfections. There was fear then, a quick quiver of it that called the adrenalin into her blood. She ceased to exist for that moment. She was no longer Sister Luke, formerly Gabrielle Van der Mal. She was, momentarily, no more than a solitary cell situated somewhere below speech level in a vast organic body which saw, spoke and thought for her and which cared for her with scrupulous charity while carrying her upward to an unknown place. The fear passed over like a moving shadow, quickly come and quickly gone. How could you be afraid of the community? she asked herself. It would be like fearing your own self or fearing number 1072.

After culpa the community recited the *De profundis*. She would enunciate each word with care, unaware that she pitched her voice a shade above the others so that she could hear herself saying in her own way, *Out of the depths I cry to Thee, O Lord* . . .

Midway in the novitiate, when the novices were strong but not strong enough, the Superior began to mete out bigger penances in the culpa. From the saying of five *Aves* for a repeated fault, the penances now became acts of humiliation performed openly in the refectory. Sister Luke tried to think of them as a final tempering before her group would make its first vows and be sent away from the mother house to smaller communities that were much closer to the lay world and to its temptations. But each time she was given a public penance, there was nothing her mind could do to help her out of a humiliation that bit to the quick.

There were four of these severe penances and quite often, in the final months, you saw all four of them going on at once in the refectory — the kissing of the feet of the ten oldest nuns, the begging of the soup, the asking for prayers from all the sisters for help in achieving the Holy Rule, and the kneeling with arms outstretched to say five *Aves*, five *Paters* and five *Glorias*.

Was there anywhere in the outside world a training and tempering comparable to this? Sister Luke tried to find an analogy. There must be disciplined lives in the world, she told herself, but whose? And to what aim? All she could think of was the ballet and its training of those special muscles which held dancers on their toe-tips for incredible periods of whirling, leaping and dropping again to those two points of pain, lightly as birds from flight. But ballerinas were trained almost from infancy. They did not have twenty-one years of natural living to undo before learning to fly.

The first time she was penanced to beg her soup, her entire past rose up in outrage. Years of impeccable service at her father's table flashed in her memory as she placed her pottery bowl on the left of the Mother Superior, knelt, clasped her hands and waited until two spoonfuls of soup had been put into her beggar's bowl, then on to the next oldest and the next, until the bowl was filled. Six nuns putting two spoonfuls each could have filled it, but that first time there were three who thoughtlessly doled out a single spoonful and then resumed their own eating. She arose and took her bowl on down the table, remembering the Meissen soup tureen at home and the silver ladle that put into each plate its full and steaming content with a single dip. When at last her bowl was filled, she returned to her place and swallowed the soup, as she knew she must, down to the last drop. She tried not to think how it had been tossed into her bowl from a dozen other bowls that had already been eaten from, and blanked out from her facial expression the revolt that rose up in her fastidious soul as she drank her dregs. One look of rebellion, she knew, would be enough to invite a repetition of the awful abasement which she was sure she could never go through again, not even for the sake of the Blessed Lord Himself.

But she did go through it several times in the final months of her novitiate. She begged her soup, she knelt to kiss the feet of the ten oldest nuns, she burned through the mortification of asking her sisters to pray for help for her, and was it more harrowing to have to stop the pulpit reader when you made that abject request than to disturb the hungry nuns by laying your beggar's bowl beside them or signaling them to put out their feet to be kissed?

Her imperfections that had brought on the penances were cut away from her as cleanly as if she had undergone surgery. She was seldom penanced for the same fault twice, but there were always others. She learned to see through her pain — beyond the strict observance of the Rule which was the inevitable result of those experiences — to something else that

53

was being taught by them. As the pride of Gabrielle Van der Mal crumbled within her and a feeling of her nothingness took its place, Sister Luke had her first haunting glimpse of humility when she looked at the prideless place within her that was being prepared for its growth.

In the last trying months before vows, she saw true humility several times but she did not know it then. Occasionally when several novices were slated for penances in the refectory, one of the professed nuns in sober startling black appeared in the white-robed penance group. Sister Luke would stare at the soup-begging nun, the involuntary exclamation, What could *she* possibly have done! almost escaping from her parted lips. Her surprised eyes would follow the dark figure of grace as it moved around the table with the slowly filling bowl. She was unaware that she looked at one of the great charitable souls of the sisterhood who had asked permission to do this mortification, to show the novices how perfect humility looked when given to God with a smile.

Thus, in that year, besides earning her nursing degree and a diploma in psychiatry, the data of struggle accumulated within her. If her reasonable mind often looked askance at the smallness of the things she struggled for, she reminded herself that nothing was trivial in the eyes of God and that the life of the cloister was made up of an infinity of small things that had an importance here undreamed of in the outside world. Each simplest act, each hidden intention, had to be cut to the Rule and polished and perfected like the tiny stones of a mysterious mosaic which had no meaning when looked at one by one, except that one by one they fitted together and suggested a pattern. The pattern was the formation of the nun but she was too close to see it.

Once on recreation when she sat cleaning beans with her sister novices, her eyes wandered around the wide circle they formed beneath the trees. She looked at the young flushed faces bent over lapfuls of beans and listened to the exclamations of the fast-fingered ones who could string more beans for Jesus than others could in the given time. No one uttered a regret for not being allowed to stroll that day through the gardens. No one looked up from her aproned lap to the flowering chestnuts and the slow drift of summer clouds above them. Their discipline showed so sweetly without stress or strain, it nearly brought tears to her eyes.

It is almost an exaggerated thing, she thought, this discipline. It is surely more than any of us could ever need in the safe communities where we shall be. . . .

She could not know then, on that summer day in 1927, that in little more than a decade their ordered world would rock and twist like the epicenter of an earthquake and that the walls she imagined would always protect them would crack in many places and fall in heaps of rubble to the ground. Some of these sisters who sat beside her would disappear in the holocaust, not to be heard from for years until, at last, a few would begin to reappear one by one . . . out of Poland, Czechoslovakia, China, out of all the sad new Godless lands called Iron Curtain where first of all the cloistered had been hunted down. They would reappear with worn pictures of saints sewn into the hems of disguising lay clothes and rosaries hidden in their shoes, and the world, stirred by their stories of endurance, would stare at news photos of those blessed objects and wonder how those alone had got them through. Because that would be all that they, the phoenix sisters, would be able to tell about their calvaries. Prayers and faith, they would say. They would have forgotten how the steel had got under their scapulars, it was so long ago that they had learned to be nuns.

She ignored her own discipline as she bent to the bean-stringing she hated. She forced her fingers to work faster in penance for her revolt against menial work and suppressed the memory of the sign the cook had nailed to the kitchen door at home: CHILDREN FORBIDDEN TO ENTER HERE.

Actually, she reflected, it was less of a strain to spend the recreation period cleaning vegetables than to walk with her sisters and try to think of something appropriate to speak about, something that would interest three other novices in the same degree that it interested you yourself. If you could only walk in pairs and speak with one at a time, she thought. It was a stern ruling, this no speech until four are together. Yet how many times had she all but foundered on that single small pebble of their Gibraltarlike discipline?

She looked across the circle at the girl who followed her in line for the weekly bath, whose eyes catching hers would sometimes reach out like hands . . . *Hold me up, Sister Luke, I'm scheduled for culpa tomorrow and I'm frightened.* Her gaze moved on to the Irish girl who always drew near to her in the recreation, smiling ever like a saint over her heartbreak that her family could not be there when she would make her vows. *It is of course too expensive a trip from Ireland to Belgium*, the Irish eyes would say. *So I'm going to be all alone with God, then . . . except of course for you, Sister Luke.* And then, when the third and fourth would join them and the oldest in the group would start the conversation, the talk would be of something safely hung up on high like the Japanese lanterns for Sister Eudoxie's jubilee or

56

those wonderful artificial flowers the cancer patients had made for the fête — something general that would not rip open the secret places of their women's hearts.

A stern ruling, she thought, but very wise. If just once any one of us let go . . . Only one in the entire congregation, she reflected, was probably strong enough to risk the human touch without becoming attached. She smiled as she thought of the Superior General, who had become the center of her universe since the day in the refectory when she had lifted her eyes and had really seen the Reverend Mother Emmanuel for the first time.

It was on one of her penance days, she remembered, when she had to beg her soup for coming late to devotions from the hospital. She had begun, as was proper, with the highest ranking, who was that day the Superior General, just returned from her annual visits to the affiliated houses in England, Holland, France and Poland. Kneeling and waiting for the two spoonfuls of soup to be doled into her bowl, she had looked up bleak with despair. She was not expecting to be looked at. Experience had taught her that the higher the nun ranked, the more assiduous she usually was in helping a younger sister to regret her faults; most Living Rules doled out the soup with disdain and frowned into space as if annoyed at the interruption. But that day the Superior General's face was bent toward her and gently smiling. It was the kind of smile Sister Luke had almost forgotten existed. It reached down and touched her and seemed to say quite plainly, *Why! You poor little thing!* It was the only time she ever came near to crying in her penance.

From that moment her captivated eyes had followed the tall spare figure whenever the Superior General was present in the

57

chapel, the refectory or the novices' recreation, and because she was looking with eyes of love, she began to see details.

She discovered that the Reverend Mother Emmanuel's back never touched the back of a chair no matter how weary she might be. It took her several weeks to gather this evidence of an inner strength that totally rejected comfort. Again and again, in study hall, recreation or in the hospital when the Reverend Mother visited her nuns at work, Sister Luke would place herself where she could get a view of the back. The Reverend Mother's long black veil always fell straight down her flat back held rigid as a cliff of granite and there was always a measurable space between it and the back support of the chair she occupied. Yet, somehow, she always looked relaxed.

In the chapel, Sister Luke saw another kind of strength. For the half hour of meditation, the Reverend Mother Emmanuel's eyes never turned first to her book of spiritual reading; she could apparently enter into immediate colloquy with God without the help of inspirational phrases. The moment she knelt at her *prie-dieu* she seemed to be regarding Him directly. Stealing looks at the venerated figure so still and lost in contemplation, Sister Luke understood how the early artists came to paint the graces descending as rays of gold toward an upturned face. It was never difficult to imagine, when the Superior General was in colloquy with God, that you saw bright bands slanting down toward her in those gray dawns before sunrise.

But it was in the recreation room that she saw the quintessence of the Superior General's power and felt most directly the regenerating force which emanated from her. The recreation, which had seemed like the final awful intensification of community life, became an adventure in humanity.

58

As with every other phase of community life, Sister Luke came upon the real meaning of the recreation slowly. She could not at first recognize those twice-daily periods of assembly as the very backbone of the instruction to overcome selfhood, nor could she realize that the recreation was the most important exercise in the difficult and delicate art of community living. Until the Reverend Mother Emmanuel appeared one day, the recreation was for Sister Luke a static sewing circle that gave her spiritual claustrophobia.

Attendance at recreation was obligatory and you always sat in a circle. The circle was obviously the formation of charity, everyone facing each other to share smiles and words, nobody left out, not even the ones like Sister Luke who wished to be. Possibly the sole relaxing feature of it, she thought, was that you could take any chair that you wished. It was the only place where seating by seniority was waived, where the rule of first come, first served prevailed, except of course for the chair beneath the crucifix which was reserved for the professed nun who presided. But every other aspect of the recreation was fixed by custom.

You came to the recreation with your workbag made of pieces of worn serge skirts which even the Vestiaire, with all her weaving arts, could no longer mend for wearing use. Your number was chain-stitched on the bag — the quick stitch, not anything time-wasting or fancy like feather- or cross-stitching. In the bag you carried the work your hands must do while you sat in the circle, for no hands might lie idly folded in the lap. The work, moreover, had to be something manual like darning or knitting. It could not be anything self-absorbing like letter-writing, sketching or reading which would take your attention from the sisters sitting around you.

Usually the sisters took stockings from their bags, the black

59

hand-knitted ones that looked strong as iron but which wore out quickly around the feet when you were ever on your feet. If all caught up with their darning and there was no knitting in progress, they took out wood spools with pins set into the tops, and wove string cords, the cords dropping down through the hole in the spool inch by inch, day by day, until there was enough length to serve as cord for the scissors that swung from every nun's belt; then it was cut off and a new one begun. The only elegant and slightly complicated work permitted in the recreation was that of the sacristy sisters, who mended altar cloths and sacred vestments.

Sometimes Sister Luke would look around the circle with a kind of desperate urgency that sought, in some one of her companions' faces, a hint of the inner rebellion she herself felt. She saw everything else but what she sought — smiles on the faces of nursing and teaching sisters who had chosen to sit next to kitchen and laundry workers, to draw them forth from shyness and encourage them to talk. She saw the Irish girls spaced far apart in the circle of charity, never choosing chairs beside each other to give themselves a respite from the patter of French which was still too quick and colloquial for their learners' ears to catch; their occasional smiles to each other were like spokes of sunlight cutting across the circle, uniting momentarily two points on its lonely impersonal circumference.

The words she had beaten back again and again since vesture, words she had dared to say only in the confessional, would speak then so loudly in her thoughts that she would look up with alarm to see if anyone else had heard. *I don't belong here. I can't even conform to the life in the recreation. I'm not strong enough . . .*

Then one day Reverend Mother Emmanuel visited the

novices' recreation and for Sister Luke the dreaded boring period was never the same again. The Superior General came in a few moments after all were seated and busy with small talk and mending. The entire circle rose instantly and bowed as she passed, not the deep formal reverence accorded her everywhere else in the convent world, but a simple head-bow, respectful and instantaneous as any salute to supreme authority sharing a recreation with juniors.

"I was detained," she said, acknowledging with her smile the authority of the bells over her as well. Then she sat down, placed her workbag on her lap and removed her handwork for the period. Sister Luke saw that it was a stocking, but when the wooden egg dropped down the long ribbed leg to the heel, she knew it was no stocking the Reverend Mother could ever have worn. There was no heel left in it, only a great oval hole such as the sabots of the garden or laundry nuns ground out of the backs of their stockings.

That was Sister Luke's only clear clue as to what happened to the recreation when the Superior General sat among them with her back never touching the back of her chair. Charity was visible in her scholarly hands expertly darning the stocking of one of their humblest sisters. Then it came alive in her voice, the same deep voice that had told them almost a year ago, "It is a life against nature," but with a personal inflection now as she singled them out one by one and spoke of affairs in their departments as if she had been working there beside them — in the laundries where those boilers were giving trouble again, in the children's hospital where the recent measles outbreak had doubled the work of the nurses — making the problems of each the concern of all. Her peculiar force that was like a fluid flowed out from her and you could follow its passage around the circle as it became visible in smiles on faces that seldom smiled, in easings of tensions and in the relaxed tones of the white-clad novices whose voices, as the day for the taking of vows approached, showed the nervous strain they were laboring under.

In subsequent recreations, Sister Luke saw that the Reverend Mother's magnetic eyes could discover struggle and doubts no matter how deeply these might be hidden. When she discovered them, she made things happen which eased them. She did not always draw the silent struggler into conversation, but seemed rather to speak to her while addressing another.

A real physician of the soul, Sister Luke would think. No doctorate in psychology could fully account for that supernatural awareness of the states of others. When she looked at the lean self-abnegating face bent over a darning egg, she was certain that she was looking at the imitation of Christ so perfected as to pass almost unperceived. The impression was so strong and it stirred her so deeply that years later, in chilly communities far removed from the mother house, Sister Luke could superimpose at will over the figure of the presiding local Mother Superior the spare outlines of the Reverend Mother Emmanuel and feel again the healing art of those dark eyes piercing through to the inner struggle.

Occasionally the Reverend Mother gave the novices a glimpse into their futures when she brought to the recreation a visiting nun from an affiliated house or from one of their missions. The visitors always had the place of honor on her right, but no matter how bursting with eagerness they might be to relate to her every achievement of their schools, hospitals or sanatoria, the Reverend Mother would not permit them to monopolize her attention. She let them talk just long enough to give the novices a foretaste of the satisfactions they too would have when they would be doers of God's work in distant places. Then, with a tact so skillful and delicate that it seemed no interruption at all, she would turn the conversation back to her novices. Her rare smile assured them that the horizons of their struggling inner worlds were for her every bit as interesting as those of the distant missions.

V

THE week of retreat before the taking of vows was over. Then the Mistress of Novices gathered up her flock and led them to the chapter hall for final instructions.

She described the ritual of the exchange of white scapulars and veils for black ones and the signing on the altar of their written promise of obedience to God and their legitimate Superiors for the period of three years, when they would then make their perpetual vows. The parchment with its holy promise would be transferred with them henceforth to wherever they might be sent and, when they died, it would be placed in their folded hands to go with them into the grave. The bronze crucifix that hung over the heart of every nun would be given to them at the altar and also the white choir cape worn always in the chapel by the professed.

The Mistress had her own cape there to show them how it went on. It had no seams or side openings. It slipped over the head and fell in loose pleats from shoulders to shoes and had a slight train at the back. The cuffs of the wide sleeves reached almost to the floor and when you made the deep hand-crossing bow to a Superior, the sleeves followed the hands and folded over like wings.

There was one other item they would receive after vows which explained the curious sound you heard in the dormitories twice each week for a few minutes after lights out. The Mistress took from her pocket a small metal ring with five chains suspended from it and a pointed hook at the end of each chain.

"This is a discipline," said the Mistress. It was the instrument of external penance. The professed must whip this device over their bare shoulders every Wednesday and Friday nights for the duration of the saying of the *Miserere*. She cautioned about excess in the use of this mortification. It was as much of an imperfection to overdo as it was to pretend to do or not to do at all.

Sister Luke looked steadily at the flagellant device. I can use that to good advantage, she thought. I can use that on my sudden hungers for oysters, on the flare-ups of carnal desire that sometimes torment my body by day and my dreams by night, on my nagging longings for the latest medical books, theaters, symphonies, mountain-climbing in the Ardennes . . . those little chains and sharp hooks will give me something else to think about.

She tried not to imagine her father's explosive reaction to such a practice but his indignant voice prevailed against her will. Neurotic women flailing themselves to take their minds off the natural life that God intended for them, she heard him cry. He had no idea, because he had never tried to lift himself out of the natural life, that it was not sex that haunted you one tenth as often as, say, a plump oyster on the half-shell which could dominate your thoughts when you knew you could never eat another one unless, like a miracle, it would appear one day on your wooden plank in the refectory.

"Private self-flagellation as a penance," said the Mistress, "is countenanced in our Order providing that it is moderate.

65

You will be doing this penance twice weekly for the remainder of your religious lives. Put the emphasis therefore on its spiritual meaning, which is real contrition for your sins, rather than on the physical force with which you apply it."

For the remainder of our religious lives . . . Sister Luke felt as if she had already lived ten religious lives. She looked back over her year and a half of trying to live the Holy Rule, not day by day, but minute by minute as you had to do. It was like remembering a protracted fever wherein you reached and reached and never quite grasped. You had babbled constantly to yourself in that fever, about what you liked most to do, to eat, to say, then had driven yourself into doing, eating or saying the exact opposite so as to please God instead of pleasing yourself. And every so often in and out of the hot tensions of that novitiate, doubts had prowled and queried, borrowing your own voice to ask, *Was I truly called? How can I know until I try it if I have the vocation for the religious life? And, even after, how can I know since the trying itself transforms and leaves you no more self to ask?* . . .

She wondered as she looked at her sister novices if her own face reflected the changes she could see in theirs. There had been a definite refining such as high fevers often give to a countenance. Even the coarse healthy faces of the novices who worked in the truck gardens had taken on a singular purity.

"Try to avoid singularization," the Mistress had told them once. "Anything that singularizes, whether inwardly or outwardly, is but the self asserting itself, a sign that we have not succeeded in suppressing the old self so that we may be born again in the Christ."

And yet, Sister Luke thought, our very life has singularized us, not one from the other but all of us from the rest of the

66

world. Even if we did not wear habits of archaic distinction, the singularization would still be seen . . . in the way we walk prim and stylized, in the way we talk with the possessives *my* and *mine* gone from our vocabularies and the words *I cannot* forever screened from our speech. And conscience, she thought, that intuitive sense of moral right and wrong which everyone is born with but which our Rule has trained and toughened with the twice daily exercise of it until it has grown from a still small voice to a functioning vital organ within us.

She glanced at two of her companions who, it was rumored, were not going to make their vows. They would probably return to the world from which, apparently, they had been unable to detach to their own conscientious satisfaction. Their fervent faces were like all the others in the row, refined to a delicacy that had not been there when they had entered as blushing postulants. How long would it take them to unlearn the nun's gliding swayless walk, the gestureless speech bereft of possessives, the habitual custody of the eyes downcast? It's going to be terribly difficult for them at first, she thought with compassion, with a year and a half of this iron discipline to undo.

Suscipe me, Domine . . .

The two hundred sisters sang them to their vows. Before advancing to the altar they lay prostrate in the center of the nave, the visible symbol of their dying to the world, to their families watching from the visitors' section and to their old selves still clothed in the novice white.

The treble choirs raised them up with the *Gloria Patri* and sent them forward to the altar in steps as slow and measured as the Gregorian chant which presently the officiating Monsignor picked up from the singing sisters and carried on in a grave baritone.

Save Thy handmaiden, O Lord, for in Thee is her hope. Let her be good and humble. Let her be exalted by obedience. Let her be bound to peace. Let her be constant in prayer. Lastly, O Lord, we beg Thee to receive graciously her offerings . . .

And mine to You, O Lord, are the things I do at the bedside of the dying when I listen to the expiring breath and watch the hands twist the coverlets. Mine to You is the certainty of Your nearness when these signs appear and the promise that I will bring quickly a priest or pastor or rabbi of the faith of the moribund upon whom he depends to bridge the gap between him and You. I have not much more, besides love, than skilled fingers, a strong back and tireless feet to offer. Mine to You, O Lord . . .

The expert hands of a professed nun put on the black scapular and buttoned it down the side. The crucifix, leather belt and rosary came next, and then the white choir cape was dropped over her shoulders to fall of its own weight in chiseled folds to the floor. She had the little pin box, reset with black-headed pins, in readiness when the dark veil was draped around her snowy coif. The ceremony closed with the antiphon *Confirma Hoc Deus* as she signed her name in religion on the paper laid out for her on the high altar.

Later, in the crowded parlor, she could not at once see her family. Tante Colette was wiping her eyes and calling, "Gabrielle, here we are!" from the edge of the crowd, but she did not turn around to that name. Patiently, politely and very slowly she circled the room until she came upon the ones who had been crying a name she no longer responded to, not even in reflex reaction.

Her father looked exactly as he had a year ago, after vesture, and he said the same words, "You are thinner, *ma petite* Gaby*.*" Only the music that lingered in her ears was different. The *Posuit Signum* was the vocal undertone that confused her now with its piercing sweetness . . . *He has set a seal on my face so I may know no other love but His.*

And then she thought to say, "It's probably the effect of the black scapular, *cher Papa.* You remember how Mama always used to say that black gives the longer line."

The effect of the black veil and scapular was visible in another way when the parlor doors closed on their families and the newly professed returned to the community. Now there were postulants and white-robed novices studying them with respect, looking up to them from below, as it were, from the place where the words *I promise* had not yet been said. Above or beyond were the fully professed, the perpetually vowed, from whom they were still separated by the traditional silence although clothed exactly like them in every respect.

No outsider could have told the difference between the first and the fully professed, but the older nuns knew in an instant who was who. The moment they spotted the newly garbed — down the long perspective of a corridor or at the head of the marble stairs — their eyes grew alert for faults. Their recognition of us is as instantaneous, Sister Luke thought, as if we carried sandwich boards over our shoulders to proclaim from back and front and in three languages that we are one-day-old professed. The sixth sense of her senior sisters puzzled her, but not for long.

She saw the first visible signs of the subjective results of profession that same day in the last recreation the newly professed were to have together before being sent away next morning to other houses. Her companions came as usual with their little black bags, but some of them, she observed, had the look of sleepwalkers. Their wide-open eyes seemed to be focused on a distant glory as they made their bows to the presiding Mistress and took the nearest unoccupied chair without, as formerly, looking about to choose a place in the circle where their presence might do the most good — next to a white-robed novice, for example, who was obviously overcome by the change in a sister who but yesterday had looked no different from herself.

Those somnambulists, Sister Luke told herself, are the potential mystics separating themselves. She had heard about this. Was it from Sister William in her lay student days? She took out her darning and remarked to her companion on the right that trotting through miles of hospital corridors certainly wore out the stockings fast, while she tried to remember the voice that had said:

"The tendency toward mysticism is always a problem in a mixed Order such as ours where work and contemplation must go hand in hand. One sees this often in the newly professed and while it is a very beautiful thing to see a young nun apparently communing directly with God, she is nevertheless lost to the community when in that rapture and someone's else mind, hands and feet must do her work meanwhile. One can never know, of course, if it is the real thing or simply one of those unconscious singularizations to which we all fall prey from time to time."

The silence of the preoccupied ones did not escape the attention of the presiding Mistress. She drew the dreamers back into the sewing circle with direct questions about their assignments, giving them lively vignettes of the Mothers Superior in those affiliated houses. Sister Luke noted with secret amusement that the Mistress found a way to liken one of those Superiors to Saint Theresa of Avila, the Spanish Carmelite who, though one of the greatest mystics, was at the same time a remarkably practical and astute woman, reputed to have said of a group of starry-eyed novices, "We don't need any more saints here, but rather plenty of strong arms for scrubbing."

The black scapular and the shining new crucifix hanging over her heart gave Sister Luke no illusion that her own spiritual condition had grown more rarefied. She felt mainly a tremendous relief that the strain of the unprofessed novitiate was over, that God in His infinite mercy had accepted her humble offerings and that henceforth, now that she was one of His, there would happen to her only what He would permit to happen. Whatever that might be, as the Mistresses said so very often, it would be for His glory and for her own good.

Later, in the refectory, the inner transformation of the newly professed was more clearly visible. Their zeal for perfection made their section of the long processional toward the tables resemble one of those mechanical marvels like Britain's trooping of the colors. With her eyes on the heels of the sister in front of her and her own advancing foot falling like an Indian's onto the exact spot vacated by the preceding, Sister Luke felt herself drawn into the perfection of her group's first appearance as professed in the community. She made ready to cross herself, like a soldier counting one, two, three, before the signal to start the prayers. When she lifted her eyes after the *Amen*, she thought she saw a look of ennui on the faces of the perpetually vowed who, though far distant at the tables adjoining the Superiors', seemed nevertheless to be keenly aware of what went on below the salt, where some of those newly professed were singularizing themselves.

She would know in a few years what a strain it was to have newly professed in the community. She too would be drawn to look at the youngest Brides, to lose the custody of her eyes to curiosity. She too would feel the pride and the pang when new blood came upon the scene, hot and eager for dedication.

But much of their brave show of perfection vanished that evening when they were apart from the community and waiting in the corridor outside the office of the Mistress of Novices. You could feel the undertow of emotion as they each rehearsed the last private talk with the Living Rule who had guided their steps to this moment of leave-taking. Only a few like Sister Luke were able to fight back the tears.

Tomorrow they would be separated to start their lives as young nuns in strange communities far from the fountainhead of their Rule. In smaller houses they would be on their own, with no more than perhaps a score of senior sisters to watch over them and help them keep their feet on the narrow path of poverty and obedience. They would be much nearer to the temptations of the world. The mother house that had cradled them in the religious life would be henceforth a fortress in memory only. They would not return to it until called in to make their final vows three years later and if, before that, they were sent overseas to a mission and made their final vows to some local Mother Superior in India, China or the Congo, they would not see the mother house until they would have earned a furlough in the home country. The Holy Rule was of course established in them, in the mind and spirit, in the muscles and the heart, but they seemed to know that it was an extremely fragile and shakable establishment, like any great alliance. And had they not, their forlorn faces seemed to say, made the greatest of all, an alliance with God?

Sister Luke had conflicting emotions about leaving the mother house. She was going to enter the School of Tropical Medicines, the first real step toward the future she had prayed for, which was a life of service to God as a missionary nurse in some faraway place. For the next eight months she would be a nun in transit, still attached to the mother house but boarded far away from it in a girls' school near the university, where a small community of nuns, professors mostly, would replace the two hundred pairs of eyes that watched over her now. She could not tell if her inner excitement was for the thought of escape from the big community to a small one where, moreover, long study hours would dispense her from much of the community life, or whether it stemmed from the realization that she was at last on her way toward that diploma in tropical medicines which was the passport her Order required for nursing supervisors in the Congo.

She thought of her visit to Sister Eudoxie, the Vestiaire, as she awaited her turn to say farewell to the Mistress of Novices. She had gone with her missal, her Little Office and her meditation books, to hand these over to the Vestiaire for packing. She had never before been inside the cavelike workroom where the old nun, known as the Cyclopean eye of the community, had spent the half century of her cloistered life mending and altering the habits of nuns and supervising a large staff of novices and postulants who mended hospital linens.

Save for the obligatory attendance at meals and devotions, Sister Eudoxie was seldom seen outside her silent workroom; she knew, nevertheless, nearly all there was to know about the private lives of her sisters. She could read in any garment she mended the total life of the one to whom it belonged and, sight unseen, could judge that nun's perfections and faults. A

73

worn place on the back of a skirt hem told her that the wearer was careless about lifting her skirt from the rear when descending stairs, a thoughtless waste of good material which translated instantly into an imperfection against poverty. Sister Eudoxie personified the Holy Rule even more than the gracious living images of it as embodied in the Mistresses, and it was whispered among the young nuns that she had, in addition to the Rule, all its bylaws, bibliographies and historical references bound into her venerable frame.

Sister Luke had stood outside the workroom door for a moment to calm her childlike rebellion at the thought of someone else packing her suitcase. When she was sure her smile showed no frayed edges, she knocked and entered, murmuring, "Praised be Jesus Christ."

The Vestiaire's eyes, sharp as the needles she threaded without aid of spectacles, looked up at her and seemed to penetrate her habit right down to the drawstrings of stockings and *serre-tête*, testing their tensions. She beckoned her to approach and picked up a tape measure. She had the card of number 1072 before her with all the bodily measurements since entry. She made a cricket sound when she measured and found Sister Luke's waist three inches less than the measure at vesture a year ago.

Sister Luke hunted words that might be safely addressed to a *monument historique*, words that would not suggest criticism of the vestiary department for having possibly issued a skirt too large, or would not seem to invite pity for having lost so much weight.

"I believe, Sister," she said, "that this skirt may have stretched a bit."

She looked at the old nun examining her loose skirt band and writing the new waist measure on the 1072 clothing card. A thought struck her as she watched the veined hands scarcely moving over the card, so tiny, so space-saving was the script. For half a century in this same small corner of the immense convent world, this sister had been content to serve the Lord with her thimble, taking in the skirt bands of struggling young ones and letting them out years after when struggle reaches the equilibrium of adjustment that allows a little fat to gather at the waist. Up and down those overhead stairs whole generations of nuns have passed on their ways to schools and hospitals all over Belgium and beyond, to India, Africa, the Orient, and all that this great pageant of Christ's work being carried to the world has meant for this old nun has been an endless succession of wicker hampers filled with clothes to be mended. She managed to conceal her emotion before Sister Eudoxie looked up.

"Tonight after the *Salve*," said Sister Eudoxie, "you will find another skirt on your dressing stand and you will leave this one there when you depart tomorrow."

Sister Luke bowed and withdrew from the presence of a self-sacrifice so complete that it stunned her. As she closed the door behind her, she prayed God to give her a wider horizon for her own sacrifice to Him.

It was her turn now to enter the office of the Mistress of Novices. The Mistress was sitting at her desk. A slight flush warmed the chilly beauty of her face, suggesting that she too, despite her rigid control, had been touched by the departure emotions. Her lips curved in a smile as she handed to Sister Luke a small leather sack with the hooked chains in it, her going-away present to the young ones she had trained to fortitude.

"Remember my words on moderation," she said.

"This is not *my* discipline, Sister. Mine is the common life, the community," said Sister Luke. It was a relief to talk frankly for once, to lay down simple words of fact without all the circumlocutions of convent etiquette. "But of course you have seen that."

"I always thought you very adaptable, Sister Luke. You were one of the few who never asked to be excused."

"I don't know that I have any merit from this, but I made myself an automaton for all the community life, except of course the devotions. It has been a constant self-beating . . ."

The Mistress shook her head.

"That is not the way, Sister. Not as an automaton," she said. "But I am glad you told me and you must believe me when I tell you I understand." She paused to consider her words, then with astonishing candor, she went on: "Once, long ago, I too found the community life a pure agony. I suffered, knowing that my forced participation could never be pleasing to God. I struggled to overcome this. I thought about the Christ who took to Himself the very humblest of companions. I told myself that quite possibly He could not abide the smell of fish or the frequently childish talk of those simple disciples. Yet . . . He lived with them and spoke with them in the picturesque parables they could understand, He who had confounded the scholars of the temple when only twelve years old. That, my sister, was the first community. That is our example."

Sister Luke wished that the Mistress had not said that. She knew she would never forget the lesson or the way it had been given. It was as if the Mistress had, for an instant, taken off her mask of discipline and had let her see the aristocratic face sensitized by centuries of breeding, its thin nostrils shrinking thinner at the mention of fish odors. Her joy for escape to a smaller community and for dispensations

76

from its common life turned to a feeling of shame and guilt.

"I have felt sometimes I was exploiting the community," she said. "Taking so much from it and giving so little back."

"Because you say that, you will learn." The Mistress gave her a last smile, then became a Living Rule again.

"Now, Sister Luke," she said, "you go forth. Have always an open heart for your Superior. As for your new community, begin with it each day before you meet it. Begin the day with a review of your sisters. Some you will like, some you will not. For those you may instinctively dislike, try to do something. Remember . . . the golden rule for antipathy is to ask to do a service for the one your spirit withdraws from. There is no surer way of conquering both yourself and her. In your new community you will be one of the youngest in the life. Take every duty you see uncovered. Replace the pot-washers when one is ill. Do all this simply. Let no one remark it, only God. And for yourself," she said more slowly, "for a doctor's daughter accustomed to comfort and social position, try to be the little donkey of Jesus who goes his way without prodding. Take up every burden without inner murmuring. Take it like that little donkey who carried the hope of the world up the stony slopes of Jerusalem."

Sister Luke emerged from the Mistress's office just like all her other companions, with tears in her eyes and clutching the lumpy little sack of chains with hooks on their ends.

They left the mother house next morning after Mass.

In the chapel, they all lost the custody of their eyes. Sister Luke lost hers to the Reverend Mother Emmanuel as she knelt gaunt and rapt at her *prie-dieu*, ignoring the wayward glances from the section of the newly professed as if she knew that they needed for their long journeys the last impressions they stole with their eyes — the silvery slants of dawnlight through the chapel windows, the motionless files of more sisters than they would ever see again in one place, the single figure in motion of the Cantatrice walking up and down between the two choirs and summoning from them an *Agnus Dei* that floated soft as fleece into the silence after the Elevation. This plain chant I will miss always, Sister Luke said silently, wherever God wills that I go.

The sisters sang them out of the chapel in their new white capes with the slight train which kept them farther apart. As they paced slowly toward the doors, they heard the opening antiphon of the *Itinerary. In viam pacis . . . and may the Angel Raphael accompany us in the way, and may we return in peace, health and joy unto our own home.*

Their papier-mâché suitcases packed by Sister Eudoxie were standing neatly in rows by the main door of the mother house. They said good-by to each other with their eyes as they climbed into their separate buses — some for short journeys within the Kingdom of Belgium, others destined for ports and railroad stations through which they would travel far out on the branches of the family tree of their congregation.

Sister Luke said the *Itinerary* silently in communion with the sisters singing them on their way from behind walls she did not need to look at to remember. *May the God of our salvation give us a prosperous journey . . .*

78

V I

THE School of Tropical Medicines was housed in a handsome château in the suburbs of Brussels. The student nuns traveled to it by trolley from the *pensionnat* run by their Order. The trip was just long enough to enable them to read four of the seven daily Offices — Matins, Lauds, Prime and Tierce — and by the time Sister Luke came to Psalm 120 of Tierce, *I lift up my eyes to the mountains* . . . she knew she was passing the café where Jean used to take his coffee when he had been a university student. But she never lifted her eyes to look. The conductor called the familiar street name while her lips moved soundlessly through passages of promise. *He shall not let thy foot slip . . . The sun shall not burn thee by day, nor the moon by night . . . The Lord shall keep thee from all evil . . .*

They were four and they always sat together in the trolley — Sister Luke and her two young companions from the mother house and Sister Pauline, who carried the carfare because she was the oldest, and who did all the talking for them when it was necessary to address car conductors and policemen.

Sister Pauline had come directly from the Congo to join the trio from the mother house. She had been promoted to supervisor and furloughed home to secure a diploma in tropical medicines. From the moment Sister Luke set eyes on her lean and leathery face, she knew she had a major problem in antipathy to overcome. The sun-faded eyes that once had been blue were colorless as ice, and the icy monosyllables with which Sister Pauline answered her eager questions about the Congo conveyed the impression that that great domain of rain forest and blistering bush belonged exclusively to her and that queries about her private property were ill-bred, if not even impudent.

"Sister Pauline is a *pisse-vinaigre*," Sister Luke had whispered to her young companions after their first encounter with the senior nun. Because they were Flemish like herself, accustomed to the sight of a small bronze statue of a pissing mannikin which was the most beloved monument in their small land, they did not think it immodest to call their sister a piss-vinegar.

Sister Pauline's possessive jealousy for the Congo seemed to be an acquired trait of all who had served there. It was even more evident in the university professors who taught them. They were all bearded medical pioneers, prematurely aged by long service in the Congo, eaten gaunt by malaria and their passionate love for the land to which their health no longer permitted a return, to which, instead, they had to send the beardless young doctors, the pale priests, the nuns and lay nurses who sat before them in classrooms kept at oven heat because they, the professors, were always shivering, even on sunny days.

The professors began each day's lectures, "If any of you thinks that he is going to see, now in 1928 when there are bicycle paths through the bush, what *we* saw in the early nineteen-hundreds . . ." and then they would tell nothing of what they had seen. But their beards would twitch and their eyes glow and if their shaking hands had not been caressing a wire model of the *Anopheles rhodesiensis* enlarged a thousand times, you would have thought it was some dark goddess that haunted their emotions rather than that mosquito to which they had given the young years of their lives, both as bodily hosts for its parasites and as research minds studying its pathological effects.

Sister Luke loved them all. For her, the lecture room was a homecoming into the world of medical thought. She could see her father behind every bearded face and hear, in each professorial voice, his own impatience with laggard minds and his scorn for squeamishness when death was not decorative and had to be described in terms of deformities of scrotum and labia. She loved most of all Dr. Goovaerts, who knew her father but did not recognize her sitting there before him in the habit of a nun. Not until she had fainted in his classroom did he realize who she was.

It was the room heat that his fever-worn body demanded which overcame her. After the healthful window-wide climate of the mother house, she found the temperature of his classroom almost insupportable. Her heavy serge, her coif and veil bore her down, and on the day when he introduced his great subject, the life cycle of the mosquito, she was sure she was running a temperature.

The doctor had been humiliating the pale young priests whom he suspected, the beardless young doctors whom he deplored and the lay nurses whom he disapproved of utterly because as soon as they got to the Congo, he informed them directly, they would fall a prey to the concupiscent colonials who counted off the white women arriving on each ship like so many bags of gold. "Women," he said, gazing at the lay

81

nurses, "as soon as they hear even the hum of a mosquito, they faint . . ."

Sister Luke fainted on his word and slipped over sideways onto the knees of Sister Pauline. She came to in the corridor outside the classroom, with Dr. Goovaerts standing above her and the senior nun kneeling beside her, loosening her guimpe. "If you can't tolerate this small heat," Sister Pauline was hissing, "I don't know how you expect to stand the Congo."

"It's another kind of heat, Sister," said her father's friend, looking down on her with recognition. "She'll get used to what's out there as you have. Moreover, she'll get the whole of my year's course in the eight months your penny-pinching poverty-vowed Order allows for you, because she was looking through her father's microscope when most children her age were turning kaleidoscopes before the eyes."

Each time, thereafter, when Dr. Goovaerts began a lecture on *Anopheles*, he said, "If a certain one of our revered Sisters will promise not to faint, I shall now tell you about the conditions most favorable to the development of the larvae of the mosquito."

And nearly every day after such a sally, on the lunch hour when the four nuns drew apart from the other students to eat their sandwiches in silence in the château park and recite Sext and None, Sister Pauline would look at her with aversion. If there was time after the Offices were said, before the school bell summoned them for microscopy, she would always turn the recreational talk to the subject of singularization. Sister Luke found it incredible that the senior nun could believe she had fainted deliberately in class to draw attention to herself.

She sought in vain to find something she might do for Sister

Pauline to counteract what seemed like a mutual antipathy. Sister Pauline was as preserved from need as was the fabled princess who slept in a block of ice — her visions of the Congo frozen behind her faded eyes and sealed in jealousy behind her thin uncommunicative lips.

The microscope classes gave Sister Luke her first real view of the Congo. Here in a long room with many windows were rows of marble-topped tables, each with a microscope under a bell glass and a box of slides that had been made in the Congo. Every afternoon for eight months she sat with one eye glued to the eyepiece and her fingers playing ceaselessly with the fine adjustment screw and illuminating mirror. Down the drawtube in the radiant field of the objective was the microscopic world of the Congo basin, the beautiful and deadly shapes which caused leprosy, sleeping sickness, yaws, malaria and elephantiasis. She stared at pinpoints of life that had been stopped and fixed on the slides as ripples of silvery thread and rods straight and curved, as bunches of grapes and strings of pearly eggs, as minute transparent worms with round or flat heads and tapered tails, and sometimes in her excitement she raised a hand to her forehead, as if to brush back a hat that had got in her way with its brim-shadow. Then her fingers, touching the damp headbands of her coif, reminded her who and how she was.

She memorized the strange forms stained faintly with blue, their breeding places in blood, lymph, stools or muscle tissue, their incubating periods, life cycles and geographical distributions, as easily as if they were special tribes with personalities as distinct as the dark people from whose ailing bodies many of the organisms had been taken.

This is the Congo that I can make mine, she would think.

83

This is the wide horizon that I prayed for in my work for God.

It was a horizon measured in micrometers but to her lens-bound eyes it looked as wide as all creation, as indeed it was. She went through box after box of slides, always ahead of the other students, and before they were ready to make their own slides, she was visiting the basement with the lab technician to draw blood from the inoculated apes, rabbits and guinea pigs kept below as hosts for the diseases they studied. Sister Pauline's colorless eyes were often upon her, registering disapproval for her lack of charity in seeming to show up, by fast accomplishment, the other students, who proceeded much more slowly and with none of her excited recognition.

If it had not been for Sister Pauline, she would have felt utterly happy doing the work that her God-given memory made easy, losing herself each day in a fascinating jungle of parasites but never losing her way. She knew that Sister Pauline was having more trouble than the others; she fumbled her glass slides and often went back to the beginning of her box as though her memory were porous. Tropical medicines depended ninety per cent on memory and the senior nun's had been impaired by the large doses of quinine which everyone took daily in the Congo. Sister Luke's compassion for her nervous sister overrode her antipathy and she tried to think of ways to help her.

When she showed the other nuns how to see the difference between the *bacille de Koch* that caused tuberculosis and the *bacille de Hansen* that caused leprosy, she raised her voice, risking being conspicuous, so Sister Pauline might hear. "They are very alike," she said, "both rod-shaped, both acid-fast, both with a slight shadow almost like an enclosing capsule

. . . but if you look closely, you'll see that the leprosy bacillus seems to be slightly fatter and longer."

She wished she could tell them that all this was easy for her because her father had made her an expert in microscopic detection of the tuberculosis bacillus before she was out of pinafores. But she was in the habit of the nun now and could not mention her past life. She suffered instead the unmerited praise of her fellow students, which often made her wish she could drop from sight through the floor.

In the evenings when she sat with her three companions studying in their large common bedroom in the *pensionnat* infirmary, she would work her way through all the tedious bypaths of convent speech to try to find a way to show her transcribed notes to Sister Pauline, who would never ask to look at them and never copy frankly from them as the two other sisters often did. It would have been so simple to say to her dour senior, "My notes are good, Sister Pauline, especially for that genus *Mycobacterium* that occupies a position midway between the bacilli and the fungi. Why don't you take a look? My drawings would clarify, I think."

Instead, she would gaze worriedly at her notebook, turn its pages over as if distressed and finally say to Sister Pauline, "Would it be asking too much to have you take a look at my notes, Sister? I'm afraid I may have some mistakes." While Sister Pauline avidly read her notes, she would leave the common study table and go to her corner of the room and sit facing the wall to study the theory. She had earlier set the stage for this singularity by informing her companions that she could never study concentratedly unless she faced a wall.

The maneuverings and the reticences, the elaborate formulae of prideless speech when you felt a justifiable pride, of charitable concealment of knowledge when you knew that yours surpassed that of others, often seemed to her like hypocrisy. Was it God's wish that his vowed ones be thus?

She studied the etiology of leprosy while the etiology of the Christian community knocked at the door of her thoughts. The science of this special way of being was all in the Gospels, she knew. But why, she wondered, did it seem so much more robust in those golden passages than in its earnest imitation? Thomas doubted and was promptly invited by the Christ to come forward and put his hand in the Wound. Robust and direct, she reflected, not anything like this indirect thing I do night after night, trying with conscious effort to win over a sister I would never wish to see again, once this course is over. Not even in a painting, she told herself vigorously.

Since she had left the mother house, her emotions seemed to have come alive the way weeds do when a stone is lifted off them. They sprang upright from the airless place where she thought she had buried them, pale rubbery stalks of like and dislike, of pride and desire, which swiftly turned green and flourishing. Her concealed hopes for Congo service were now a passionate obsession. Her initial instinctive mistrust of Sister Pauline had become an antipathy she could no longer counterbalance with forced smiles of humility and charitable deceits about helping with the homework. Her twice-daily examinations of conscience told her clearly that something was wrong. A fortnight before the final tests, she decided to take her troubles to the local Mother Superior.

Mother Marcella was a woman of great interior richness who ruled her small community with enchanting grace. It had been easy for Sister Luke to keep an open heart for this Superior, whom she had admired from the first moment of meeting. Though dispensed from the community recreation, she had gone sometimes in the evening to hear the brilliant talk of Mother Marcella and her score of professor nuns. It gave her a foretaste of what she imagined the Congo communities to be — small groups of matched minds, witty, intelligent, almost worldly at times.

Equally broad in her application of the Rule as she was in her ideas, Mother Marcella gave liberal dispensations to the four transient sisters confided to her care, allowing them to rise one hour later than the community because of their late study hours and permitting speech among them after the grand silence. She seemed especially deft in her choice of their spiritual reading. Each Saturday in their pews they found a book with pages marked which she wished them to read and meditate for the week. Her selections pointed up their weak spots as she had observed them — a chapter on humility for the proud, on obedience for the headstrong, on faith for the doubters. Sister Luke found chapters on humility marked the most often for her.

On the evening when she stood outside the door of Mother Marcella's study, Sister Luke was aware that her humility had a slight shading of the heroic. She had never before gone to a Superior to discuss her relations with a sister. She was ready to admit her antipathy and her defeat in all attempts to overcome it. She would follow whatever advice the Mother Superior might give, she told herself firmly, even if it meant darning Sister Pauline's stockings for the remainder of their time together or shining her shoes each week. Nothing in the quiet hallway told her that she was standing at a crossroads of her religious life.

She knocked, entered with a bow and lifted two fingers to her lips requesting permission to speak.

"*Benedicite*," said Mother Marcella.

87

"*Dominus.*" Sister Luke looked up. The large crucifix behind the Superior's chair gave the impression it was meant to convey, that she was not kneeling before a woman.

"I am in trouble, *ma Mère*. I've come to ask the grace of your counsel." The Superior encouraged her with a nod to go on. "It is Sister Pauline. My conscience is not at peace because of her."

With scientific detachment, she recited the growth of her antipathy and each of the steps she had taken in vain to overcome it. She avoided any mention of Sister Pauline's icy conduct toward her and stressed what she believed was her senior's need for help in the course. "In all humility, *ma Mère*, I believe I could help her if she would permit friendship. What should I do?"

Mother Marcella's eyes gleamed while she was speaking, as if she were hearing a twice-told tale and knew the end before it came. She waited a few moments before replying. Her silence was a little disturbing; Sister Luke had never seen her falter for the decisive word. She looked at the hand lying lightly over the crucifix that hung beneath the Superior's bib on a level with her eyes. The long white fingers moved up and down the ebony, seeming to take thought from the touch.

"You are intelligent, Sister," said the Superior at last. "You have broad ideas. I know that you can face things I would not say to others. I should not even tell you that Sister Pauline has already come to me." She hesitated, then said, "The antipathy you describe is mutual."

Sister Luke looked steadily into the Superior's eyes.

"She apparently has many complaints," said Mother Marcella. "In sum, she thinks you are an intellectual snob. She says you have no humility and does not believe that you can ever achieve it. She even wonders why you ever came to the convent."

"I am ashamed, *ma Mère*. For her and for me. All this sounds very childish when you tell it."

"It is not precisely childish. One might say uncharitable on the part of the older nun, but not childish," said Mother Marcella. "Her antipathy, I believe, is based on fear. She worries that she will not pass the examinations or, if she does, that she will be far below you in grade. You can understand how difficult it can be for an older sister to be superseded by a first-professed, as Sister Pauline most certainly will be, from all I have been told of your progress."

Sister Luke felt her heartbeat quicken. The small room, furnished frugally with desk, chair and a tall bookcase from which were drawn their spiritual readings, seemed to close in about her like a box. The Mother Superior gazed at her as if hoping that she herself would speak and suggest the thought she appeared to be taking up and putting down. Her silence was eloquent with indecision. Then Sister Luke saw the hand tighten about the crucifix.

"You have been given a truly great opportunity to make a sacrifice for God," said Mother Marcella. "He dowered you with a precious gift, a brain retentive, muscular and articulate. You asked what you might do." Again she fell silent, weighing her words. "Would you, Sister Luke, be big enough, tall enough, to fail your examinations to show humility?"

She swayed on her knees as if the floor had moved. She stared with shock at her Superior. The luminous eyes set deep in sculptured sockets held her with infinite compassion, knowing the full measure of what had been asked. But had she the right? Sister Luke asked herself wildly. Had anyone except the Superior General herself the right to suggest such a thing? Her hands beneath her scapular seemed to twist out the answer. Anyone has the right, she told herself, anyone at all in our peculiar God-vowed world, if it is seen that you lack humility or need strengthening in what little you have of it. You had this coming to you. It was inevitable from the start. You were even proud of your submission when you came to this room to confess defeat.

"*Ma Mère*," she whispered, "I would be willing, if . . ." her scapular moved visibly above her wringing hands ". . . if the mother house knows of it and approves." Bargaining again with Him, said the inner voice, never the perfection of all, as He wishes.

"Then it would not be for God alone," said the Superior as Sister Luke knew she would say. "It would be, as we say, a humility with hooks, a humility that takes something back for the sacrifice. In this case, the satisfaction of knowing that the mother house knows."

"Courage needs witnesses," Sister Luke said involuntarily. Her father used to say that. *Le courage a besoin des témoins*, he would say and discount all the bemedaled heroes to point out the unknown real one who had died alone, unseen, near the ground.

"Yes," said Mother Marcella. "Real humility, on the other hand, passes unperceived between God and the soul."

She had one more question. It was one she was going to be asking for the rest of her religious life, in all sorts of places and circumstances and always on her knees.

"How can I know He would want this from me?"

"Go and ask Him," said the Superior.

Sister Luke bowed her head for the benediction. All the struggles she had passed through were but a prelude to what

90

lay ahead. She went immediately to the chapel and buried her face in her hands.

She tried to look at the sacrifice that had been suggested to her by one who quite possibly could have been God's chosen instrument. She saw herself standing before Dr. Goovaerts and the examining board, making wrong answers to questions while her father's friend gazed at her with unbelief and disgust. She saw herself looking down a microscope at the filaroid worm *Loa loa* and writing *Wuchereria bancrofti* on the blank ticket attached to her slide. Her father's face came clear into the field of the objective, bewildered, shocked and shamed by her failure.

"Oh God," she whispered, "it would be wasting all those months of Your time." But her training told her that He would be happy if it were in humility for Him. She knew that this was indisputable. She knew too that she was weighing an opportunity she would never have again. Out of His eternal time, she reminded herself, God chooses His moment to offer the most perfect alliance with each individual soul. And this is mine, she thought. I can take it or I can leave it. If I take it, He might make no sign whatsoever. On the other hand, He might shower me with graces and bring me close to sainthood. If I don't take it . . .

"This I cannot do, O Lord."

Then she saw in the mirror the Superior had held up to her, the inner awful mirror of the mirrorless convent world, all the cords that bound her to the selves of pride from which she had fancied herself detached. They were no silken cords. They were cable-thick and they ran out from her like jungle lianas extending even into the distance of childhood, when pride of family was born in the phrase *la famille du docteur* which set her apart socially from the children of mere businessmen. She followed each long trailer to its end and saw maturer things she nourished still — her pride of intellect, of judgment, of her ability to achieve whatever she set out to do.

"Must I now do this for You, O my God? Do You really ask it?" She tasted the tears in her hands and waited.

There was an abyss of silence in the chapel. Christ would not speak to her, she knew, but He might inspire. If He wished, He might answer through her conscience. But even then, she thought, you could never know truly whether it was your imagination, your own desire cloaked, or His inspiring. Only the great pure souls could be sure. I should never have tried to be a nun. The path is too steep for my strength. . . .

With her tears she tasted the most poignant experience of the nun — the deep silence between Christ and the soul in trouble. She waited but her conscience told her nothing. It lay heavy and mute within her, an organ in trauma.

The Mistress of Novices spoke out of memory. "You have only one aim, one constant dedication, one unique desire in the religious life," she said. "It is to please God. Nothing else matters, absolutely nothing else. We have spoken often of the lilies of the field created by God for His pleasure alone. That is your example. Though you toil in kitchens, schoolrooms and hospitals and produce many good works in His name, He is pleased only in how you grow inwardly. That is why He gave us those lilies of the field to consider."

The kitchen, laundry and gardener nuns who seldom came in contact with human beings in the world were lilies of the field. Their lives in Christ called for no choice because their tubs, tools and casseroles presented none. They joked at their heavy work and were gay. They had the ideal conscience of the nun, a conscience with nothing on it, like a child's before conscience awakens. *Une conscience légère*, they called it in the convent. I'll never have it again, she thought.

The mirror was always there between her tear-wet palms and the eyes she pressed shut with them. In giant magnification she now saw bright red disks sliding over the silver and she said to God, This is bird blood and this next is monkey blood and here now is human blood and you can see, Blessed Lord, how swiftly I can tell them apart . . . as I must do down there when I trace these tropical diseases through the blood of chickens, cattle and monkey pets that your natives come in contact with, and also your priests and civil administrators isolated in lonely posts in the bush. Would I not please you in taking this knowledge where it is needed? O God, don't ask me to give up the Congo . . .

The abyss of silence was awful in its depth, width and height. Her heartbeat hammered into it like asking drums and no sound came back out of it.

While she waited, she had her first deep experience of real humility as she saw how little she had of it. After all the struggling, after all the systematic slayings of small prides one by one, day after day for two years, she had touched only the outer edges of that jungle where I, Me and Mine flourished in a thousand forms. She had never known that she had this inborn sense of her own worth, a form of pride so deeply buried in her that she had never seen it until now when she was asking if, for the sake of humility to God alone, she could do the thing that would make her seem worthless in the eyes of the medical world.

"Humility." She whispered the soft syllables longingly.

The Irish girls once taught her a couplet from one of their country's poets:

93

Humility, that low, sweet root
From which all heavenly virtues shoot.

That was long ago in the mother house. That was when she had been an infant in the religious life and had thought that humility was a bowing and a bending and a begging of the soup. After a long while she left the chapel.

The last two weeks of the course were so fearful in their intensity and took so much out of all the students that Sister Luke's pallor passed unnoticed. She was preparing for two examinations, one of herself in humility and the other, easier one in tropical medicines.

Each day she walked beside Sister Pauline from the trolley stop to the university gate, with the two younger sisters following close behind them, and she would feel nothing about her silent partner except pity for her obvious state of nerves. Never once did she relate Sister Pauline in any way to her own inner torment.

In classes she studied with concentration. Even had she known what would be the outcome of her examination of self, even had she known that she would find the strength to fail deliberately, she would have gone on studying. Her nun's training in making full use of every moment of God's time would have made it impossible for her to fritter away the final weeks in pretended attention. She was there to study. Whatever the task of the moment, it must be done as perfectly as possible.

Dr. Goovaerts grew almost savage as he took them through the last big review of the total course. His fevered eyes swept over the rows of pallid people who wanted to go to the Congo, cherishing them for their choice though he acted as if he despised them all. He seemed to be trying to kill them then and there with the fevers, the dysenteries, the tropical skin ulcerations, the nematode, tapeworm and fluke infections he flung at them, first in great subject headings, then in long lists of crippling polysyllables — *trypanosomiasis, frambesia, ancylostomiasis, lymphopathia venereum* . . . You could hear memories bending and breaking in the room. When he stopped for breath and listened to the scratching of their pens, he pulled at his beard as if he would throw that at them too in his red-eyed eagerness that they should have the whole of him, they who were taking over his malignant and wonderful world.

Occasionally in the final days he fell in step beside Sister Luke after class and asked her, as a doctor to the daughter of a doctor, how he had performed, and once her heart stopped when he told her that he had telephoned to her father to tell him about her own performance in the course.

That had to be in it too, she thought afterwards. Papa had to be told that I was living up to the reputation of the family. And she saw him smiling and nodding as he held the receiver to his ear, listening to his old friend saying, Your daughter isn't doing too badly . . . not badly at all, in fact.

Then she saw with her father's eyes of the world the incredible sacrifice that had been suggested to her. It would be beyond any mentality outside the cloister to understand the simple logic of it. The simple logic, she went over it again and again, is that I am still proud and that I add to Christ's sorrows by being so. I was going to try to be a good nun, the best if I could. I kept looking for ways. Now a way has been pointed out. I need only say in the oral exams that the tsetse fly seems to have a tendency to alight on white instead of on black, though I know that its tendency to come down on

95

the black skins is the reason why good colonials dress their native workers in white as much as possible. Which is why sleeping sickness is relatively rare among Europeans and a scourge among the Blacks. I need only begin with an unproved but often observed thing like that, then go on to proved facts and say, in deliberate misstatement, that yaws is a form of syphilis because it is caused by a spirochete and is contagious. All the facts I know about the mosquito I could say opposite. The adult mosquito lives on fruit and plant juices, but the female requires a blood meal for the maturation of its eggs, not necessarily human or mammalian blood but maybe avian or reptilian blood. I could say that the mosquito never breeds in birds and snakes.

I could say, O Lord, that enlargement of the lymphatic glands is not one of the most characteristic visible signs of the first stages of sleeping sickness though I have looked at hundreds of photos of glandular enlargement in early stages and have that primary symptom fixed in my mind forever. *What am I going to say? Will You tell me when the time comes?*

Her whole being rocked with the inner disturbance. She seemed to split apart into two debating teams with several selves on either side. That she could bear up under the constant contending was proof of the strength already instilled in her by the convent training. But this she could not realize.

She skipped most of the final study hours and spent the time in the chapel. There was always that abyss of silence. The vigil light became the red eye of Dr. Goovaerts, growing larger and redder as she stared at it and waited for some Voice other than her own or her professor's. Will you please name for the board, Sister, the intermediate hosts of the parasite *Onchocerca* and give us a brief symptomatology? *It is an ordinary life lived extraordinarily,* said the Mistress of Novices; *this is the essence of our way and we will remind you of it often until your own experiencing becomes your constant reminder.* . . . *Messieurs les Docteurs*, it is an ordinary life lived extraordinarily . . . and the red eye widened and the professor shouted, I am not asking you about the life cycle of the nun, Sister . . . The *Onchocerca* produces tumors of the skin varying in size from a pea to a hen's egg . . . O God, I *must* say that unless You prompt me otherwise.

"Is it wise to go so often to the chapel?" asked Sister Pauline. "It would seem to me that we serve the Lord best at this time by staying close to our studies. Can you imagine what a scandal it would be for the mother house if any one of us failed?"

"I can imagine only too well, Sister." She looked at the vinegary countenance, surprised to see real anxiety reflected in it. "I have put it in God's hands," she added in a gentler tone.

"Very laudable, of course. But surely He expects us to come halfway to help Him during those eight days of examination. Moreover," said Sister Pauline, "the mother house will offer tomorrow's Mass for our intention. The help we need will be asked for us."

It gave Sister Luke an odd turn to hear this. The eight months away from the mother house had not dimmed her memory of its psalmodizing sisters and the purity and perfection with which they offered up their daily Mass. Perhaps this very night in the recreation, the Reverend Mother Emmanuel would be reminding them that tomorrow would begin the days of test for four of their sisters and some of the artist or clerical nuns would doubtless be saying, "That must be atrocious, *Révérende Mère* . . . to have to learn all about

97

those fleas and flies in so short a time." Tomorrow, Sister Luke thought, they will sing their hearts into the *Kyrie* for us . . . for me.

She opened her text and read: *In the tsetse fly, trypanosomes will be found in the gut, mouth parts and salivary glands, in all of which sites they multiply.* She had no idea what she was going to do.

She didn't know until her turn came for the orals before the examining board. Dr. Goovaerts, with six doctors beside him at the long table, gave no sign of preference or recognition when she came in the door. But when she was seated opposite the row of bearded faces, his eyes flashed her a look of connivance. "I shall defer to my eminent colleagues for the first question," he said. His challenging tone seemed to say, Trip this one up if you can, my friends.

The malariologist cleared his throat and delivered the first question with the solemnity of a death sentence.

"The board would like to hear from the Sister a résumé of the special clinical types of pernicious, as differentiated from chronic or latent, malaria, naming no less than four of its forms as discoverable through their symptoms."

She counted five of the forms on her fingers beneath the scapular — cerebral, algid, bilious remittent fever, blackwater fever and the bronchopneumonic form — while the doctor continued, "You may take your time with this, Sister. *We* have been working on it since the eighteen-eighties."

She took time to say inwardly, *Thy will* . . . Then she began to speak.

She knew she had passed the examinations before the official results were published. On the eighth and final day, Dr. Goovaerts walked toward the door with the four sisters. His aside to Sister Luke was delivered in an offhand manner.

"You may telephone your father tonight and tell him to have a platter of oysters delivered to the convent for you," he said.

"We are not permitted to use the telephone for personal messages, *Monsieur le Docteur*," replied Sister Pauline for her.

He lifted his hat as he walked away to his car. His glance of amusement told Sister Luke that he would telephone to her father himself.

The rule of silence kept Sister Pauline from asking any questions about those baffling oysters but her eyes told what she thought about doctors who addressed nuns in code and nuns who invited such intimacies. That night in the recreation, Mother Marcella announced to the assemblage that all four sisters had passed the examination. She handed out the diplomas sent special delivery from the university. Each diploma guaranteed a post in the colonies. Sister Luke wondered, as she received hers, if she had given it to herself or if God had.

The Mother Superior drew her apart and said, "I do not know if I should regret my suggestion to you, Sister. It was an inspiration of the moment. You passed fourth in the class of eighty."

"And I do not know, *ma Mère*, who inspired the answers to the questions." She looked at her parchment. "Nevertheless, this is not mine. It belongs to the congregation and any salary earned through it."

"Ah yes, the congregation will profit, Sister Luke." The Superior was silent for a moment. "But your failure," she said wistfully, "would have been a gift to God."

V I I

THE letter from the mother house did not explain why Sister Luke was not to be sent directly to the Congo. She was to be attached for an indefinite time to the mental diseases sanatorium run by her Order in southern Belgium.

She told herself that her diploma in psychiatric nursing must be the reason for her assignment, that the Superior General doubtless wished her to have actual practice in mental nursing so as to make her more valuable in the Congo service. She reread in her tropical medicines text the pages on tropical neurasthenias and mental changes resulting from pellagra and tried to persuade herself that she was guessing rightly about something she had no right even to guess about. In the convent, you went where you were told to go.

She could not resist asking Sister Pauline on their last recreation together if there was much insanity in the Congo. Sister Pauline was a changed woman since she had received her diploma. All the vinegar had gone out of her face.

"Everybody is a little crazy in the Congo, my sister," she said. "There is something about the country itself that deranges. The grandeur of everything, the tremendous horizons . . . ah, those horizons! But of course that is not what you asked."

Her face when she talked about the land to which she was

returning made Sister Luke think of the photographs in the convent magazine of nuns returning for their second or third tour of duty in the missions. Grouped under captions — *2ᵉ départ, 3ᵉ départ* — the white-bibbed busts capped stiffly with coifs framed faces of such sudden life as to give the impression that the departing ones had thrust them through a hole in the paper to look at you with a secret smile.

"There is not much insanity as we know it," said Sister Pauline. "I would say that our natives are more normal than any race on earth . . . except when they drink the mysterious beer they brew from roots, maybe manioc, no one knows for sure and no one can ever find out. Then sometimes they go berserk if they cannot dance it off."

She paused as if she heard the drums. There was that secret smile. Then she went on: "They call it *simba*, though it is nothing at all like the famous Simba Beer the Belgians brew in the Katanga. Only the name's the same. *Simba* — lion in their language."

"*Simba*," said Sister Luke. Her first word in Kiswahili was as easy as a sigh to say.

She left the *pensionnat* directly from the refectory after breakfast. Farewells were never said in the convent except by the Mother Superior, who always accompanied the departing one to the door of the house and there gave her benediction. But the nuns nevertheless made little signs to her as she passed, discreet hand waves when the Superior's back was turned and smiles that said very clearly, We shall miss you.

Mother Marcella embraced her on both cheeks just inside the front door, the first time anyone had touched her since the sisterly embraces at vesture. She knelt for the benediction. Then the Superior opened the door, looked out to see if the chaperone was there, and smiled farewell.

Her chaperone was one of the odd little ladies who lived like swallows in the crannies of all the convent houses except the mother house. They were all elderly and without family. Considered by the Order too sprightly to be relegated to the old folks' home, they were permitted to live with the nuns and perform light tasks such as chaperoning them to and from the dentist, fetching stamps or something from the pharmacy, or sitting by the telephones when the nuns were all in the chapel. They had their food, their tiny rooms, and they were provided with black garments which they wore like a uniform of gentility. Most of all they liked to chaperone a nun through city streets. In their eyes the sisters were the salt of the earth and they showed this by their constant surveillance of them in public.

One called Sophie had a taxi already summoned. She looked to see if Sister Luke had on her black gloves for travel, smoothed her own, which were exactly like those the nuns wore, and opened the taxi door. Sophie instructed the driver to take the shortest route to the railroad station. No roundabout for us who are vowed to poverty, said her sharp eyes watching the taximeter.

At the station, Sophie signaled her to wait by the door while she queued up for a ticket. She watched the old lady elbow her way ahead of two stragglers in the line so as to get her nun onto the train in time to find a window seat in the crowded third class. Sophie was happily unaware that nuns always found seats in trains. The habit, the exterior sign, made people draw away from you, preferring to sit anywhere than beside a nun. Sometimes when incoming passengers looked into the compartment and saw you sitting there, they did not bother to lower their voices when they said, "Not here!

There's a black crow," as they walked past. To be called a black crow always gave Sister Luke a little twist of pain.

Her new madhouse world hidden away in a corner of Belgium might have been not only on another continent, like the Congo, but even on another planet, so strange and unearthly were all its sights, sounds and customs. It was a self-sustaining village-sized enclosure surrounded by high walls inside of which prowled the female inmates muttering and cursing — the charity cases in their subdivision crying, "I spit on you!" to the tallest nuns Sister Luke had ever seen, and the paying cases in their section calling their habited guardians "Species of crow!" "Species of sorceress!" Except for the dangerously demented, nobody here was physically restrained.

The Superior, Mother Christophe, was a magnificent nun. An Englishwoman in the prime of life, she ruled her inverted world of a thousand deranged females and a hundred overworked nuns with courage and poise. She never dramatized, always minimized, and taught her nuns to do likewise. She herself conducted Sister Luke through the many installations and gave in fluent French with a very engaging accent the facts and figures of her domain and the names and peculiarities of every patient they met en route.

Sister Luke's first impression of her new community was that everyone in it was larger than life and had the most dominating eyes she had ever looked into. Every nun's eyes looked up and out, which in itself was such a reversal of cloister practice as to make their habits seem like masquerade. Their attention to exterior signs, sounds and changes of sounds was developed to a phenomenal degree since their very lives depended on sharp and constant observation. Suddenly she understood a thing that had puzzled her since her novitiate days in the mother house. When outside nuns had come there for a retreat, the local sisters had always been able to point out the alienists to the young ones, saying, "That one and that one come from our insane asylum." Their sharp attention to every sound and movement around them set them apart from sisters whose lives had been spent suppressing exteriorized awareness. In the mother house refectory, she remembered how when a fork was dropped, theirs were the only eyes that turned to the source of the sound.

The practical lay nurses who assisted them had the same sharp observation. They looked like female giants — stout farm girls trained by the nuns but not diplomaed in psychiatry. Two of them were with every nun in the gardens, standing nearby with arms folded while she controlled and kept at a distance with a level stare the wild-eyed women who cursed them with the voices of importuning lovers.

"Our practical nurses," said Mother Christophe, "can stand only a four-hour shift, but our sisters take unlimited duty, sometimes remaining for eight or ten hours at a stretch with brief relief for meals and prayers."

They started with a tour of the *observatoire*, where all incoming patients were kept for a week or two under observation until the type and extent of the derangement were known. Here were the top alienists of Belgium, many of them known by name to Sister Luke. From there, Mother Christophe led her to the pavilion of the paying patients, mentioning names that could be found in the Almanach de Gotha. Each of the nondangerous — alcoholics, epileptics and semi-agitated — had a special apartment luxuriously furnished. Sister Luke looked at a baroness peaceably eating the geraniums in her window box and heard her Superior say calmly, "We'll plant others tomorrow." In another apartment, a young woman was on her knees eating from a plate on the floor.

"That is the Countess de V.," said Mother Christophe. "She thinks she is a dog and will not touch food unless it is given to her on that coarse dish which must always be placed on the floor. She is a brilliant woman otherwise, as you will discover. You will be attached to this pavilion."

Beyond the private apartments, but part of the wing, was a long corridor of padded cells for the dangerous lunatics. Each cell had an inch-thick window with louvered opening at the top. The Superior spoke to those who looked out on them as they passed. "This one," she said, indicating a handsome blonde whose china-blue eyes smiled sweetly at her, "thinks she is Archangel Gabriel and we call her that. *Bon jour, Archange*," she said. When they had moved on, she said, "You may never enter that cell alone. Always two or three."

At the end of the long corridor of padded cells were the bathrooms where the major treatment of the violent cases was given. Through the hermetically sealed windows Sister Luke looked in upon a purgatorial scene. There were twelve tubs in the room, each covered by a stout canvas or by a wooden hatch that screwed down, each cover with a hole at one end through which protruded a madwoman's head. A dull subhuman roar could be heard through the small hole in the door into which fitted the triangular notched key that opened all the knobless doors in this section. A single nun sat in the middle of the bath scene watching the twelve tubs.

"When we go in," said Mother Christophe, "you'll not be able to hear me. This is the treatment for our dangerously demented. We coat them with vaseline and put them in water maintained automatically at constant temperature and keep them there, according to doctors' orders, four to eight hours

a day. Because the atmosphere in there is so disturbing, we want to provide an occasional relief for the sister, who often stays on for eight or ten hours. This is why we needed you. You are momentarily the only sister in transit who possesses the degree in psychiatry necessary for working in this community."

"I understand, *ma Mère*," said Sister Luke. She tried to keep her sudden relief from showing. Mother Christophe read instantly the emotion she had not concealed.

"You are still very young to go to the Congo," she said, "though we know your heart is already there." Her pleasant tone showed she held no rancor for having had to receive a reluctant nun. "Our Reverend Mother Emmanuel perhaps would not have spared you to us, had you been a little older, a little more in the mold. This vineyard, meanwhile, will be an excellent proving ground."

The Superior opened the door. The total lamentations were now loosed in the room. It was almost impossible to believe that only twelve maniacs could produce those waves of singing, cursing and praying that mounted in crazy laughter, broke and began again, with rhythmless terrible beat, without end. Sister Luke looked at the back of the seated nun who could endure eight or more hours sealed up with insanity in this humid tiled room.

The nun, following the movements of eyes in the tubs, turned, stood up and made her deep hand-crossing bow to her Superior. The antique salutation so full of grace stopped the howls from the tubs for an instant while the wild eyes watched. Then the howling resumed while the nun wrote her name on a slip of paper and showed it with a smile to Sister Luke. *Soeur Marie de Jésus* was written on the paper in a script as delicate as Valenciennes lace.

A chic type, Sister Luke thought, with a courage beyond anything I've seen. She felt an instant bond with the tall nun standing beside her with her eyes ever on the neck-holes of the tub covers, turning only for an instant to the paper on which she wrote, *They try for ways to suicide. That thumping you hear is their heels beating up and down. They beat their heels raw and feel nothing.* Sister Luke could not hear the drumming heels.

Sister Marie led them to the door and let them out with her skeleton key, locking herself in with her maniacs and their terrible cries. Only a nun could do it, Sister Luke thought.

The comparative silence of the padded cell corridor made her ears ring. The Archangel Gabriel thrust her face against the glass and called out *"Au revoir, chérie!"* as she went by. It was so long since she had been called *chérie* that she blushed.

She was trembling when she emerged from the pavilion. There was a flicker of the odd presentiment she always had when death was near. The specialized awareness was something she had known ever since she could remember and it often made trouble for her with doctors when their diagnoses were hopeful and she would shake her head and say, "If you will excuse me, Doctor, I believe we should call a priest."

She looked at the twelve-foot fence surrounding the begonia beds in the private patients' gardens and saw them sauntering about, and thought, There are a dozen people in this place who could die at any moment. She tried to shake off her foreboding but the great dark eyes of Sister Marie and the china-blue eyes of the patient called Archangel Gabriel remained in her thoughts. She remembered this afterwards. She had already met two of the three persons who were going to live indefinitely in her memory though one of them was to

die; the third was the tall elderly woman with heavy ankles coming toward them now through the begonia beds.

The woman had a brown paper bag on her head. Her walk caught Sister Luke's attention even more than the bag. It was the convent walk, swayless and smooth. The patient advanced with downcast eyes in imitation of a nun approaching a Superior. That of course was one of the faculties of the deranged, she recalled, as she watched the perfect imitative reverence the madwoman made to Mother Christophe. When the patient looked up, her face under the brown paper bag had the gentleness of a child's and, like a child's, was without crease or crow's-foot.

"That was the Abbess," said Mother Christophe afterwards. "She is an easy patient so long as you keep her supplied with paper bags. She wears one summer and winter, day and night."

Sister Luke ventured a comment. "One would imagine, *ma Mère*, that she had been a nun."

"She was," said the Superior. "She is laicized now, of course. Once she was an Abbess in a contemplative order."

Sister Luke cast a startled look back at the paper-coifed woman who had once been a Living Rule. The Abbess had a finger to her lips as a fellow inmate chattered at her. She was maintaining the rule of silence.

Sister Luke became used to it after a while.

She learned that sedatives were to be given only as a last resort and then as sparingly as possible, that the approach even to a dangerous patient was through gentle persuasive reasoning and that everything *they* did was to be accepted as if it were normal. She accustomed herself to praying in chapel with her eyes wide open when it was her turn to chaperone in-

mates to Mass, and she learned to use her eyes as her experienced sisters did — like swiveling lenses that moved from antic to antic, suppressing by anticipation the attention-getting tricks of her charges without having any of those queer gyrations enter into her brain as impressions calling for action.

It took her some time to know all her sisters since half of them slept by day in this wracked world that had to have wide-awake eyes upon it twenty-four hours around the clock. She often looked for the enlarged moth eyes of Sister Marie, but that brave one was switched to night duty shortly after her arrival and it was a month before she encountered her again, except in the recreation room conversations.

"When Sister Marie returns to day duty," the nuns told her, "then none other of us needs to sit in the patients' section in chapel. You know she is there with them and that nothing can happen."

It was in her eyes, they said. She had only to look at a madwoman making ready to fling into song at the Elevation and the impulse died under her gaze. She never said no to a patient who wished to go to Mass. She believed that mere exposure to the Holy Eucharist helped, in some way, the human wrecks she cared for, and she would sit with twenty or thirty of them and not a sound would ever be heard except the cracking of the joints of the old ones as they flung their arms into the air in ecstatic imitation of the priestly gestures at the altar.

Mother Christophe permitted her nuns to talk shop in the recreation long enough for them to unwind from the tensions of the day but not long enough to become involved in the more bizarre half of the double lives they led. Sister Luke followed the talk with burning interest. Except for her few visits to the recreation in the *pensionnat*, this was her first real ex-

perience of a recreation with Living Rules. She discovered that they had specialties in their perfecting — some concentrating on the poverty vow, some on obedience and some on charity. It was odd to hear them speak of these ancient struggles in self-perfecting almost in the same breath with which they discussed aspects of precocious dementias, responses to delusional systems, and all the types of hallucinations which they had to seem to share with their patients in order to be able to reason with them.

This ideal of trying to reason with lesioned brains seemed to Sister Luke, in the beginning, almost a folly in itself. The toll it took from the nuns was never visible when she was working with them in the wards, where lunatic eyes were upon them all, but in the evenings when they appeared in recreation, their faces were as bleached as their coifs and, except for their powerful eyes, seemed to be of a piece with them. Her father would have called it nonsensical to spend so much energy on their cases when one round of hypos would have done the trick of quietening. But, she reminded herself, that was not the way of nuns, who believed that in each mumbling human vegetable they tended there lived a soul undamaged which might, just possibly, be reached through patience, courage and constant care.

In such a setting, until you became accustomed, the weekly culpa sounded like something being read off a crumbling parchment from the Middle Ages. A walk with precipitation when a madwoman was pursuing you was still a walk with precipitation, to be proclaimed in open session before all your sisters, along with the vainglory and overconfidence which had got you into that situation in the first place. A meditation missed because a patient had you locked in the bathroom of her private apartment was your imperfection for forgetting the nearness of meditation time when you entered that apartment, knowing from experience the time-consuming strategies required to effect a quiet exit. No nun of course ever gave the reasons for lateness or obligations missed. But you knew them when the low voices named the faults, cutting them clean from a context to which you had often been a startled witness.

Every Wednesday and Friday night in the nuns' dormitory, the senior began the *Miserere* after lights out; but only in the first days when you heard the clink of chains you knew were falling over bare backs in this place of so many other sacrifices did you think that you were listening (and contributing to) the sound of excess — pure, heroic and unique in a modern world that elsewhere chose the careful middle way of tepid souls. The familiar cloister assumed only briefly the aspect of a living museum conserving the penitential ways of mankind when Christ was nearer. Then, like the hallucinations you dealt with daily, the troubling vision faded. You swung your scourge, thought of your sins and murmured the psalm through to the final lines, *Then shalt Thou accept the prescribed sacrifices, oblations and holocausts* . . . after which you could put your discipline back into its leather bag and climb onto your straw sack to the great reward of closing your eyes.

VIII

FROM her first day on duty, Sister Luke felt herself drawn to the two patients who were at the opposite poles of mental derangement — the Abbess, with the single mania which made her only gently queer, and the Archangel Gabriel, who was a diagnosed case of dementia praecox in its schizophrenic form.

The Abbess's peculiarity was poverty. In the contemplative order where once she had ranked high, the practice of poverty was a strict rule but never, apparently, strict enough to suit her. She was suspected of practicing many secret self-denials and was regarded as a saint by her nuns until the day they found her in the convent library with many rare manuscripts in it carefully cut up into inch-square bits. She told her shocked nuns that those glowing illuminated manuscripts had been troubling her conscience. All that gold was a sign of lack of poverty, so she destroyed the parchments as seemed proper.

For poverty's sake she now slept on the floor in the middle of her private apartment, on a mattress she had long since shredded into small squares, along with every sheet and blanket subsequently given to her. She called her fluffed-up pile of mattress-stuffing and rags her dunghill, and the only desire she had left was to die like Job on his dunghill. In addition to her mania, her chart recorded a heart disease that contributed to a dropsy which would have immobilized most women of her age; but the Abbess took her daily walk at the hour when, as a nun, she had made her obligatory stroll in the cloister.

Sister Luke never saw the mad side of the old nun because she never contradicted her or tried to get her off her scrap heap onto a bed. The Abbess called her "my child," as if she were one of her nuns, and waited for her daily visit so she could exhibit the latest poem she had written, or sing in a trained contralto a song she had composed in the night. Sometimes the Abbess spoke about life in the convent, the struggles and self-denials about which the world knew so little, and she would ask Sister Luke lucid questions about her own spiritual progress, as if she were a functioning Superior again. Once, on an impulse, Sister Luke told her about her hopes for a Congo assignment.

"That will be of course as God wills," said the Abbess. "But you must continue praying for it and I, meanwhile, will add my prayers to yours." It gave Sister Luke a curious consolation each time she saw the Abbess present in the chapel and praying with fervor. Even when she was on the eve of one of her periodic attacks, she performed her religious duties with great grace and sanctity.

The Archangel Gabriel on the other hand could never be trusted anywhere but inside her padded cell or in the tub under a screwed-down hatch. She was exactly what her chart stated — a schizophrenic with all the familiar observable states of stupor, incoherence and impulsive acts. It took three of the practical nurses to wrestle her into the sacklike garment called a *maillot* that encased her whole body from neck to ankles and left just the feet free so she could hop with small steps down the corridor to the baths. Even so, when she hopped past the desk where Sister Luke was on duty, she would always pause and call out "*Allô, chérie!*" with joyful recognition.

Sister Luke was certain that one day she would penetrate the weird inner world of the Archangel, which seemed to be peopled mainly by male angels and winged stallions. When coherent, the Archangel would talk sanely about her farm. The winged stallions of her mania then became the Percheron horses she used to breed — a draft beast far superior to the Clydesdales and the Shires, she said proudly, no matter how much the English bragged about their too heavily fetlocked breeds. Fetlocks, she told Sister Luke, were no good in furrows.

"Sister Luke is the little friend of the Archangel," said the nuns in recreation. Their nods of approval for her having gained the confidence of one of their most difficult cases would ordinarily have embarrassed her. The fact that they did not failed to warn her that she nursed a secret pride for her ability with the deranged.

Pride never lasted long in the convent. But very often its owners were brought to their falls in such roundabout ways that it took a lot of piecing together, afterwards, to be able to see the relation of the fall to the fault.

Sister Luke believed that she was being the little donkey of the community when she offered to take the night watch for Sister Marie on the evening of Mother Christophe's name-day fête. There was to be a party in the recreation with the special indulgence of cakes and chocolate for the occasion.

Mother Christophe looked at her sharply when she made her request to see if it was for reasons of personal attachment, which would have brought an instant veto to the unusual offer.

"You are young to be alone at that desk in the wing of the

dangerous patients," said the Superior. "Since it was Sister Marie's duty, I've already given permission to the two practical nurses to attend the party."

"The patients know me, *ma Mère*."

Mother Christophe pondered a moment. "Very well, then. But only from eight to nine tonight, after which Sister Marie will resume."

The padded cell corridor was quiet. Sister Luke walked past the heavy windows and looked in upon each patient. Tranquilized by their baths, most of them were in their beds. The Archangel's eyes were wide open but they gave no sign of recognition.

Sister Luke went back to her desk and sat down, putting from her thoughts the overtones of almost a personal anxiety in Sister Marie's voice when she had said, "You will promise, Sister, to ring this bell if any one of them raps for attention?"

It was pleasant to be alone, a treat as rare in the convent as were the cakes and chocolate being consumed in the recreation room. She took from beneath her scapular Tante Colette's last letter and reread the lines that had amused her: *Your father is incensed that they waste you in that idiot asylum after taking that strenuous course. What can you possibly learn in such a place?* Obedience, she thought. That's what I'll try to explain next time I'm permitted to write a letter home. There was a gentle rapping on one of the cell windows.

It was the Archangel standing at her window in her long white nightgown and asking plaintively, like an overgrown child, for a drink of water.

"I'm thirsty, dearie," she whispered upward toward the louvers, showing awareness of people around her who slept and should not be disturbed. Sister Luke searched the blue eyes. They had no more wildness than a summer sky. "A thirst of all the devils," said the Archangel. The colloquial phrase had a persuasive familiarity.

Sister Luke went to the tap and drew a paper cup of water. It seemed ridiculous for so small a matter to ring the bell and bring Sister Marie and two assistants out of a party that came but once a year. She could open the door just a crack, hand in the paper cup and shut it quickly while the Archangel drank. The thirsty one could keep the cup. It was not anything she could break and slit her veins with. The worst she could do would be to eat it afterwards, she thought. Two years of obedience fell away from her as she walked toward the cell alone.

She took the skeleton key in her left hand and the cup in her right. The Archangel waited as relaxed as a sleepy child. Her blue eyes on the paper cup seemed not to have noticed that only one stood outside the door. Sister Luke slid the key in the lock, turned the latch and kept her eyes on the Archangel's face as she thrust the cup through the crack. The next instant, her whole body followed the cup.

The steel fingers that had closed about her wrist yanked her off her feet and through the slight opening that her flying body widened in passing. Before she landed, the Archangel had her veil stripped off. The starched coif and headbands gave way like tissue paper while she was still on her knees. The guimpe choked, then it was off. She lunged upward, caught one of the wild arms and clung to it while the other reached for her scapular and tore it away. There wasn't a sound except the crazed whisper, *"Chérie! Chérie!"* and once the clink of her belt, key ring and crucifix falling together on the padded floor. She thought of the skeleton key still in the

116

door, mercifully not attached to her belt. Twice as she wrestled from wall to wall, she kicked the door open wider. Her prayers were continuous gasps, her heart bleeding out for mercy. She wasn't fighting for her own life but for the lives of the fifteen others in that corridor and for the old Abbess on her heap of rags in the apartments beyond. It took several moments for the Archangel to get her skirts off, the tough top serge first, then the petticoats. Stripped then of the encumbering habit, she was lighter and faster on her feet than the ponderous maniac nearly twice her size. She feinted, dodged and kicked and the Archangel whispered *"Chérie!"* as she tried to get both arms around her at the same time. God, O God. Just the holy name, no time or breath for more. God, O God . . . The Archangel stooped to pull off a stocking. The strength she prayed for came to her then. She thrust the madwoman backward and off balance and for an instant was free of the flying arms. In that instant she got out the door and slammed it shut.

She had no idea how long she clung to the long iron key her hand had frozen to but could not pull from the lock. The Archangel's face distorted with grief was flattened against the glass one inch from her own.

Gradually Sister Luke forced her eyes into focus and saw her shredded habit scattered over the padded floor, and then the belt, the key ring and crucifix lying in a heap in one corner of the cell. The sight of the leather belt, with which a thwarted maniac could choke herself, gave her the strength to move. She stumbled down the corridor and rang the bell.

Sister Marie and two female stalwarts appeared so promptly it seemed as if they must have been there when she pressed the button. Sister Marie looked at her without surprise, judgment or shock and reached for a sheet to cover her up. The two practical nurses waited with folded arms, incurious, unexcited, as if it were a common event to relieve a bareheaded nun, stripped of her habit, with two blacked eyes and scarcely any voice.

As soon as she could gasp "The Archangel . . ." the aides walked down the corridor unfolding their arms as they went.

Sister Marie wrapped the sheet around her like a toga. Her compassionate eyes examined bruises and scratches as she covered them. With merciful delicacy, she made no reference to the deep inner wound of failure in obedience which Sister Luke had inflicted upon herself.

"Pride got me in . . . prayer got me out," Sister Luke whispered.

"Don't try to talk," said Sister Marie as she pulled up a corner of the sheet and looped it around her bared head, stiffening her trembling chin with the knot she tucked firmly beneath it. "Myself, I would probably have done the same thing." Sister Marie picked up the telephone and called the infirmary to bring a stretcher.

Sister Luke began to sob, not for the scandal of her situation, nor for the pain of her bruises, but for that extra charity from the tall calm sister who had identified herself with pride and disobedience to share her shame. Tears stung her puffed eyelids as she watched the two practical nurses coming back down the corridor with the pieces of her destroyed habit. There, neatly stacked in their big red hands, was the result of two years of trying to please God with obedience. She shuddered at the thought of Sister Eudoxie eventually receiving those scraps of black and white, which were not even big enough to be made into sewing bags but possibly only into potholders for the kitchen nuns. She looked up at Sister Marie.

"This . . ." she managed to say, "could never happen to you."

The powerful eyes stopped the emotion that thickened her voice. Two points of light darted from them, fixed her and held her safe from the further faults of personal attachment and of prophecy.

"Only the Almighty God can know that," said Sister Marie. She put out her arms and took the torn habit from the aides flat on her upturned palms as if it were still a whole garment. The gesture recalled to Sister Luke the Living Rules of the mother house coming toward her before vows with her new black veil and scapular held just so and she began to cry again, but without a sound now.

The extraordinary discreetness of the convent fell over the affair. It seemed as though nothing had happened. Save for the interview with the Mother Superior, the whole thing might have been one of those dark dreams that caused nuns to toss and moan on their straw sacks at night.

Mother Christophe heard her culpa in private, which was the custom for exceptional faults. The Superior listened without comment to the truths about herself that she had uncovered during the three days she lay in the infirmary. Her salient characteristics had ugly names like pride, personal judgment and sense of heroism. She listed them in a toneless monotone as if her voice had died upon discovery of them. No notes were taken, but she knew as she shaped each halting word that she herself was dictating the incident report which would go forward to the mother house to be read, weighed and judged by Reverend Mother Emmanuel. Once during the long culpa she remembered how just a few months ago she had begged another Superior to inform the mother house of another kind of struggle, and she almost said aloud to Mother Christophe, Had I succeeded in humility for Him then, would this be happening to me now?

She was returned to the community penanced to beg her soup for eight days, an unheard-of duration for this extreme mortification, but even that did not seem to be happening when she knelt with her beggar bowl and made the rounds of the refectory day after day. Her sisters charitably ignored the green-blue condition of her eyelids, the bound wrists holding up the bowl, and even the brand-new habit which, ordinarily, would have drawn their women's eyes quicker than the bruises and sprains to which they were accustomed in that community. Not a single eye slanted toward her in curiosity. It made her feel like a ghost.

On duty, it was the same. The Superior did not transfer her to another wing but wisely reassigned her to the place where she had learned a lesson that could not be improved upon. The Archangel called out *"Allô, chérie"* each day as she hopped past the desk on the way to the baths, as if that were the closest she had ever come or could come to the sister of her choice. Even the practical-nurse aides suppressed their gusty admiration for muscles and bravery and refrained from comment when she reappeared, as though they too had entered into the conspiracy of compassion which bound the total community to silence and left her alone, as it were, the only living being in it with a memory.

But not quite . . . there was the Abbess. Sister Luke sent her assistant to attend the old nun until the last trace of blacked eyes had vanished. She used the polished brass lid of the inkwell as a mirror to determine when this moment had arrived, noting the imperfection in her conscience notebook as a reminder for next week's culpa and writing firmly beside it: *For charity's sake, not to disturb a patient unduly*. One of these fine days, she thought wryly, maybe I'll learn with God's help where the Rule ends and charity begins and not have to fill my notebook with these split hairs . . .

The Abbess was waiting for her. Sister Luke guessed at once that her heart must be troubling her again for she had made an armchair of her scrap heap and was sitting straight up in it, her long thin torso like a ramrod above the edemic legs stretched out fat and heavy.

"I missed you very much, my child," the Abbess said. Her sweet sensitive face showed concern. "Did she hurt you?" the old nun asked quietly.

Sister Luke knelt swiftly to take her pulse. How could she have known? How through panes of unbreakable glass separated by corridors and a social hall could she have heard the sounds of scuffle in a padded cell? One could conclude only that this was another facet of her long nun's life preserved undamaged in the disease-ridden body and mind — the ability to feel an atmosphere and know what was going on with it.

"No, Sister, no . . . I only hurt myself."

The Abbess never spoke of it again. But day after day thereafter, she entertained Sister Luke with discussions on dogma as lucid as any ever heard in a retreat, or, for recreational relief, with the exquisite songs and sonnets she composed. Sister Luke had the impression that the old nun, out of her great knowledge of the soul, was making a conscious effort to draw her forth from silence and self-reproach, to make her smile again.

She actually did smile on the last afternoon of her month of day duty when she heard herself saying to the Abbess a happy colloquialism straight out of her childhood, as if at long last she had recovered again the light conscience that a nun must have in order to endure. Afterwards, Sister Luke remembered bitterly that when she had said *Everything will roll on wheels tonight!* she had been thinking of the joy of relieving Sister Marie after her month of night duty, and of the way her sister's weary eyes would glow with gratitude when she would appear exactly on time.

The Abbess had one special request before she went off duty. She wished Sister Luke to take her to the attic to see her garments in storage. "I'll probably not see you during your month of night vigil . . . and who knows . . ."

She followed the Abbess to the attic. Late afternoon sun came through the gabled windows, reflected up from the sand-scrubbed floor to the white pine shelves neatly stacked with the clothing that patients in the pavilion had been wearing when brought in. Each pile of clothing was numbered and inventoried and on top lay the special objects that owners had clung to at the moment of mental breakdown — ice skates with long curved blades, parasols, old-fashioned box cameras, satin slippers with Louis Quatorze heels, silver-framed photos of parents, of villas, horses, dogs and yachts, and here and there a great Edwardian lace hat with ostrich plumes drooping over the brim. Sister Luke had never reacted before to the attic, except to admire the order in which it was kept by the nuns. Now it made her think of death. It seemed like a strange graveyard where no bodies were buried, only clothes sweetly scented with camphor to keep the moths away.

The Abbess moved down the long lines of shelves searching for her number. She hardly looked at the clothing of the world. Her eyes, like a Superior's on inspection, passed over the gleaming folds of silks and velvets to the walls behind and the rafters above, looking for a cobweb or a speck of dust. Presently she halted before an austere pile of simple grays and blacks. One by one she unfolded the garments of her order, the black scapular of finest spun wool, the linen guimpe and the long gray dress and then the coarse hair shirt that was worn beneath it. She shook them out lovingly and held them up for Sister Luke to see.

"This is what you will dress me in when I go to meet our heavenly Groom," she said softly.

Sister Luke nodded agreement but could not speak. She watched the lean fingers stroking the only materials they had never tried to tear into inch-square bits, then folding each garment back again with practiced ease in its traditional folds.

"I wanted you to see," said the Abbess, "before you start night duty. We could not come up here then."

Sister Luke followed her as they went back to the garret stairs. The ingrained habit of the madhouse never to turn your back on a patient, no matter how trusted, gave her a momentary feeling of shame as she walked behind the gentle old nun who, so often of late, had seemed as sane as any of her guardians. She studied the shapeless ankles; they looked heavier above the slippered feet that barely cleared the floor.

At the door to her apartment, the Abbess turned and thanked her with a beautiful smile. Then she said, "I will pray that your vigil tonight will be without incident."

"Don't worry, Sister. Everything will roll on wheels tonight!"

Everything will roll on wheels, she said again to herself as she walked between the begonia beds in the moonlight. There were never any problems when you took over the duty after a sister as conscientious as Sister Marie. She would have notes written in her lacelike script telling which patients in the dormitory were tied down with bound sheets and which ones were without restraints for that night. Patients who had visited the toilets would be listed and those who had asked for a cup of water. Any other nun would take advantage of the dispensation to speak during the grand silence on matters of duty and change-over. But not Sister Marie, she thought, not that perfect nun.

The duplex pavilion with its gabled roof looked like a toy house set down in the center of the wire-enclosed gardens. Because she had come a few moments too early, she stood looking at it in the moonlight, mentally lifting away the façade. Downstairs was the big social hall for patients, the private rooms for special cases like the Abbess and the countess, the corridor of padded cells and the treatment tubs beyond. Hermetically sealed glass doors and partitions closed off each section from the other, but you could look through them without moving from the central desk. Two aides were on duty, one awake and the other asleep, and a single nun who never slept — Sister Henri that night — was on duty in the office where the alarm bell was. At the rear of the hall, behind a knobless door of unbreakable glass, a flight of stairs went up to the big dormitory stretching the width of the building where slept the nonsuicides, the patients who had seizures only once or twice a year and were well known by the nuns. Up there was Sister Marie with her back to the glass door and her eyes on the twenty beds spaced around three sides of the room. The washbasins were along the fourth wall behind her, and in a cubicle beyond these slept a practical nurse whom Sister Marie could awaken if for any reason she had to leave the dormitory.

With her imagination Sister Luke set the five quiet guardians into motion — made Sister Henri downstairs signal the practical nurse that she was leaving her desk. The nurse awoke her sleeping companion, pointed to her post and took the place of the nun while Sister Henri went upstairs and looked through the glass, as the floor chief always did twice each night, to see that all was well with the nun on vigil in the dormitory. The figures moved in her imagination like chessmen, forward and back, each with a place to go, no spot left uncovered for more than a moment. She smiled as she slipped her notched key into the front door lock and entered the quiet house to become a part of its smooth-running perfection.

Sister Henri smiled back at her, glanced at a watch and wrote her entrance time in the log — one minute to one in the morning. The practical nurse behind a glass partition looked at her not as at a person but as at a shape in motion within her range of vision, then resumed her steady watch over the padded cells. Sister Luke opened the door at the back of the hall, shut it soundlessly behind her and climbed the stairs, automatically lifting her long skirts from the front as she mounted.

As she fitted her key into the glass door at the head of the stairs, she looked through it and took in the whole room at a glance — the twenty beds with their motionless forms, the dimmed lights above and, on the desk, the shaded lamp which made Sister Marie's back look like a silhouette cut from black paper, a slice of shadow without dimension leaning forward against the light, leaning . . . but the head was not right! It was lying forward on the arms.

Her heart missed a beat as she rattled her key to make the head lift before she entered the room, to awaken Sister Marie and spare her the ignominy of being found asleep on duty. "I've got to pay her back," she said wildly to herself, "pay back that charity she gave to me . . . pay it back with this noisy entrance, with this door clicking sharply shut behind me." She shook her key ring and prayed "O God, let her wake up all by herself."

She lingered by the light switch, fumbling at it audibly and staring at the dark silhouette that would not move. Then she switched on the bright lights and saw the ebony knife-handle sticking out of the back of Sister Marie's black scapular.

Her horror-filled eyes swept the dormitory. The motionless lumps under covers never moved but here and there she caught a sarcastic grin, a leer, a glint from eyes wide awake, watching to see what she would do.

"I'll do exactly what Sister Marie would do," she whispered frantically to herself, adding, as Sister Marie would have done, ". . . with the help of God Almighty." She walked calmly to the desk, dropped her trembling fingers over her sister's pulse and pretended to read the page of notes on which the dead hand lay. Then she pressed the alarm bell, which was not heard in the dormitory.

Sister Henri and one assistant appeared from below, their faces rising like two blanched moons behind the glass door. Then they were inside the dormitory moving with such studied calm that it looked like slow motion, the practical nurse going to the cubicle beyond the basins to awaken the aide sleeping there, then the two of them returning side by side down the long room, unhurried, like lethargic giants. Sister Henri made a lifting motion.

They never looked at the knife-handle as they bent to lift the chair with Sister Marie sitting in it. They tipped the chair slightly backward as they raised it up, making her arms drop naturally into her lap and her head fall forward in a drowsy nod. Sister Henri, clutching her crucifix with one hand, opened the door for the aides and stepped back as they passed through. The bright lights showed up the white knuckles on her crucifix hand while the other closed the door with a barely audible click. Then she came toward Sister Luke, whose habit alone seemed to be holding her up.

"We'll have another chair for you in a few moments," said Sister Henri in a voice meant to reach beyond the desk. She lowered her tone and added, "Unless you would prefer to be relieved this night, as indeed you may."

"Thank you, Sister, I prefer to stay." Sister Luke forced her voice up and said, "I'll not need a chair tonight," as she faced the room squarely while Sister Henri made her silent exit.

Both nuns knew that nothing more could happen. The knife — stolen from a pantry or smuggled in — had been used. It was no longer in the dormitory. Only that leering aware-ness in the few who had seen the violent act, and the memory, in just one of those twenty deranged brains, of having com-mitted it, needed to be subdued, to be confused by calm and eventually blotted out altogether. As if nothing had hap-pened . . .

The discipline supported her that night. The Rule took over like a separate organ of command having no contact with her mind or emotions, existing independently of these with its own set of precise acts and facial expressions. She stepped backward and dimmed the lights. She stepped forward to the desk, picked up Sister Marie's notes, looked from them to each numbered bed listed upon them in two columns, one headed *W.C.* and one *H_2O Given.* Something in her screamed when she remembered that the hand that wrote what she was reading had been warm when she had touched it, but the Rule let no sound emerge. A thought formed halfway — *May-*

be if 1 hadn't stood in the moonlight for the perfection of ar-
riving exactly on the minute . . . and the Rule suppressed
the rest of it.

She read on, holding up the log without a quiver, looking
from it to the beds containing patients in precautionary
bindings — only three of those. Then she began to patrol the
room forward and back, clicking her beads as she paced
slowly with her eyes uplifted to the great mirrors hung aslant
at each end under the ceiling. The mirror toward which she
paced gave her the view of the three beds along the end wall
to which her back was turned and of the beds against the long
wall as she passed them one by one.

Her form was centered in the mirror she faced, very clear
against the white rectangles of beds. It was a reflection of any
nun pacing back and forth on a quiet night, seeming to tell
her rosary. It was the Rule walking.

She watched the Rule walking through the whole of that
night and through the thirty that followed which became one
with it. Pacing the dim-lit dormitory, she watched how the
Rule turned the nun as on wheels when someone in a bed
·stirred in the mirrored reflection; how it held her there in
calm when a wild woman climbed from the bed, grimaced
her way and padded off to the toilet; how it turned her again
and made her resume her walk when the patient stepped into
the mirror and walked catlike behind the veiled figure until
she came to the empty bed and climbed into it, without being
looked at or told to.

Shafts of daylight penetrated the long night watch. For
those intervals she could rest her eyes from the spellbinding
mirrors. Her relief sister came each morning a little before
seven, which gave her time to shower and put on a fresh
guimpe before attending late Mass with the patients. There

was sleep until three in the afternoon and then breakfast alone in the refectory, followed by two hours in the chapel to read the daily devotions straight through from Matins to Vespers, since devotions when on duty with the demented were forbidden though not the semblance of saying them.

Dispensed from community life during her solitary month, she never once felt that she did not belong to it or that it no longer existed. She did not have to see or hear the community to know what was going on in it. Experience informed her.

She knew exactly how the Mother Superior made the grave announcement that their beloved Sister Marie de Jésus had given her soul back to God. That was in the chapter hall the morning after the event, when the nuns were assembled for spiritual reading. She knew how the nuns stared, their shock and heartbreak showing only momentarily and no head turning to the sisters known to have been called to the infirmary the night before, no questions asked then or thereafter, no wasting of God's time with conjecture. No drama, no singularization . . . a Living Rule permitted to die as she had lived, in quiet self-effacement. They would render that to her — even the sisters who had prepared her body for the posthumous last rites, even the one who had withdrawn the ebony-handled knife. Yet, she knew, it was not a cold uncaring. In their thoughts Sister Marie would be present for the thirty days after her death, while the small cross lay on the refectory table at her place, which was set each mealtime with her napkin, wooden plank and water glass. The two sisters who flanked the empty place never passed soup tureens or bread baskets over it. As these came down the table from hand to hand, they stopped with the nun on one side of the vacancy. The serving nun stepped forward, picked them up and handed them, from the rear, to the nun on the other side of the place

129

where nobody was sitting. She could see it very clearly all the way from the refectory to the kitchen, where, for those thirty days, the ration Sister Marie would have consumed was measured out with scrupulous accuracy and given to the poor.

Toward the end of the long vigil, one night when the beds were quiet and she allowed her eyes to dwell in thought on the dark-veiled silhouette in the mirrors, she felt a thrill of admiration for that solitary form patrolling without visible strain or vainglory a demented dreamland of fearful potential. The thrill flew like an electric shock through her exhausted nerves. "The Rule thus achieved is very beautiful," she said to herself. "In motion it is like a simple walking with God."

Then her gaze moved to a mirrored bed where an arm was flinging off the covers. *Bed five . . . her menstruation is due . . . probably restless with a little pain in her sleep.* Her watchful eyes flashed every other message to her brain except the awareness that she had just been looking at herself.

She was earning the Congo in that month-long night but she had no idea of this when it ended. She had crossed out that hope long ago.

The remainder of her time in the asylum community passed without events or attachments, or any special inner or outer torments. Work and prayer dovetailed so closely as to leave no crack for thought. Much later, when she had experienced other plateau periods and could compare these with this first one, she knew that they must have been her intervals of effortless, perfect conformity. They lay like irregularly spaced steppingstones through her memories of struggle — the places where she had never had to watch her feet or her thoughts.

In the spring of 1932 she was called back to the mother house with the remaining sisters of her group to make her final vows. She walked into the home convent with her head erect and her wide blue eyes looking up and out, flicking toward every sound she heard in that nearly soundless place.

She sensed immediately an atmosphere of which she had been unaware when she had lived there as an awed postulant and novice. It was impossible to analyze but it had to do with peace and perfection. She saw its effect on the many sisters who came there for other reasons than to make their vows, on nervous nuns perhaps just informed that they were to be promoted to Superiors, on nuns about to be transferred to the other side of the world, and even on the mediocre nuns who plodded in. Their first deep breath of the mother house atmosphere seemed to put color into their pale cheeks. Behind the scene of all the coming and going, you sensed the powerful presence of the Reverend Mother Emmanuel in her small bare office, interviewing the incoming sisters one by one. It was rare that you saw a sister emerge from that office without tears in her eyes and a smile lifting all the tired lines of her face.

Her group of first-professed, now preparing for final vows, seemed smaller than it was three years ago, but neither she nor any of her companions turned around to count, or even to look at one another as they sat in a circle with the Mistress of Novices. No side glances of curiosity, no whispered queries — *How did it go with you? Did you have a Superior you liked?* Each seemed to be alone in the room with the Mistress.

"You are all here," said the Mistress, "except Sister Monique, who died and said her perpetual vows on her deathbed, Sisters Rose and Bernadette, who were put back three months at their own request, Sister Vitalie, who was advised to wait

131

by our Reverend Mother Emmanuel, and Sister Godefrieda, who has gone out."

Then you could almost hear the clicking of their thoughts. Am *I* ready? Am I worthy? Should I also have the courage of those who asked to be put back? This time it's not for three years, it's for good.

"Perpetual," Sister Luke said to herself as if reading a crossroads sign she had come to sooner than expected. Her hand clung to her crucifix in the manner of the perpetually vowed. That evening she went to the Mistress.

"I believe it would be better if I wait," she said. "There is still much struggle. Too much, it seems to me."

"No, Sister Luke, I would not counsel postponement for you. You have to struggle. So do we all." The Mistress gazed at her thoughtfully. "We know how you were proved this past year, Sister Luke, and we know that you did everything to surmount the difficulties that came your way. As you will continue to do, because you have a fighting soul. For such, there can never be too much struggle."

She leaned slightly across the desk. It was unusual to see a Living Rule betray eagerness.

"We need combative souls, Sister Luke, not simply the phlegmatic ones who accept everything without question. You are one of us who has a taste for struggle. God would not have put you to such tests were this not so. You must count on His graces. Never forget that He tests His real friends more severely than the lukewarm ones."

"Oh, it's not for fear of further proving that I ask to be put back . . ." Sister Luke faltered. It was so long since she had spoken of personal feelings, it was like a venture in a foreign language. "For me . . . for one such as I, Sister . . . it is the

Rule that is difficult. It is the constant struggle away from the natural. The supernatural life . . ." She gave up.

"The supernatural life . . ." The Mistress smiled as she picked up her unfinished thought. "Yes, it does seem audacious when we name it so. In the world that phrase is associated with magic and a wave of the wand. It is not thought that man can achieve such a life, only angels perhaps. But we have our Holy Rule. It is a way to the Christ. The stern slow way to sanctity, but a very sure one. We know it can be achieved by the help of His graces."

Sister Luke felt the persuasive pull of the dark eyes that reminded her suddenly of Sister Marie's.

"Remember, Sister," said the Mistress very softly, "you would not be here had you not been called. When you were accepted for vesture by the Superior General, it was a sign that you were one of His chosen."

The familiar words heard so often during her novitiate gave her for the first time a startling and unfamiliar impression. It was as if she had been asking Christ to wait a little before making that final step toward Him.

"Right now," the Mistress continued, "you feel perhaps unworthy, inadequate to meet that call. Possibly many times in prayer you have asked Him what He wishes of you, as we all do. Ah, how very often." She clasped her hands. Her voice dropped so low she might have been talking to herself. "Sometimes, God lets us know why we were called. Sometimes not. Meanwhile, the vows keep us where we want to be — near to Him in poverty, chastity and obedience."

At the end of a ten days' retreat, Sister Luke made her final vows in the only way her strictly honest soul could formulate them. As she lay face down on the carpet, she whispered for

God's ear alone the words she was sure He knew were in her heart. "I cannot promise You until death . . . but I shall try . . ."

Next morning she was summoned to the Superior General's office and informed that she would not be returning to the asylum community. She was to report to the Vestiaire to be measured for the white cotton habit of the Congo nuns.

In a daze she heard the beginning of the Reverend Mother Emmanuel's brief precise instructions, but from the moment she said, "I suggest while you're waiting for all your shots and vaccinations, you take from our library a Kiswahili grammar and begin to study the language," there were two voices in the room. From the place in her mind where she had hidden it away, the word *simba* leaped softly as a cat. *Simba,* said her inner voice over and over again while the Reverend Mother Emmanuel was saying, "You must never lose the awareness that in yourself you are nothing, you are only an instrument. An instrument is nothing until it is lifted. No one knows how it is lifted. It may be the prayers of some poor bedridden sister who had apostolic ambitions and longed for the missions, who accepts her affliction without murmur, that you may go . . ."

I X

A COMMERCIAL photographer from Antwerp took a picture of the departure for the Congo. Months later, when she looked at it printed in the little magazine of the congregation, Sister Luke imagined she had known then everything that was going to happen to her on that white ship trimmed for the tropics.

The camera had centered on the section of the ship's rail where the nuns stood, herself and Sister Augustine, professor of Latin and the humanities, who was making her second departure and showed it in her slightly haughty expression.

Her own face in the photograph looked like a small triangle of white stone severely incised with fixed eyes and a slit of a mouth tightly drawn. That must have been when the band started playing the Brabançonne, she thought . . . and then it all came back — the surging splendor of her country's send-off to sons and daughters bound for the colonies, the whipping flags and tossed confetti, the world catching her up at that moment as if to say, *You too! You are outward bound for adventure!* — catching her on the wave of its own emotion and nearly drowning her in that unfamiliar medium until she saw below her on the crowded quay the Gothic figure of the Reverend Mother Emmanuel . . .

The Reverend Mother Emmanuel seemed to be waving like all the others. Then she saw the figure-eight motion of the long hand. It circled tirelessly, sending little signs of the cross over the widening space between ship and shore. The white sleeve hung like a banner from her wrist and made the benedictions visible long after other flags blurred with distance.

Voices from the pier carried over the water. "Don't forget to come back rich." "Don't forget to come back." "Don't forget . . ." The white sleeve signaled, "Don't forget you are only an instrument. Never lose the awareness that in yourself you are nothing. The one who does your work will be an unknown praying for you. Only an instrument, remember . . ." Slowly the ship turned.

The spires of the cathedral swung into view pointing up from a gray huddle of waterfront hotels and seafood restaurants. Beyond the spires she saw the mansard roof of the hospital where her father was making his rounds, doubtless telling everyone that his daughter was sailing that morning for the colonies. "Don't be proud of me," she whispered. "This is really flight. I'm glad to get away. It will be so much easier out there to remember that I am nothing." She looked steadily at the roof until it vanished. Then Sister Augustine plucked her sleeve and she turned away from the rail.

The silent summons brought her back into the orbit of the mother house. She followed the senior nun to the cabin and knelt with her to pray. It was not going to be difficult to keep near to God in the midst of shipboard life, not when you had an experienced companion to show you how. In the curtained cabin, her only wayward thought as she murmured the responses concerned the beauty of Sister Augustine's Latin. The twentieth-century world seemed far away when you heard her *Deus qui Abraham puerum tuum, de Ur Chaldeo-*

rum eductum, per omnes suae peregrinationis . . . the vowel
sounds flowing from her thin lips as if this were the everyday
language.

But right outside her cabin door, the modern world in glittering microcosm lay in wait for her. Its music struck the first
notes of a waltz as she and Sister Augustine, bound to silence,
stepped from the cabin into a lounge full of people who were
introducing themselves, pairing up for dinner and bridge
partners, their faces laughing and lively with anticipation of
a long voyage with nothing to do except to pursue pleasure.
The waltz was one she knew. She had not heard it for four
and one half years but its words were suddenly all there
singing in her memory.

Inattentive as a deaf-mute, Sister Augustine moved through
the lounge and led the way to the promenade deck. Her prim
nod indicated that they would make a tour of their new cloister before settling in deck chairs to read the Office. Sister
Luke realized that her companion had made her debut into
the world so long ago, she had forgotten its impact after the
sequestered years of preparation. It was going to be as if Sister Luke traveled alone on her first real journey in the world
since vesture.

In the world. The phrase drummed in her thoughts as
she tried to match her companion's sober pace. How many
times had she heard it in the convent? Perhaps a thousand. *In
the world* was the phrase of separation. It meant out there,
beyond these walls. It meant everywhere else except here
and everyone else except us. It meant this ship now.

Before she had gone halfway around the scrubbed decks,
she knew that everything she had renounced was there on
board to be looked at and listened to again, and again to be
set aside, if she could. The familiar music pursued her, reviv-

ing dance partners out of her past. The passengers smiled, inviting speech. The bulletin boards listed motion pictures she longed to see. Eighteen days of this, she thought. It was to be the sternest of all her tests of detachment.

You were expected to live on that ship as if still behind walls. Your meditations were not supposed to be colored by excitement every time you looked up at the blue flag of the Congo with its single gold star. And, if they were, you must have the strength to say, "I am nothing, only an instrument," and cease seeing yourself surrounded by Blacks in the lonely bush and see instead the pale hand that was lifting you, the hand of a sister perhaps who might at that moment be spitting blood in the mother house infirmary while she prayed for the missions. You knew you betrayed her sacrifice each time you let parts of yourself escape to dream among the dancers, to keep score on the deck-tennis players, to eavesdrop on the bearded colonials whose roving eyes measured the bare-backed women the sunny skies off Spain brought forth upon the decks.

There was no chapel on the ship, only a library momentarily transformed into one each morning when two Jesuit passengers said Mass there. Then it became a place of temptation furnished with deep leather chairs and books about which you must try not to have a flicker of curiosity.

"I miss the chapel," she said to Sister Augustine during one of their recreation periods. She was going to add that a nun without a chapel was a little like a fish out of water, but thought better of it when she saw her sister's smile of mild surprise.

"But we carry our chapels in our hearts, Sister Luke," she said.

During the first week she walked the deck so often she

might have been going on foot to the Congo. Sometimes she held her Office open, trying to read. Sometimes her hands were clasped beneath her scapular like two wrestling shapes wanting to get away from each other to swing in compensation to the body's sway as the ship lifted and dipped through the easy sea.

Off Tenerife, when she and Sister Augustine put on their tropical whites, she had the impression that everything would be easier. She imagined it would be less difficult to meditate on the open decks in those whites that would refract the sun's rays instead of drawing them in, like the blacks, to fill the body with disturbing warmth. But as soon as she stepped on deck, she knew that the change of habit would make nothing easier, least of all her concentration. The feeling of lightness invaded her thoughts. She could have played tennis like a whirlwind in those weightless cottons, and each time she passed the courts a ghost with squinting competitive eyes slipped out from beneath her scapular and ran toward the nets with veil and skirts flying, to show up every player there including the two Jesuits, who were fast with the rubber rings.

Sister Augustine was as unaware of her divided state as she was of the world around her. Geared to the clockwork of the mother house, she signaled by dropping her knitting and picking up her Office the times for meditations and prayers. Sister Luke knew from her rapt expression that she really was meditating when she stared out over the sea. She was not finding images of loved ones framed in the cat's-paws the wind ruffled up.

The nights brought other distractions. They retired to their cabin at eight-thirty and undressed without looking at each other, as if there were a cell wall between the two berths. They said the evening prayers and the *Salve Regina* and were in bed with lights out by nine. Then the night life of the ship began.

You heard the ballroom music first. It drifted through the passageways in the changing tempos of waltzes, polkas and fox-trots with intermittent flurries of hand-claps calling for encores. The rustle of ice in champagne buckets, in the lounge just outside the cabin door, announced the intermissions.

Much later, after the music ended, there were shufflings and whispers from the promenade deck and sometimes against the porthole curtain the shadow of two heads thrown into silhouette by the moon. "Don't watch that shadow play," said the nun inside you and you looked away quickly while there was still a space of moonlight between the two profiles.

You looked at the white guimpe and scapular swinging from a clothes hanger against the dark paneled door. It was a pendulum that counted the rolls of the ship. By staring at it, you could make it draw your thought so that when you at last fell asleep, you would not dream again that you were still in the world, a young girl with flying hair and unfettered impulses.

There was one image which Sister Luke could always put between herself and the distractions. It was the native service to which she was destined. She saw the bush station often between the lines of the medical books she studied. It was in a place that could never stir a worldly association because everything there was totally new to her experience. The people were black. The music was drums. Even the thorn trees could never recall any tree she had ever sat under before.

She had seen so many photos of the Congo missions in the convent magazine that it took no effort of the imagination to build her own. Hers was in a clearing among outlandish trees, a pavilion with thatched roof and a veranda around the four sides of it. Two bicycles leaned against the stairs, one of them hers. Beyond the main building were the conical huts where lived the black boys she was training to be male nurses. There was just one other nun with her in the bush clinic, a facsimile of Sister Marie. Each time her imagination cast up the picture, she thanked God that that was to be her lot instead of one of those hospitals for whites in the bustling cities of the Congo where the majority of the nursing sisters were stationed.

Afterwards, she wondered why the voice of religious experience had not spoken within her from the moment she began using that bush station as a screen. In retrospect, it was so perfectly clear that as long as the world could distract her, she was not done with it. She would be kept in it until her detachment from it was perfected.

Off Dakar, a radiogram came to the ship addressed to Sister Augustine and delivered to her in the dining saloon. She thanked the steward with a smile, slipped the message beneath her scapular and tucked her napkin under her chin. Sister Luke looked on with unconcealed admiration.

The radiogram had to be from the mother house or from family. Only a death announcement would be considered important enough to be radioed; anything else could wait for letter transmittal.

Sister Augustine gave her a lesson in detachment. She lifted her wine glass, took delicate sips and sent a smile of utmost sweetness across the table, nodding as if to say, "Do likewise, my sister. This is our time for rejoicing."

Sister Luke remembered the years of refectory meals when heartbreak, discouragement and fatigues were concealed and all the nuns came to table to celebrate in serene silence the bounty that God put before them. She picked up her wine glass and turned it slowly. She smiled back at her companion as though saying, "It's a good wine. We are blessed with the dispensation to drink of it freely on shipboard so as not to singularize ourselves in the eyes of passengers by drinking water."

They ate in silence as always, anticipating each other's needs for salt, more bread, a bit of horse-radish, passing these back and forth with practiced grace and little nods which occasionally caught the eyes of diners at nearby tables and made them stare musingly at the two white sisters who seemed able to read each other's thoughts.

Sister Luke looked at her companion with envy. Sister Augustine's withdrawn face ignored everything that came to her from the outside, including the radiogram beneath her scapular. The wheedling dinner music, the bursts of laughter and fragments of vivid table talk floated into her silence but captured no part of her. She was safe in the convent refectory listening to the voice of the pulpit reader.

When they finished dessert, Sister Augustine folded her napkin and announced the time for recreational speech by saying softly, "Praised be Jesus Christ." She thought a moment before she withdrew the radiogram. Weighing the indelicacy of reading a personal message in the presence of a sister . . . Sister Luke knew that much about her veiled thoughts. She smiled at the fine-spun delicacy of convent etiquette.

"If you will permit," said Sister Augustine, "I will read the message here where there is good light."

She opened the envelope with a fruit knife and spread it flat on the table. Sister Luke watched her lips forming each word as nuns were taught to read, thoughtfully and without skipping. When her companion looked up, she knew by the flash of sympathy in the usually impersonal eyes that the message concerned herself.

"You must prepare for what may be a little disappointment, Sister Luke. Your assignment has been changed. You are to report for work in the hospital for Europeans in . . ."

In a city with streets and stores, with newspapers and telephones. In a bustling bit of Belgium set down near the copper mines of the Haut Katanga . . . Her disappointment cut like a knife. Only her training in concealment of emotions kept her from crying out. Her bush station flew apart as she took a last look at it. The trees and hills of her dream changed into smokestacks and slag heaps while Sister Augustine folded the radiogram corner to corner with care.

"Apparently," said her companion, "one of our sisters was stricken with lung trouble, which always writes *finis* to service in the tropics. So, there was a place on the government payroll which our Reverend Mother Emmanuel has chosen you to fill."

Sister Luke waited until she could speak calmly. Then she said, "When God orders, He gives . . ." and she thought how bitterness, shock, even a flash of rebellion were laid low by such words of obedience. And, something always happened when you said them. Like the *All for Jesus* of student days, they shifted the emphasis.

Presently she thought of herself on a payroll, earning a salary which would be paid into the coffers of her congregation for her services. It was strange to think of herself being worth money, being one of those earning sisters who worked in the world, were paid by the world and yet must not be of it. She had often studied the sisters who, although never named or singled out, were known to be earners in the congregation.

143

She had wondered what they did about pride when they realized that their salaries helped to pay for the vast charitable activities of their Order. Could you transmute pride into humble thanksgiving when you knew that orphans and old folks, unmarried mothers and even your own aged and ailing sisters depended in part upon you for their daily bread?

She looked over the dining saloon. She had forgotten to put people into her new picture. She gazed at the passengers who were now her potential patients. She felt the pull of their worldliness as she realized that she knew these people whom she might have met time and time again in her father's drawing room. She knew their intrigues and love affairs. She could have told just which of those gusty colonials had sired a mulatto in the bush. She could have put a yellow flower in the corsage of every woman who was deceiving her husband aboard that ship. Yellow, she thought, the color of cuckoldry. "Name of God," she whispered to herself, "how did I remember that? How . . . after all the years of no color except black and white?"

"I think," said Sister Augustine, "that we should go first to the cabin and say a prayer to ask our Lord for His graces to help you shoulder your disappointment."

She caught the eye of an army officer as she passed his table. Had she been looking down as she should have been, she would not have seen his frank glance of admiration. Seeing it, she remembered yet another hazard of work in the world which every young nun had to face sooner or later. It was the curious tendency of men to fall in love with nuns, a fact which even the Rule recognized in its strict injunction that sisters must always be in pairs when in the presence of the opposite sex.

She was praying before she reached her cabin. It was the

144

kind of swift spontaneous prayer she had always been able to make before she had boarded that ship. She talked directly to God as though He instead of Sister Augustine accompanied her down the passageways.

"You cannot let me be a worldly nun, Blessed Lord. You know my all-or-nothing soul. You know that I would flee the convent tomorrow if I thought that this lingering worldiness would stamp me always. Dear God, they are the most unhappy of Your servants, those half-caught, half-given. Help me to be not like that. Don't humiliate me further by showing me that I am. You've taken away the bush station and put me back in the world, but You must put into me as well the strength to ignore its temptations. You have ordered . . . Now You must give . . ."

She passed the bulletin board outside the purser's office without looking to see what motion picture was to be played that night, the first time she had not cast longing eyes toward the entertainment schedule.

In the Gulf of Guinea off French West Africa, they crossed the Equator. The life of the ship turned lunatic. A colonial with beard dyed green came forth as King Neptune. Everybody was in bathing suit or masquerade except the two nuns who stood at a safe distance from the swimming pool where every passenger crossing the Equator for the first time was dragged for a ducking.

Sister Luke looked more often away from the horseplay than at it. She gazed beyond the port rail toward where the coast of Africa would soon show above the watery horizon. It would be just a series of brown humps, Sister Augustine had said, very disappointing to the newcomers. But as soon as you get inland a way . . .

145

They would debark at Lobito in the Portuguese Congo and take the train from there to the Katanga Province in their own colony, which was eighty times the size of Belgium. It was a three-day train ride with few stations en route and nothing much to see in them except natives and occasionally a tamed lion walking about unchained. It would be hot and dusty in the *wagon-lit* because September was near the end of the dry season when the whole of the central belt would be gasping in drought. "But ah, my sister, when the rains come," said Sister Augustine . . . and then her inner clock informed her that the hour for recreational talk had come to an end. And she left the rains hanging there in a sky as black as tar.

The nearness of Africa shrunk the world around Sister Luke. She stood hours on end at the port rail waiting for its first brown humps to appear. The faculty for self-examination, which a nun does as naturally and as ceaselessly as she breathes, holding up each thought and act and asking herself if it was to please God that she thought this or did that, came alive again as she scanned the bright horizon. It made her inner world as exciting as the jungle land she was trying to lift prematurely over the edge of the sea.

On their last night aboard, the nuns were invited to the captain's dinner. They shined their shoes for the occasion and put on fresh guimpes so starchy they crackled to the touch. The prospect of a gala dinner with speech permitted sent a flush to Sister Luke's cheeks. Like a Cinderella of sorts, she could live a special life until the clock struck, save that hers would strike three hours before midnight and it would make no sound. It would be a sign from Sister Augustine that the hour of the grand silence was at hand.

The captain seated them in places of honor and proceeded at once to tell his other guests what the colony owed to its missionaries. He had been carrying them out to Africa for eighteen years as an officer and earlier, as a cabin boy, he had sailed with the first nuns ever to set foot on Congo soil, the first white women many of the natives had ever seen.

"That was in the eighteen-nineties," he said, "and the Blacks were waiting for them on the beach with spears pointing seaward." He lifted his beard with the back of his hand and grinned. "Those tribesmen were the reception committee sent down by the Fathers working at the inland mission, but the Reverend Sisters didn't know that when they walked down the gangplank with their black cotton umbrellas in their hands. Four of them that first time. I remember their names . . . Sisters Clarella, Marie-Joannita, Polydore and Brigitta."

Sister Luke forgot she was sitting at a banquet table. She forgot she could speak freely for once to the Congo specialists seated about her — doctors, army men and engineers and their wives — who had the answers to questions she had stored up. She listened with glowing eyes to the memories of a cabin boy who had helped carry the tin trunks of the pioneering sisters down to the beach. She saw the sisters clutching their umbrellas as they walked in pairs toward the naked tribesmen who were to be their guard of honor for the long trek upstream.

"But you'd have thought one of the Fathers would have come to the port," said the doctor's wife, shaking her head as if to say, These men, these impossible, egotistical men . . .

"Ah yes, but it was a thirty-five-day trip out from Antwerp then and ship arrivals were never certain. That original old port of Banana was a sandspit between salt marshes. No place to camp out for indefinite waits . . ."

The first four sisters walked across the sandspit and got

into the hammock-shaped contraptions the natives carried and she saw them lifted up and borne away through mangrove swamps to the place where the dugout canoes were moored.

"And they looked," said the captain turned cabin boy again, "exactly as composed as if riding down L'Avenue de France."

Their sisters followed. They came in larger groups at the turn of the century when the Matadi-Leopoldville railway was under construction and fifteen thousand Blacks were laboring on the tracks and dying off in numbers both alarming and embarrassing to the railway company, and those first nuns set up the clinics and then moved on, ever forward and inland as the Fathers beckoned.

The procession moved through her mind as she listened. Sometimes it halted to regard the scenery and she heard the voice of Reverend Mother Emmanuel reading from a yellowed letter written by one of those sisters named Clarella, Marie-Joannita, Polydore or Brigitta. "We did well to arm ourselves with the Sign of the Cross and to commend our souls to our guardian angels. If one does not have a solid head, it is prudent not to look from one side to the other while the train goes through the frightening gorges and seems to rush over mountains of stone. One moment you are rolling through vertical partitions in rocks opened by dynamite; the next, you race over a mountain's flank that drops straight to the muddy waves of the River Congo . . ."

Sometimes the procession halted to comment on the native children who followed the pioneering sisters like flies and she heard again her Superior's reading voice — "They belong to the most savage tribes of the upper Katanga. In the first days after our arrival, I surprised several in the act of eating sand, others who smacked their lips over dead rats, earthworms or slugs. They are all tattooed with dreadful incisions from head to foot. From the moral point of view, they are pitiable. Lying and theft seem to be such a part of their natures as to be considered talents, if not even virtues. In our beginnings here, they ran out each night and devastated our corn-field . . ."

On through the years the procession moved and grew in numbers. The pavilions changed from hasty wood enclosures to buildings of brick and stone. At some time, perhaps when they had proved their staying power, the nuns were given tropical whites and they ceased perspiring to a degree that had formerly made blisters on the paper over which they bent to record the strange sights of the evangelizing frontier.

At some point in the captain's reminiscences, Sister Luke found herself in the procession. A thrill of pride caught her unaware. She looked down at the table to hide her blush as she saw herself bringing up the rear of that long line of stalwart sisters that was woven like a white thread into the immense tapestry of the Congo.

It was only one of many, and a single thread, to be sure; but it was tough and continuous. Other sisters would follow her. Like herself, they would come out to the colony with the same kind of termite-proof tin trunks those first sisters had carried, and the same number of guimpes, chemises and pieces of underwear in them. The same work bags chain-stitched with a number, a shoe-shine outfit and two textbooks each, which Sister Eudoxie, who packed all the trunks in the mother house, would verify — to make sure the books were medical for the nurses and educational for the teachers. And in their hearts, quite likely, there would be the same simple prayer that chanted in her own . . . "O God, let me do some good . . ." as the captain talked on and on.

Five minutes before nine she was walking back to the cabin with Sister Augustine. She couldn't recall if her senior had plucked her sleeve or lifted her eyebrows or what she had said to her host and the guests when she withdrew. She had the queer impression that Sisters Clarella, Marie-Joannita, Polydore and Brigitta had been sitting at that banquet table in their black habits burned rusty green, with their faded cotton umbrellas hooked over the backs of their chairs.

"Lobito tomorrow at dawn, *Deo gratias*," said Sister Augustine.

X

THE stucco station appeared quite suddenly out of the Congo night. It was lit brightly and full of cotton-clad natives cheering and waving, with a few whites among them so sun-tanned as to be indistinguishable as Europeans at first glance.

Sister Luke stood at the train window that had three days of dust piled in its corners. This was her destination, her convent city, the copper capital of the upper Katanga. It looked no more like Belgium than had any other of the lonely towns passed en route. Sister Augustine pointed to two coifs at the rear of the crowded platform and stood up beside her as the train came to a halt.

She tried to see the faces of the nuns come to meet them, one of them Mother Mathilde, her new Superior, the ruler of her days henceforth. But there was too much motion between her and them, too many stranger sights than coifs to catch the eye. A black-faced band wearing red tarbushes and khaki shorts marched into the station. Then the blare of the Brabançonne stopped all motion save that of the huge winged ants dashing themselves against the lamps.

The two coifs were the only identical headgear in the mixed crowd. They brought back the departure from Antwerp twenty-one days before and made Sister Luke reflect that although she had gone halfway around the world, she had really only passed from convent to convent — bracketed there and now here by two coifs and the strains of the national anthem. Yet, as she studied the crowd and saw details like necklaces strung with teeth and coins, hair oiled shiny and twisted into tufts and bared chests scarred darkly with tattoo incisions, she could tell herself that no matter what convent life could be like in this new setting, it could never be exactly like what she had known before.

And it was not. The moment the anthem ended, their carriage door was snatched open from the outside. A wiry Negro in makeshift uniform cried "Mama Augustine!" and helped them both from the compartment, lifting up their skirts from the rear as if he too had read their Rule. She recognized, from Sister Augustine's talks, Kalulu, the convent factotum, the Congolese version of the genteel old ladies who chaperoned nuns in the homeland. She smelled the Congo night as soon as she stepped on the platform. The jacaranda trees which heralded the beginning of spring in the upper Katanga were in bloom.

There was another beginning going on around her which she could not recognize because she had disciplined herself not to eavesdrop on the businessmen, mining experts and government officials who had made hers one of the first full trains to come up from the port since the world money crisis of 1929. After three years of financial stagnation, the wheels of the Belgian Congo were starting to turn again.

The coifs came toward her through the crowd. The face of her new Superior was a Frans Hals portrait, peaceful, joyous and positive. She looks too gentle to be a Superior, Sister Luke thought. Then she felt the firm Flemish cheek laid against hers.

Mother Mathilde allowed no traditional bows in this public place. She gave them a disarming smile, said, "We are so glad you have come," and led the way to the convent Ford parked behind the station. She motioned Sister Luke to sit beside her in the back seat, and her aide and Sister Augustine up front with Kalulu. As the car started, she reached over and took the hand of her new nun in hers. She held it quietly in her lap as they drove through wide streets under darkly arching trees. Like the Reverend Mother Emmanuel, here was one who could venture the human touch, Sister Luke thought. Her heart opened up to her new Superior as she gazed straight ahead at the two white veils beside a kinky black head.

The night widened when they came out from the tunnel of trees. The uncovered Ford chattered under a canopy of stars she felt she might touch with her free hand. The city she had dreaded petered out quickly and there seemed to be nothing ahead except an immense dry darkness smelling of dust and mimosas. Now and again when Kalulu slipped out of gear to coast and save motor fuel, she heard the shrill song of cicadas and a faint staccato background sound which she realized with quickened emotion was drum talk.

Then a familiar music chimed through the Congo night. Five strokes of a chapel bell announced the beginning of the grand silence in the only place on the dark plateau which would remain voiceless until dawn. The convent was a series of shadowy blocks set against the starshine and it had no walls.

The cloister in the Congo was not like anything she had imagined. The first morning she saw her sisters lined up for showers, she thought she was looking at Siamese cats. The parts of their faces normally covered by headbands were creamy white and all the rest was burned dark by the African sun. Each face seemed to be wearing a little brown triangular mask with the broad end just above the eyebrows and tapering to a point at the chin.

The next unexpected sight was of a single face, all black and male, peering into the refectory from a serving window that gave onto the convent kitchen. Never before had she known a man to look upon nuns at their meals. André not only looked, but weighed and judged as well, and ordered up the best servings for his favorites. This she learned later when she had her turn as serving nun. Always the tenderest and most perfect portion was for Mother Mathilde, whom André idolized and at whose place he set each morning a little bunch of marguerites in a tumbler, which the Superior dared not order removed for austerity's sake, for fear of hurting his feelings.

The black boys who replaced the pot-washer, cooking and laundry nuns back home taught her who was who in the community even before she learned the names of her sisters and whether they worked in school, nursery or hospital. The tricks the boys played upon the sisters momentarily fallen in their esteem spotlighted the nuns' characteristics. If a sister with a passion for cleanliness humiliated André before all the others by handing back a fork that looked unclean, she paid for her forgetfulness of native prestige for as much as a week thereafter. André would set her place without a fork, knowing she could ask for nothing at the refectory table but must wait until some sister observed her lack and asked for her, knowing also that the sisters were generally too weary with overwork to note immediately what went on around them.

A sister made irritable by the heat might speak sharply to one of the laundry boys. The sleeve of her chemise would then be torn in the laundering, almost out but not quite, and it would be hung in perfect shape in her cell with the rent not observable until the next dawn when she reached for it hurriedly and found it unwearable. Since the bells gave no time for mending before Mass, she had then to take back from her laundry bag the mussed habit of the previous day. You could read the crumpled habits appearing in the chapel and know which sisters had offended the feelings of Boula, or Rutshuru, or André, or any one of their wives, sisters or brothers.

Or, you could read the reproach of a cleaning boy in the form of a ball made of dust, insect wings and the fuzzy drift from blossoming trees, named curiously a pussy-cat, and as visible as a small gray cat sitting on the stone floor beneath the bed of a nun who had spoken too quickly or had chided in public the boy who swept the convent and swabbed the floors each day.

Even Mother Mathilde might mention the pussy-cat in the recreation, lightly, as if in jest, but the nun under whose bed the gray ball reposed never took it lightly. "Something I said or did to him," she would say thoughtfully. "I cannot think what, *chère Mère*, but of course I offended his prestige somewhere, somehow . . ."

The recreations were held outdoors in a rococo kiosk centered in the cloister garden. Sister Luke looked at the bats and winged ants flying about, at the magenta bougainvillea hanging like a bishop's sash over the garden gate, and reminded herself that no matter what she was seeing or hearing, she was still in a convent. In the first days, it was often difficult to believe.

The convent was a brick bungalow which opened directly onto a wide dusty street, one end of which led to the city and the other to the bush. Behind the nuns' house was the small garden with kiosk, and beyond the rustic chapel of the sisterhood and the refectory. All the buildings had galvanized iron roofs lined on the inside with wood, but with enough space between to accommodate lizards and snakes which occasionally dropped through the knotholes in the wood.

On one side of the convent stood the big government hospital, as modern as anything in Belgium, and on the other the boarding and day schools for children of the colonials, and an immense nursery for the care of white infants whose parents were stationed in unhealthy or dangerous posts in the bush. Less than twenty nuns ran these establishments, in addition to giving the prescribed time to the daily devotions which followed the schedule of the mother house.

Until she saw the boys whom the sisters had trained to assist them, Sister Luke wondered how so few nursing and teaching nuns could handle such a city-sized task. *Les évolués,* the colony called these natives — the ones evolved or in process of evolving. Many had gone to the missionary schools, Catholic and Protestant, which were peppered all through the Congo. They had emerged with a new language — French — and a white man's craft which set them apart from their brothers still running half naked in the bush. The black boys were everywhere throughout schools, nursery and hospital, working as clerks, typists, baby-sitters and practical nurses and, like the selected few who worked inside the convent and laid upon the backs of the nuns the extra cross of their personal and passionate preferences, they worked best for the sisters they liked.

Sister Luke was keenly aware of their black eyes upon her when she made the rounds of her new community. They seemed to be taking her apart, examining the depth of her smile, the sincerity of each spoken word. Her heart went out to them but she was careful not to show it too soon. She did not know that already a favorable report had passed over the Congolese grapevine direct from Kalulu after his encounter with her in the railroad station.

"Young enough to bear children," Kalulu had broadcast. "Held hands with Big Mama Mathilde on way back to sister house, therefore esteemed. Said thank you in our tongue when I helped from car, but how much more Kiswahili she understands I cannot say. Talks little. Looks much." Boula the laundry boy had added to the publicity the number he found stamped on her guimpes, which, he reminded his listeners, was the same as that of Mama Marie-Polycarpe who used to tour the bush and bring back news of their villages. And André had rounded out the picture with his observation from the refectory serving window: "Only pretends, like us, to take quinine. Pinches finger over the dish and puts nothing on the tongue while making meanwhile a very bitter expression."

The hospital boys were as deft as women at their bed-making and bandage rolling. They passed barefoot through the pavilions in utter silence as their fathers had passed through the jungle, startling her when they came up from behind with trays poised lightly on their big black palms. The native nurses prepared her somewhat for the Congolese assistants in surgery and, eventually, for the skilled laboratory technicians with whom she made her refresher course in tropical medicines. These were the real *évolués*, the end results of a medical education that was going to produce full-fledged Negro doctors within the next few years.

Before beginning her studies with them in the government laboratories, she was sent by Mother Mathilde to visit the hospital for natives run by her Order in the section of town from which she had heard the drum talk on the night of

arrival. Here she saw in flashback, as it were, the beginnings of the native training in white man's ways.

To the maternity clinic came black women carrying newborn babes to be inspected by the nuns. Behind each young mother walked the husband carrying in a bowl the placenta, which was also shown to the nursing sister, who could tell at a glance if all the afterbirth had been expelled.

"Until we taught them to bring in the placenta," said the maternity sister, "we often had cases of puerperal fever in the mothers." She lifted a purple membrane with forceps and examined it. "It took us a long time to make them understand why this was as important to come out in entirety as the baby."

"One would think they'd all wish to come here for delivery," said Sister Luke.

"Not all of them trust us that much . . . yet. Many still feel safer delivering themselves in the bush. They scoop out a hole, crouch over it and *voilà!* In time and with patience, we'll overcome this centuries-old practice. But one thing in their asepsis is as good as ours. Look." The nun pointed to an infant being weighed. There was some sort of dark powder on the dried tip of the little black umbilical cord.

"Pulverized charcoal," she said. "In all the years we've been here, we've never seen one baby brought in with any suppuration of the cord. How they learned that charcoal is sterile and water-absorbent, we'll never know. They simply pat it on when the cord is severed. Not even a bandage required."

Sister Luke looked at the three black husbands carrying placentas. One in the line wore the matched shorts and shirt of the *Force Publique;* the others were covered by loincloths. The clay bowls holding the afterbirths were fine examples of native handicraft. The husbands' eyes rolled whitely toward the receiving table to see if all went well with the man showing to the sister a thing usually left for the jackals to consume.

She thought of Kalulu tinkering knowingly with the spark plugs of the convent Ford, of the black boys in her hospital already adept with many strange tools and of the colored technicians whom she had seen in the government laboratories examining slides sent in from the whole Katanga and identifying the bacilli faster than she believed she would be able to do when she joined them. It excited her to realize that here before her eyes were the fellow tribesmen of those laboratory *évolués*, making the first fearful steps toward civilization with flyblown placentas in their outstretched hands. The bush is that close, she thought.

The bush came closer when she saw what it could do to the white man who had to learn to live in it by will alone. After her refresher course, she took up her post as chief nurse in the European hospital staffed by her nursing sisters. The bacteria she had injected into apes and guinea pigs were now visible in their human hosts in the forms of fevers, rashes and hideous ulcerating sores. In the emergency ward she looked at scalps torn by wild beasts, at hands and feet gangrenous with thorn wounds, at savage gashes from crocodile encounters, and she had no feeling that she was confined within four walls of a city hospital, sentenced to a long tour of routine nursing.

The doctor was also a new experience. Chief surgeon, obstetrician, tuberculosis, cancer and malaria expert, Dr. Fortunati was a witch doctor in the eyes of the black nurses, a Beelzebub in the eyes of the nuns and a genius in her eyes. He began operating before five each morning to escape the heat and he wore out his nun assistants almost as fast as Mother Mathilde could supply them.

Sister Luke examined his postoperatives. He had to have God on his side to have pulled through some of the cases she charted. She longed to see him operate and in due time the opportunity came. The nun assisting him fell ill and Mother Mathilde asked her if she could take on the additional job in surgery meanwhile.

"You must always leave surgery the moment operations are over," said the Superior. "Don't ever linger to discuss a case, as you will certainly be tempted to do because he is an ace, as you know. But remember, he is also a man, a bachelor and an agnostic. In short, an Italian with hot blood." Her gentle face, so pure in its goodness that it seemed as if a prematurely aged child were looking at you, turned momentarily worldly. "Don't ever think for an instant, Sister, that your habit will protect you." She traced a firm sign of the cross on Sister Luke's forehead before sending her forth to the man who was to become a dominant influence in her cloistered life.

In the beginning she knew him mainly as a pair of blood-shot eyes in a sallow masked face and as the source of a nause-ating garlic odor. The garlic mixed with the ether she ad-ministered in the dark dawns on a fasting stomach before Mass. She fought her nausea while he fought for the life on the table.

For the first few weeks pride supported her. She could look around the surgery and see it performing like a precision bal-let. She had already improved on the training of the native as-sistants, given them style. The boy who stood behind the doc-tor and swabbed his forehead with a piece of ice wrapped in gauze took cues from her nods. An instrument boy replaced the nun who usually passed scalpels, hemostats and catgut from trays which she arranged earlier in the exact sequence

160

the operation would require. When a doctor from the mines assisted, she had a boy trained to assist him.

But one morning Dr. Fortunati asked her to assist. Then she was directly opposite him across the table, her head bent close to his, his garlic breath stifling her nostrils with each tense order he gave. Waves of nausea assailed her and a cold sweat broke out on her forehead. She knew then why so many surgery nuns had been done in after a term of assisting this garlic-eating genius.

But not I, she promised herself, I'm not too timid or too modest to speak to him, or too unearthly proud of my ability to swallow back nausea and endure. Anger sustained her for the remainder of the operation. When it was over, the doctor complimented her and asked how her health was since she had taken over the double duties.

"I can continue, *Monsieur le Docteur,* until the replacement arrives from the mother house. But on one condition only."

"Which is, Reverend Sister?"

"That you promise not to eat garlic on the nights before you operate."

It was the only time she ever heard him laugh. His mask was still on. His breath blew through the gauze and made her back away before she saw his gloved hands reaching out as if to take her by the shoulders to shake her.

"That's what Madame Lamartine says! Only she says it every night before dinner." His laughter pealed through the surgery, youthful and fresh like a small boy's. She knew he was referring to his mistress and that he was taking an enormous liberty with her in so doing. She turned her back on his laughter and pulled off her gloves. She heard the doctor say-

161

ing as she hurried toward the door, "For *you*, Reverend Sister, I agree . . ."

He kept his word. She began to assist him regularly although it meant rising at four on the mornings when two operations were scheduled, because the summer heats came down with the November rains and after seven o'clock the surgery was a Turkish bath.

Her chief boy, Emil, who headed the native staff in the hospital, now accompanied each stretcher to surgery and recited the vital statistics of the cases his assistants lifted upon the table.

"All pre-op medication given, Mama Luke. All lab work done and okay. No temperature. No apprehension. No dental plates. Blood pressure one-forty over seventy." His aide stood beside him, lifting the pages of the chart as Emil spoke, holding them before her eyes to read and confirm, but never touching her when he saw she was sterile.

The doctor seldom looked at the charts when she approved them. His dependence on her judgment was a tribute she tried to accept with humility, but in the pre-op tempo of those queer humid dawns, it was often difficult to remember that she was a nun first, and then a surgical nurse.

As he operated, Dr. Fortunati taught her everything he knew, taking her step by step through each technique as he cut, clamped and stitched. Very often they were in the midst of an operation when the chapel bells rang for six o'clock Mass. But she went right on with him, knowing that in time the Father would come to the hospital with the communion for the patients and that Sister Marie-Rose, on duty at the desk, would nod toward surgery when she was there.

The black altar boy holding candle and bell would stop first outside the surgery door. At the sound of the chimes, the boy who mopped the doctor's forehead would swing open the door so she could pass through without touching, and she would kneel, receive the Host and be back at the operating table in a matter of seconds.

The doctor never looked at her then. These were the only times he made no sardonic comment on the religious life. His momentary silence gave her enough time to say to herself, "He is with me and I am with Him." Then the doctor resumed his explanatory monologue.

He called her for every emergency and there were many in her first months. He sent Emil to fetch her out of chapel when he could not find her in the hospital. She knew that in time her sisters would talk, since more than half were professors with little understanding of medical crises. Once when the doctor summoned her for a matter she thought could have waited another five minutes and permitted her to finish an Office with the sisterhood, she mentioned the fact. Dr. Fortunati turned on her sharply.

"*You* may be in a convent but I am not," he said. "When I want you I want you. You are paid by the government and therefore at its disposition. They don't pay you to pray but to assist me." His eyes were bloodshot and weary after a week end party in the Kivu. "If your Superior allows you to work for two, it means that you have to give twice the time to the hospital, and it means one less at prayers."

She knew he was right. It was exactly what her father would have said, what he probably had said many a time when he operated in hospitals run by nuns, save that he would have spoken his piece and stalked out.

Afterwards, she reported the doctor's rebuke to her Superior. Mother Mathilde was a nurse herself, one who knew moreover the savage dedication of the doctor when he had a flickering life on the table. It was not difficult to make her understand the problem of nun versus nurse which had begun to worry her.

"In addition to this, *ma Mère*, I think about my sisters," she said. "My frequent absences from the community must seem to the teaching nuns perhaps a bit bizarre, even sought-after . . ." She trusted Mother Mathilde to read the rest of her thought, so she spoke it. "They'll start to talk, *ma Mère*, and though I know it will be for charity's sake, talk often starts trouble. In every community where I have been, events have singularized me and in some way set me apart from my sisters. I have prayed so hard it would not happen here. But now, this one they call Beelzebub causes me to be the one less at prayers, with your permission always. But still . . . so visible a subtraction from our small community . . ."

She watched Mother Mathilde composing her thoughts, making a rough draft of them so as not to waste time hunting words. This was the habit of every nun. Presently her Superior said:

"For the moment, Sister, you can do only what you have to do. Ask God to inspire you to act rightly. I have written again to the mother house begging another nurse, for you cannot hold those two jobs indefinitely." She paused, stroking her crucifix. "I am not thinking of our sisters. If they speak, it is for reasons of charity. It is that they wish to keep you close to God. I am not thinking even of your missed sleep which sooner or later is bound to affect your health in this climate. Physically, you are strong, but what is that with us? Health is expendable, even we are expendable. But the spiritual life is not ours to spend. This belongs to God. My concern is for what may be happening to your spiritual life, my sister."

Mother Mathilde leaned forward slightly, detaching herself

as it were from the crucifix hanging above her chair. Her gentle face was that of a friend, very human and warm. "Momentarily, I have permitted a situation to exist which forces you to starve your spiritual life. You starve it with a prayer snatched here and there, with a meditation shortened by emergency, with a rosary recited between pavilions when one part of you is thinking of the patients you have just left and those you are going to see."

"But I am strong, *ma Mère*."

"Only God knows who among us is strong and who is weak," said Mother Mathilde. "You appear to be graced with spiritual strength. This I count on, but I of course can never know for certain. Only your own conscience, Sister, can tell you how long you can continue without too great strain on your inner life."

Sister Luke remembered a parting advice from the Mistress of Novices. "You can cheat me. You can cheat your Superiors and cheat, with pretense, all your sisters. But there is One whom you can never cheat. You cannot cheat God."

"I can see," said Mother Mathilde as if picking up her thought, "only the visible palpable thing which every sister sees. I can never say that you do not do a meditation because you are not present when the community meditates. I cannot say you are not praying when your pew is vacant at Mass. I know always, because you are obedient, exactly where you are and what doing. When Father Stephen leaves us in chapel to take the Host to the hospital, I know that presently you will receive your communion, but I know also that under those circumstances, you cannot have time to reflect and make your act of thanksgiving fully." She smiled ruefully. "It is not easy, Sister, to serve God and Dr. Fortunati simultaneously."

Sister Luke knew exactly what she meant. There was always

the risk of the nurse carrying away the nun. It was the very problem that had brought her to Mother Mathilde, but now she saw the challenge in the situation. I'm strong, she thought, I can live on snatched prayers and curtailed meditations and manage that hospital with one hand and Beelzebub with the other for as long as she remains understaffed . . .

"With God's graces, I can carry on without risk, *ma Mère*."

"For the moment, I have no choice but to permit it." Mother Mathilde looked her straight in the eyes. "But remember, Sister, your soul was put in my care. Whatever risk to it may be inherent in this trying situation is mine as well as yours."

Sister Luke returned to the hospital filled with inner excitement. She had never before felt so close to a Superior. Her last words delivered with a smile of ineffable trust had gone straight to her heart. "Mine as well as yours . . ." Mother Mathilde shared the risk. *The risk of me*, Sister Luke thought with emotion.

Suddenly she saw the dimensions of that risk. Her love of the medical practice, fed and encouraged by Dr. Fortunati, could become an attachment very difficult for her conscience to cope with. And, when the doctor sent for her, was there not sometimes a secret satisfaction in being singled out from all the other sisters, a sort of sweet feeding after all the years of struggling to pass unperceived? She crossed the foyer on the way to the wards and another aspect of that risk was there before her eyes. Two wives of her colonial patients were waiting to tell her their sides of the stories she had already heard from their husbands babbling in fever.

As chief nurse of the hospital, she was more exposed to worldly affairs than she had ever been since entering the convent, and here in the colonies those affairs were often matters

166

about which a nun was supposed to know nothing. Yet she had discovered, as she gave sympathy and advice, that she knew enough about gambling, drinking and illicit love affairs to be able, quite often, to win a man away from them and back to his Creator when the shadow of death hung over his bed. And how often, she asked herself, when she had secured permission from some godless old colonial to call a priest for absolution, had she remembered to say, Someone's else prayers achieved this, I am only an instrument.

The risk of me, she thought again and her self-confidence turned to dismay. She stepped into the dispensary, the only place in the hospital where she could be alone. She looked out the windows at the vast horizons of Africa. The sky was blackening and making ready to release the daily deluge. Risk was out there, too. Presently there would be flash floods that caught the unwary and carried him down to quicksands that gave no footing. The way I could be carried if I'm not exceedingly watchful, she thought. *Blessed Lord, help me to be everything she trusts me to be . . .*

The dispensary door opened. "Mama Luke . . ." Emil's black face signaled emergency. She made her heart keep in step with her unhurried walk instead of running ahead as it usually did when Beelzebub called from surgery.

The table was empty and the operating lamp not lit. The doctor was putting on a linen street jacket. He smiled and asked her if she could do without him for a three-day week end while he went up to the Kivu to fish.

"There's nothing risky around here at the moment," he said. It was odd to hear him using the word she had just been weighing. "You'll have lots of time to catch up on your prayers while I'm gone."

"And if an emergency does come up, what then?" She asked

the question routinely as she ran through her mind the serious cases in the pavilions.

"Get a medic from the mines," he said easily. "Keep on with the morphine for the terminal cancer . . . he'll probably die but we're expecting that. Keep the drip on the three gangrenes. Don't touch the dressings on our skin graft even if they start to smell . . . just leave it alone. That's my technique to get good results." He looked at her standing quietly before him with hands folded beneath her scapular. "And get a bit of rest yourself, Sister. I've used you pretty hard in recent months."

She stayed in the surgery after he was gone, checking over the things she would have time to do while he was away. The pharmacy clean-up, work on hospital records, making a rough draft of the government report that had to be as exact as a bank statement, taking another slide of that mysterious ulceration case in Contagious and trying to identify the bacillus . . . She caught herself thinking only of the work. I'll live my full religious life with the community as well, she promised herself. Chapel, refectory, recreation . . .

The telephone buzzed. It was Sister Aurélie from the men's pavilion advising that the cancer case was failing fast.

"I'll get a Father right over." She rang the brotherhood that was just a few blocks distant and smiled with relief when she heard Father André's voice. He was her great friend and spiritual adviser as well, a man so universally loved in the colony that even Freemasons held up their infants to receive his benediction when he passed.

"Just give me time to get the old Ford cranked, Sister. Wait for me by the main door."

The bells rang as she hung up, calling all sisters to chapel

168

for prayers. If the bells had not been fixed in her mind as the call of Christ, she would have said at that moment that they had a mocking tone. Once again, and this time on the heels of a firm resolution, she would have to miss a community devotion. She telephoned to Mother Mathilde and received her permission to stay on duty.

Expecting the rattle of the brotherhood's Ford, she did not recognize Father André when he appeared around the street corner. She gazed at the four men bearing a chair on their shoulders and at the priest slumped sideways in it, seeming to doze. You often saw missionary Fathers returning like that from a long tour of the bush, motionless with exhaustion, looking a little like apostolic statues with the long beards which all the Congo Fathers wore because the natives, who had seen God only in holy pictures, expected anyone coming in His name to look like Him. *The physiognomy of the métier* . . . She smiled as she remembered her father's phrase and watched the cortege come down the street. Then she saw that the four men bearing the chair were not natives. They were the shaven-headed brothers of Father André's order.

She hurried forward as they turned in at the hospital gate. A brother said, "His Ford left in gear when he cranked . . . smashed him against a stone wall." Her shocked glance took in the splintered leg hanging askew, the blood-drenched white cotton trouser and the bicycle clip he had forgotten to remove, which served as partial tourniquet and had probably kept him from bleeding to death. She gave orders as she led the way to the treatment room. Emil sped to get Mother Mathilde. Sister Aurélie telephoned to summon another priest for the cancer patient and a doctor from the mines.

She had the white cotton trouser slit and sterile compresses

169

applied when Emil reappeared with the Superior. "If we'd only had time to get him sterile so we could do this in the surgery," she whispered.

Mother Mathilde gave her the comprehending glance of nurse to nurse and rolled up her long white sleeves. Emil saw her examine the torn veins and began to set up the tray for blood transfusion while Mother Mathilde tested for blood type, then found the brother with matching blood and prepared the apparatus for direct transfusion from donor to receiver. Sister Aurélie came in, reported calmly that there wasn't a doctor to be found at the mines, in the town or in any government office, and took her place at the table.

The three nuns worked like a single being with six hands, preparing transfusion and anesthetic. Sister Luke lost her calm just once, when Father André came out of his swoon and said he wished to confess himself before they gave him any narcotics. She looked with rage at his pain-twisted face and almost shouted, "What have *you* got to confess? . . . With *your* purity you're always ready to meet your Creator . . ." but she bit her lip and kept silent. Her hand shook as she worked the transfusion needle into his arm. Microscopic imperfections against his Rule, she thought savagely. She knew the agony her hands would cause him when presently she must try to reduce the fracture.

The three brothers at the head of the table worked over the spotless soul of Father André while the nuns at the foot worked over the difficult transfusion with double syringe and laid bare the macerated tibia and torn flesh. There was no praying at their end of the table. They were all nurses then, swift and expert, fearless and sure in the strength of their medical knowledge. Father André confessed himself humbly in the presence of everyone. As only the very great and simple souls can do, Sister Luke thought, and she nodded to Mother Mathilde to start the narcosis.

All her surgery-room boys came up around her as she prepared to go into the wound. She had sent no one to call, but they were there with sterile gowns and gloves from surgery, but no masks. They even knew the nuns would have no time to remove the coifs and put on the nursing veils over which masks could be worn. Silent, efficient, like a black shadow dance she herself had originated and trained, they shook out the gowns and dressed her and Sister Aurélie, snapped open the gloves and pulled them on their upraised hands.

The tibia had a compound fracture, the ankle tendons were mashed and the leg muscles a shapeless red pulp. One of the boys began to break the tubes containing sterile catgut, as if he read her mind and knew she was going to suture. She was sure it was a case for amputation only, but something drove her on to do the best she could. Mother Mathilde ran the slow narcosis, watched heartbeat and color changes in Father André's face, and called out the numbers of the sutures needed, first for the deep stitches, then the finer catguts for the veins.

I stitch, she snips, she watches and calls, and here are the three of us nuns turned totally nurses for this hour — Mother Mathilde, Sister Aurélie and I, and what was that risk I was pondering this morning? Was it not for a performance such as that that we were trained, bent and molded, every whit as much as for staying close to walls in wide places and never running, always walking, never frowning, always smiling?

She stitched. Sister Aurélie snipped. Mother Mathilde called the suture numbers to the boys. Presently they began laying back the ribbons of skin over the red pulp their hands had re-formed into the shapes of the *extensor digitorum*

171

longus, the *tibialis anterior* and the *peroneus longus* muscles. A boy had the gutter mold ready. They lifted what was left of the leg into it. Then they laid dressings carefully over the best that they could do without amputation and Sister Luke caught Mother Mathilde's eyes upon her when she looked up to see how the intravenous was running.

Three days later she saw the same look in Dr. Fortunati's eyes when he removed the dressings and examined her handiwork. It was a glance of pure professional admiration.

"I did what I could," she said, "what conscience and the grace of God told me to do . . . but I couldn't amputate as indicated, being only a nurse." She heard herself saying I, I . . . and flushed. "Mother Mathilde and Sister Aurélie assisted me."

She staggered a little as she helped him change the dressing. She had sat up for three nights with Father André and had listened to him wander in fever. Even in delirium, the Father had thought only of God, his fellow traveler in the bush. Sometimes he had imagined that she was one of his brothers from the monastery and had given her a saintly exhortation meant for the ears of men only. As she had sat through the vigils, she had made up the day's devotions, beginning with Prime and reading straight through to Matins and Lauds, and Emil had shuttled back and forth like a black bobbin between her and Mother Mathilde, weaving them tightly together with bulletins of health from the bedside and dispensations to remain on vigil from the office of the Mother Superior.

"Nothing more could have been done, Sister." The doctor straightened up with a satisfied sigh. "You have not only saved the Father but also his leg. In forty-eight hours we can put a continuous drop on it. It might take a year . . . but he'll walk again."

She stiffened before the rush of pride his words gave her, and when she told herself promptly after that she was only an instrument, she couldn't see the sister back home in the mother house who coughed as she prayed for the missions . . . but only the bed on which that sister lay, a soft white hospital bed that gave no rustle of straw when she turned over on her side to sleep and sleep and sleep.

X I

THE changing colors of the altar cloths from the violet of Advent, through the whites and golds of Christmas and on to the purples of Lent, told of the passing year.

Or, there were the four letters she was permitted to write annually to her family, of four pages each and not a sentence more except with special permission which she seldom sought; instead, she shrunk her bold square handwriting down to the spidery lace that gave more lines to the page and saw herself finally writing just like all the other missionary sisters.

There was the continuous drop on Father André's leg for three months after his accident and then bimonthly X-rays of slowly mending tissues which always gave her a struggle with pride. And, every so often, Mother Mathilde reported that she had written to the mother house for the nursing reinforcement that never came.

Afterwards, when Sister Luke looked back on her first Congo year, she saw but one really important experience in it. It was nothing she could report to her family as a major impression. You had to be a nun to see it that way. God caught up with her and gave her one more chance to recite her vows without reservation. Then, when she was safely in

174

His pocket, He let her see with shattering clarity how little humility she had. She repeated her vows on what she hoped and prayed was her deathbed, struck down with a dysentery that left no desire to live or even the memory of what it had been like to be alive without the agonizing pain that tore the will to shreds.

When she discovered her condition, she hid it as long as she could. It was a humiliation, a loss of a working hand in the community, a waste of God's time through her own carelessness, she believed. She traced her malady to tropical fruits which had possibly been stung by the fruit fly.

Twice weekly when she went to the native hospital to take lumbar punctures, a serving boy showed his ardor by waiting for her at the clinic door with a bowl of iced fruit, usually mangos he had traded in the native market. It was his way of saying, I like you. The chilly golden flesh of the mangos was delicious to eat in the humid forenoons when you had a dozen lumbar punctures lined up and the sensitive tests of spinal fluids to make afterwards, in quest of the trypanosomes of sleeping sickness.

The dysentery was the fulminant type, quick and acute. The day she collapsed in surgery seemed to be her last. The doctor raged at her as he put her on a stretcher.

"You should have told sooner, you proud little fool." His face hung close. "How many stools in the past twenty-four hours?"

"More than thirty," she whispered and saw his sallow face go gray.

They carried her to the convent infirmary. In a haze of pain and exhaustion she swallowed what the doctor ordered and felt the needle-prick of his opium injections. The black face of Emil, the doctor's yellow face and the delicate ovals of

Mother Mathilde's and Sister Aurélie's hung alternately over her until late in the night, and she guessed she must be passing the bright-red gelatinous mucus of the last stage when she heard Mother Mathilde tell the doctor she would summon priest and sisters.

She was floating above the bed, looking down on a young nun dying there, when she heard the sisters at three o'clock in the morning coming along the path from dormitory to infirmary, singing the *Miserere* softly in the cricket-shrill African night. She saw all twenty sisters with lighted candles in their hands and old Father Stephen at the end of the procession carrying the Viaticum, with Mother Mathilde and her senior nun beside him with the holy oils. You die so beautifully when you are a nun, she thought. She looked down again upon the bed where the dying one lay, so young, so heroic, so humbly waiting with folded hands for a bit of parchment to be placed between them — a promise signed on an altar years ago and in a distant place.

She listened to the *Miserere* plead that she would have strength to ask God for His mercy, confess her iniquities and offer up to Him a contrite and humbled heart. Coming toward the dying, the sisters sang their hopes for her. Going away, they would sing the *Te Deum* to thank God for accepting her nothingness. All this for me, she thought. And even more. Next day a cable would inform the mother house of her death and shortly after, every convent in the entire congregation would make the Stations of the Cross in her name. She saw the processionals winding through all the European houses, on to the Orient and back again through India and the Congo . . . ah, those beautiful processionals that had always caught her by the throat, even when she had been participant in them and occasionally, like these oncoming sisters, had been routed from sleep at some unearthly hour to wind around a dying nun a shroud of heavenly song.

There was a smile on her lips when Father Stephen entered her room, raised the Viaticum and intoned the opening phrase of extreme unction.

"Peace to this house," he sang in a rich baritone.

"And to all who live herein," responded her sisters, holding their little candles before their faces . . .

But she recovered. She knew why, even before she returned to the community to be congratulated by her sisters for her readiness to die. One by one during the weeks she lay in the hospital, her conscience turned up the humiliating truths of her illness. Her entire preparation to die had been a fraud, an indulgence in heroism and self-pity. The smile the sisters had seen and called courageous had been for gratification at the thought of a thousand nuns circling the globe in a memorial procession in her name. Had there been a single moment, even in that most solemn ceremony of last rites, when her heart had been truly humbled and every thought bent directly toward God?

Her self-examination grew more relentless as she gained strength. She made it as meticulously as she had prepared slides for the microscope, looked down the tube and named what she saw. You walk, you talk, you even write like a nun. But you are not a nun, not yet. The mold has shaped you to look like one, but inside that deceptive shell still flourishes pride and vainglory, worldliness and self-love.

On a scorching afternoon when the winged ants flew thickly around the recreation kiosk, she returned to the community. From the sickbed she brought one fixed idea — that God would pursue her with humiliations until she learned humility. Her first hour with her sisters confirmed this belief. She shrunk with shame when they congratulated her on her courage before death. When she could stand their praise no longer, she said, "It wasn't courage." She hunted for something other than her own truth to say. "It was more of a . . . a snobbism."

The nuns knew what she meant. Sometimes, the more lowly and humble you made yourself, the more superior you felt. Some of the nuns were shocked by her frankness, others admired it. Mother Mathilde tapped twice on the arm of her chair to indicate that she would take over the talk.

"Sister Luke didn't die," she said quietly, "because her mission is not yet accomplished. Moreover, my sisters, it was not she who was tested, but us, the community." She nodded emphatically. "Ah yes, God was only testing us to see if we were willing to give up a number." Her smile embraced the circle and reminded them that they were all only numbers. "One number less in our understaffed community would have been a heavy cross for us to bear at this time."

Not one sister less, not one nun with a known name and background less . . . just one number less, Sister Luke thought. She looked up at her Superior, who never forgot first principles of the religious life. Be nothing before you can be something. She saw some of her sisters squirming inwardly under the anonymity Mother Mathilde had thrust upon them all. But upon me mostly, she thought.

She trained her dressing boys soon after she returned to work and made Emil her deputy. Both innovations brought the spotlight of singularity upon her.

The chief in charge of nursing in the hospital had always had a nun as deputy, as she had been given Sister Aurélie. But

178

why a nun? Why not, she asked herself, old black Emil, who has seen generations of us pass through this hospital and knows as much about nursing as any of us?

"I'd like to make him my deputy," she informed Mother Mathilde. "Then we can free Sister Aurélie for total time in the maternity pavilion. Were Emil my deputy, moreover, all punishment of the colored staff would be dealt out by him instead of by the nuns and I think this would be good. Only a handful of us for those three hundred beds . . . we have more to worry about than the trace of *simba* on a black boy's breath, *ma Mère*."

Mother Mathilde thought for a moment, seeming to weigh the intention rather than the suggestions. Sister Luke felt the probe of her bright eyes. Desire for change, merely for the sake of doing something different, was one of the big temptations of every nun. It could catch you on even such little things as having to fold your habit in exactly the same way, day after day, year after year, for no other reason than that the Rule said thus and thus and not so and so. And your occasional rebellions, boiling up with the force of almost a physical passion and as difficult to overcome, reminded you that obedience was no mouselike virtue, easily captured and kept. Sister Luke knew that all this had passed through her Superior's mind before she gave her consent.

"Very well," she said at last. "And I myself will inform the doctor, who could have no objections, as far as I can see."

Sister Luke returned to the hospital to hand over to a black man a responsibility nearly equal to her own. She called together all her registered male nurses and technicians, most of whom had had four years of study and were fluent in French, and all her messengers, cleaning boys and kitchen staff. She told them that from that day forward, Emil was to be their

Capita. Knowing how the Blacks loved the idea of hierarchy and understood it through their own tribal traditions, she explained that she was setting up a line of authority.

"When you have some problem, you will now tell it to Emil, your Capita," she said. "He will tell me. I will consult with Big Mama Mathilde and she, in turn, will ask God for guidance. Thus, all problems will be handled henceforth."

Their faces beamed. It would be easier to tell their troubles to Emil and have him translate them for white understanding. The sudden longings to return to the bush village, the tabus and fears always difficult to express in any language other than their own . . . now they saw these going up, through Emil, straight up the line to God and back again, justly decided.

"Also," said Sister Luke, "there will be no more punishment ordered by the sisters. Your Capita will henceforth decide each case and himself decree the punishment."

This made an even greater impression. Her boys looked with renewed respect on Emil, a caste Negro like themselves, the oldest among them and the longest in the hospital, now most justly elevated to a worthy position. Punishment was always a ticklish business. Like the doling out of the dry ration which constituted part of their pay, punishment must also, to make it acceptable, be weighed and dealt out with exactitude. Sister Luke listened to the ripples of approval that passed through the room when she finished speaking.

She would have been astonished had anyone told her that her innovation was in reality a small stroke added to the vast blueprint of a future Congo which planned to turn the children of cannibals into full-fledged doctors, priests and engineers within the next two decades. She knew almost nothing about colonial policies. She knew only that without the aid of her black boys, she couldn't have run her hospital.

She would never even have known that her name and the news of her prestige-giving promotion of Emil started on its way to the bush that same night, had not one of her sisters been able to read the drums. In the recreation kiosk as she sat under the electric light dodging bats and fanning off winged ants, she heard a visiting sister from the Kipushi bush station compliment Mother Mathilde for something having to do with the hospital administration.

"And who, may I ask, is Mama Luke?" said the visiting sister, looking around the circle while the drums talked softly from the native town.

Emil became her shadow. When she asked for extra night duty, he found out from the bulletin board and took it also. When she went across town to the native hospital, he rode with her in the convent Ford, carrying the instruments which had never before been entrusted to a black man.

From him she learned more about the Congo and its twelve million Blacks, of whom the majority were Bantus like himself, than if she had made many safaris. Emil told her of the rivers she had never seen and of the spirits inhabiting their whirlpools, of the rain forests and the mountains where the great baboons lived, and he named the tribes belonging to those regions . . . Baluba, Batembo, Batetela, Balamba, Bayeke, Basuku . . . the smile or scorn on his thick black lips telling which he considered admirable or otherwise. Sometimes when they drove through the market place, he would point out a native who looked to her eyes like any other and tell her that he was a Bangala, as anyone could see from the coxcomb tattoo that lifted in lumps down the middle of his forehead; or that that one trading an ebony statue was either a Bakuba or a Tutshiokwi — tribes known for their good sculptors.

She in turn told him whatever he wished to know about her people, which was not very much. Emil had been so long with the whites, first in missionary schools and then in the hospital, that he seemed to take them for granted, neither to be feared nor revered, but simply to be respected because they knew more than he. Only the "white mamas" puzzled him, he once confessed. Where were their husbands?

When she tried to explain, she discovered how incomprehensible to the mentality of the bush native was the idea of chastity. Even to one as evolved as Emil, who had words like appendectomy in his vocabulary (and probably could have performed one after all the operations he had assisted), the concept of a mystic marriage was impossible to explain without getting into the subject of polygamy — as had happened to one of the nuns who had tried to make the seeming solitary situation of so many white sisters understandable to a Negro with five wives.

Eventually, Sister Luke solved the dilemma by telling Emil that indeed she had a husband who was in Heaven and that she had made him a promise never to marry again. Emil understood promise. He understood widow. Grave with sympathy, he nodded and never spoke of it again.

Emil helped her to work out her plan to give specialized training to some of her male nurses. Observation had taught her that the Congolese was an excellent routine worker. Once shown how to do a thing, he would follow the original teaching without a hair's deviation. There was a saying in the convent, she explained to Emil, which would automatically put the seal of approval on their efforts. No task is difficult, went the maxim, once it is fully perceived; the big merit lies in seeing the task and in comprehending what it consists of.

Instruct to capacity was the watchword of the Congo in the 1930's. The whole country was standing on the threshold of a phenomenal upsurge which was to double its white population within a few years and quintuple the number of Blacks drawn in from the bush to its hospitals, mines and textile mills, to become, like her own boys, a first generation to work with whites, eat their foods, copy their customs and eventually to enter into that queer lonely society of the *évolués* which was neither black nor white but some kind of gray mixture like clay before it is fired. Hundreds of other Europeans were doing the same thing as she at that time — pushing, encouraging, putting into the natives as much knowledge as they could absorb. The only difference was that the others knew they were in step with the times. They read newspapers and lived in the new world rising visibly around them out of the ancient bush and jungle.

Sister Luke merely saw her boys follow with eager eyes the progress of their Capita as Emil pushed the dressing cart from bed to bed and handed her what she called for. She asked Emil to select the four brightest; then she summoned them to a conference.

When you had something to tell or show to the natives, you always made a little drama to give an added value to the piece of white man's knowledge you were going to impart. The boys came into the dressing room and saw Emil lying on the table heavily bandaged. Sister Luke waited until their startled chatter died down; then she told them that this was Monsieur X just recovering from a hernia operation.

"I am going to change his dressings," she said. "Then I am

183

going to teach you to do it. This is practice, but the day will come when you four will be the *corps élite* of our nursing staff, entrusted with the change of dressings of all our male patients."

Not a boy moved, but she felt them draw back instinctively, and knew why. No black man, no matter how skilled, ever touched the wound of a white man. It was one of the unwritten laws which made no sense when you recalled that many of the younger patients had grown up in the Congo and had had black boy guardians who had removed chiggers from under their toenails and had patted mud on their bruises and scratches.

"We do everything with forceps," she said. She picked up a forceps from the dressing cart. "Never touch a patient, see. Never touch a dressing, even with sterile gloves." She made a frame of overlapping towels around the black abdomen of Emil, then with forceps began lifting in slow motion the first layer of dressings. The boys drew closer to the table.

For a week she trained them in secret and they practiced on each other under Emil's supervision when she was making the rounds with the doctor. Then one morning she told them they were ready. Sterile-gowned and gloved, they preceded her with the dressing cart to the men's pavilion.

They were practical nurses with four years' schooling. They knew every white man lying in the rooms, had carried trays in to them and bedpans out, had watched over them in fevers and over the apparatuses that fed them blood or glucose; but they went to pieces outside the door where Sister Luke flagged them to a stop. Fear of the new thing they were about to do made their faces go gray. There was a quick chatter of Kiswahili among them, as of birds warning each other.

Sister Luke called their names calmly, made each pick up the object he was responsible for.

"Mafuta, the sterile towels. Banza, the kidney basin. Edouard and Illunga . . . forceps," she ordered sternly, then smiled. "We'll go over it again before we enter. You are going to dress a deep thigh wound. Mafuta places towels around it, edges overlapping so no sheet shows. Edouard assisted by Illunga lifts off the dressings with forceps, drops them into the kidney basin Banza holds ready. They remove as far as the collodion gauze, which you know is bright yellow. Then they step back. I come forward, lift the gauze, look at the stitches, remove them if ready. Emil passes medication if needed. Then, you again . . ." She did not tell them that she had prepared the patient also for this innovation and had selected for their debut the most easygoing colonial, who thought it would be amusing to have her boys dress his wound instead of a nun. She nodded for them to put everything back on the cart. "Now we are ready," she said, giving her boys a smile of trust before leading the way into the room.

Within a fortnight she had a production-line system of dressing changes which enabled her to dress twenty-five postoperatives in an hour and have a full report on each ready for the doctor when he made his rounds at eight-thirty. When he saw the dressing boys in action, Dr. Fortunati looked from them to her with something of the same expression he had had when he inspected her work on Father André's leg. This time he said, "So . . . you're a teacher, too, Sister Luke!"

Perhaps if he had not bragged to the mine doctors of how efficiently things were running in *his* hospital and how they ought to have a nun to show them how to utilize the black manpower in their own medical center, there would have been no spotlight. The colony was a small place for gossip, especially when the talk was confined to the copper boom town with its white population of born entrepreneurs who reveled in innovation. News of a nun who had a trained circus of dressing boys got around. The Apostolic Delegate of the province telephoned to Mother Mathilde to inform her that one of her nuns had apparently gone out of the mold and was being named by name in public places.

You could be named as a white sister, or a gray or a blue sister, as a Dominican, a Franciscan, a Benedictine or an Ursuline — if the public knew enough to read coif and habit and place you in the congregation to which you belonged. You could be called a teaching sister, or a nursing sister, or an evangelizing or a visiting sister. But outside your own walls, your own sphere of work and co-workers black and white, you were not supposed to be called by your name in Christ. There was nothing written on it; it simply was not done. And if it was, it meant that you had somehow singularized yourself.

Sister Luke knew when Mother Mathilde came to the men's pavilion to watch her dressing boys in action that it was for a reason other than routine inspection. A shadow lay beneath her never-failing smile, imperceptible to any but the perceiving eyes of a nun. The boys thought she had come to admire them and performed beautifully. They were dressing a cancer postoperative. In swift silence, with a style precise and elegant, Edouard plucked up the soiled dressings with forceps, suspended them for the fraction of an instant over the kidney basin as if saying to Banza, Yes, it must be held exactly there and no place else — then dropped the dressings into it without looking to see where they fell. Illunga unrolled the sterile dressings on the cart. Mafuta opened the lid of the soiled dressing container each time the kidney basin

186

was full. They all stepped back like soldiers when Edouard came to the collodion gauze. Emil summoned Sister Luke to the bedside with a glance.

"What teamwork, *Révérende Mère*," said the patient. "You must be proud of your nuns." He turned his head on the pillow and smiled at Mother Mathilde. "We could do with a little of this organization in the textile mills."

Sister Luke lifted the gauze and inspected the clamps on the large abdominal incision. Ordinarily she would have told the boys why they were not yet ready for removal, but she dared not trust her voice. It would not be the sure steady one they knew. Like her heart, it would tremble with the awareness she had plucked from the air when she stood by Mother Mathilde. She had erred, she had failed her Superior somehow. It meant nothing that Mother Mathilde's voice and manner betrayed no more than appreciative interest in a nursing job well done, for no nun ever rebuked another in the presence of others.

If I have failed her, Sister Luke thought. O God, let it be anyone else . . . the doctor, a patient, any or all of my sisters, but not her . . . not her. She signed abruptly to Mafuta for a clean collodion gauze, laid it on the wound and stepped back. The boys moved in to complete the dressing.

"I must go now, Monsieur," said Mother Mathilde. "I leave you indeed in capable hands."

As was customary, Sister Luke accompanied her to the door of the pavilion. The Superior paused in an alcove apart from the traffic of the corridor.

"Your only fault, Sister," she said softly, "was in failing to tell me about this in advance. I see now that you are not responsible for a certain acclaim this work has brought. It would have been noted eventually no matter which sister in-

187

spired it. But earlier, when our Delegate telephoned me to ask me why one of my nuns sought to singularize herself, I had no answer."

From its effect upon her, the mild reproach might have been delivered with a lash. She trembled and wanted to strike back at the purple-sashed Delegate who had made her Superior suffer with the knowledge that one of her nuns had not confided in her. She knew exactly the sort of polite aggrieved words he must have spoken. She had had a brush with him once and had discovered him to be, as far as she could see or sense, curiously untouched by the largeness of the Congo.

"I should have told you, *ma Mère*," she whispered. "I think perhaps I wanted to surprise you . . ." She stopped before her voice would break.

"I have my answer now, Sister," said Mother Mathilde very firmly and loyally. "I shall telephone to our Delegate, perhaps even invite him to come see how we make both ends meet, lacking sufficient nursing sisters." Her parting smile made it all seem a very small matter.

But it was not a small matter, not when you were a nun. Though but a sin of omission, the most forgivable, you nevertheless had to connect it to all the others that had gone before. You had to put it into the context of your religious life.

The more failings she put into the context, the more depressed she became. The doctor was the first to see a change in her. One morning after operations, he detained her in surgery. He showed her the final X-ray of Father André's leg and gave her a photo print of it for a keepsake.

"To remind you always," he said, "that you are an excellent nurse." He watched her slip the photo without comment into her pocket. Then he said, "But you know something,

Sister? You're much too stark and disciplined a person. Something in your life here has made you so. I remember how you were when you first came out to the colony. Recently, I've watched you tighten, fold in upon yourself, and I cannot think why. What is it, Sister?"

Caught off guard, she flushed. That this irreligious layman had guessed her inner struggle nearly brought tears. She turned quickly and left the surgery, but his sharp face grown suddenly sympathetic was difficult to banish from her thoughts. And the way he had talked to her — as if she were a human being in the world, beset like any other with troubles that a friend might be able to understand and help to iron out.

She knew that if she were the kind of docile nun who thought every emotion worth reporting to the Superior, she should go to Mother Mathilde and tell of her reactions to the doctor's personal remarks. She stood for a moment undecided. She heard very distinctly the voice of the Mistress of Novices saying, "Every failure to a Superior, no matter how small or how innocently committed, is a tug at your sleeve from the world, trying to pull you back to it."

But she was never to know if she would have gone that day. Duty came toward her down the hospital corridor in the form of Father Vermeuhlen, the famous priest of the leper colony, and Etienne, the town's coiffeur. Etienne was there to dress the hair of the banker's wife and Father Vermeuhlen had come for his annual precautionary check. The saint and the sinner, she thought as she watched them approach.

XII

FATHER VERMEUHLEN looked like one of the elder apostles walking down the corridor. Even had she not been expecting him, she would have recognized instantly the priest called the white saint of the leper colony. Sister Monique, professor of art in the school, had once described him as Michelangelo's Moses in motion, to explain why every bush native fell to his knees at his approach.

He was a giant of a man, dressed in white cotton soutane and an immense sun topee, and heavy high-laced boots that bespoke long treks through tick country. A snowy beard fell far down over his broad chest, and his eyebrows, arching thickly over the most beautiful and kindly eyes she had ever looked into, were coal-black.

"Father Vermeuhlen, you are expected," she said. He towered over her like an immaculate monument. She smiled up at him. "I'm new since your last check. I'm Sister Luke."

"Sister Luke." His voice was deep, trained to reach only to the ears of his listeners. "I've heard about you . . ." His dark eyes twinkled.

"The drums, Sister," said the fox-eared coiffeur she had forgotten to look at or greet. "Father reads them like newspapers."

"Monsieur Etienne." She forced a smile for the pomaded

190

little man she always tried to avoid but could not now because he was with the saint who avoided no one, not even the leprous Blacks with whom he lived. "Your client Madame Goossens is in room twenty-two of Maternity. If you wish, I'll get Emil to show you the way."

"Ah no, Sister, thank you. I know my way." He twisted his mustache and winked at her. "There's not a room in the colony I haven't been in, except" — he bowed — "those in your contagious pavilion you isolate so strictly."

And the nuns' dormitory, she thought, thankful that at least one segment of the colony's womanhood was out of reach of his prying eyes. He was like a dirty little bird, picking, pecking and dropping. She disliked him because he always made her retaliate in thought.

Etienne looked up at Father Vermeuhlen. "Good luck on the tests, Father. If you'd like a little trimming and combing of the beard while you're here, I'd be happy to do it, *pro Deo*, of course."

The Father chuckled and shook his head. "My boys would never approve such changes."

Nor would I, thought Sister Luke. She shuddered at the image of the Assyrian curl Etienne would like to give to the beautiful beard and made no reply when he trotted off toward Maternity saying, not asking, "You'll come later, Sister, to tell Madame how beautiful I've made her for her ordeal."

She walked in silence with Father Vermeuhlen to the laboratory to start the tests which would take two weeks to complete. Later that day, when she heard his story, she thanked her guardian angel that she had not spoken the thought that made her heart forget its woes as she matched his long steps down the corridor. You'll conduct one or two Masses while you're here, she was thinking. With that wonderful voice you'll sing the Sacrifice as it must have been sung in the days of old, as it is still sung by the monks of Solemnes, with thought and purity, without hurry or mumble.

In the laboratory, Father Vermeuhlen removed his topee. It gave her a start to see that his hair was as white as his beard. It made his black eyebrows and dark shining eyes doubly strange, as if age had come with sudden whiteness only to certain parts of him. She prepared the slides while she wondered what in his saintly life could have given shock. He lived alone in the bush village far off the beaten track, caring for the bodies as well as for the souls of his miserable black lepers. More than a hundred of them, the doctor had told her, most of them in the advanced stage when even their own tribes throw them out to die. She had never asked why he had chosen so risky a field because, being a nun, it was perfectly obvious to her that he had chosen it for love of God alone. As she would have chosen the place of deepest suffering if God had willed it and if nuns had had choice.

"I'll take your nasal secretions first, Father."

He tilted back his massive head and shut his eyes. She said a little prayer as she made the smears.

Etienne found her at the desk that afternoon studying the case record of Father Vermeuhlen.

"You didn't come, Sister," he said aggrieved.

"I was busy." She smiled because the Rule said always smile and act with grace and politeness.

"I made her beautiful for her ordeal."

"It will not be an ordeal, Monsieur Etienne. She will have a perfectly normal delivery."

"Ah that . . . perhaps. But if she gives birth to another daughter . . ." Etienne leaned over the desk. "That is the ordeal I speak of, Sister. If it is not a son *this* time, Monsieur

192

Goossens will cut his throat. Or hers." She couldn't stare him down. He went right on talking. "Or even he might be driven to try elsewhere. You know how he prays for a son to inherit that banking business. Madame also. She just was telling me with tears in her eyes."

"She will accept God's will. If she weeps now, it is simply the strain of the final hours, or possibly because you, Monsieur, were too deeply sympathetic." She heard with dismay the sarcasm in her voice. The coiffeur missed it completely.

"Sympathetic." He bowed as for a compliment and looked at the chart. "As I am for that saintly Vermeuhlen who lives out his life of penance without a murmur."

"Penance?" Despite her will for silence, the word escaped her on a tone of surprise.

"But you who are caring for him should know his story, Sister." The coiffeur looked around to see if anyone could overhear. She knew she should stop him but she could not. An astonishing compassion came into his voice and his flying hands folded in woe as he talked. He gave her not the colony gossip he carried around in his little black bag along with curling irons, razors and unguents, but a secret knowledge he had stumbled upon when he was a young man in the colony, and stammered over now as he told her because he did not tell it often.

Many years ago, he related, one of the Fathers — a Salesian or a Père de Scheut — was making a tour of the jungle on an apostolic mission. In a certain village he found a white man, then about forty years old, who was playing with some Bantu children and seemed to be alone with the tribe and quite unexplainable. The white man came toward the priest with love and a sort of apprehension in his eyes and asked him to visit his hut that evening for a talk. They had apparently

193

talked straight through the night. The white man told that he also had once been a priest, that he had come out to the Congo in the early days before there were roads and telephones. For months on end his work kept him isolated from his brothers, from all contacts with civilization. A terrible loneliness started to gnaw. After two years, he despaired. He walked off into the bush one day and made no further effort to communicate with his distant mission, which eventually gave him up as lost, captured by cannibals or eaten by a prowling cat, a common enough event at that time. Whether out of pity, or loneliness, or love, the coiffeur said respectfully, he lived with a native woman and had three children by her.

"Nobody knows, of course, what the Father said, but rumor had it that a few weeks later, the white man appeared at one of the bush missions and left three black children there to be cared for and educated by the nuns." Etienne paused. She asked God to forgive her for listening, for wanting him to go on. "Then, the ex-priest disappeared."

Months later the bush hummed with the news that the white man had reappeared, back from Europe, from Rome most probably, and that he was a priest again. Apparently he had asked his higher hierarchy for permission to devote the rest of his life to lepers as penance for his sins, and this had been granted to him along with permission to say the Mass again.

"But he may never say Mass outside the leper colony," Etienne whispered. "He is adored there, Sister. You should see. Once, I accompanied a fashionable hunting party that passed by the colony. The others were afraid, but I went in . . ." Words failed him. He looked about to cry. "You should go, Sister . . ."

When he was gone she sat staring at the charts, trying to make the clinical notations come into focus. *Nasal negative. Blood negative. Physical — no thickening of nerves; perfect cutaneous sensibility.* The first entries were almost illegible with age. This was expiation on the grand scale. It was the kind of penance God granted only to the chosen few.

The doctor came down the corridor looking for her. She was unaware that he stood before her desk until he made the little *Psst* sound used by nuns to attract each other's attention. She looked up.

"You can enter the physical," he said. "All negative so far. It's a miracle." She couldn't conceal her rush of relief. He studied her for a moment, then said, "I see you know his story."

She nodded and saw the sardonic look that always came over his face when he considered the religious life.

"I suppose, Sister, that such total and utterly insane sacrifice makes complete sense to you."

"Yes it does, Doctor," she said quietly. "I envy him. God must love him greatly . . ."

Twice yearly after that Father Vermeuhlen came to submit his body to the small indignities of the leprosy check — at the end of the summer rainy season in March and at the end of the winter drought in September. He came from beyond Kipushi, partway by pirogue paddled by his boys, then picked up at a certain place along the river by the car of the Vicar General.

Each time she filed his clinical report with negative results, Sister Luke wondered apprehensively how long it could go on. The doctor said, "Just give him time, Sister," with anger in his voice and a curious look of love on his face.

195

In the months between visits she thought about him. He seemed to be the happiest soul she had encountered in the religious life and certainly the kindest man she had ever known in or out of habit. Once he said to her, "Kindness resembles God the closest and disarms man the quickest," and although he was explaining why nothing ever happened to him when, alone and unarmed, he visited unfriendly tribes to gather in their lepers, she knew that he was telling her his credo, the sole rule by which he lived and caused others to live when he was with them. The doctor was always a changed man when Father Vermeuhlen was under the hospital roof. And the coiffeur, who always visited with him (gazing ever wistfully at the beautiful beard), told stories stripped clean of scandal, anecdotes of colony life that could have been related in the nuns' recreation.

She drew closer to the Father after she began to live in the hospital, visiting with him when she made her rounds and talking as she had not talked with a human being in years.

Six months after her first meeting with him, Mother Mathilde transferred her from the nuns' dormitory to a small room in the hospital. Since, according to some mysterious convent tradition, the dormitory was always locked during the day, the move to the hospital was the only way for her to get the occasional afternoon nap the doctor advised, if — as he told the Superior — they expected to keep her on her feet. She was still working sixteen-hour days, and on nights before assisting in surgery often got no more than four or five hours of sleep.

It was an extraordinary dispensation to sleep apart from the sisterhood. Sister Luke saw no connection between it and a queer breakdown she had had one morning in the refectory when, of a sudden, her coffee bowl had slipped from her hands and splashed brown all over her white habit. She was alone in the refectory having a late breakfast, after two operations. She forgot the black face of André looking in through the serving window. She stared aghast at the broken bowl for which she must do a penance, then dropped her face in her hands and wept uncontrollably. André was terrified, never having seen a nun cry. He reported at once to Mother Mathilde.

When the order had come, along with the urging to try to slip off duty for a nap when work permitted, Sister Luke was too surprised to speak. Mother Mathilde's worried expression acknowledged the risk of partial separation from the community.

"It's a solution born of necessity and you may well believe how earnestly I asked God's guidance before telling you. Each hour I dispense you from community life, even your all too few sleeping hours, is a deprivation . . . for us," she smiled a little sadly, "and especially for you, Sister Luke."

"I understand, *ma Mère*." She understood more than her Superior intended. Mother Mathilde was again sharing a risk, possibly a double-edged one this time. Nothing was more visible than a nun's empty cell at night, and when, in the recreation, her Superior would casually remark that a nursing sister was sleeping pro tem in the hospital to facilitate the work, there would be veiled looks her way suggesting favoritism.

For it was no deprivation in the convent to sleep apart. It was on the contrary a special grace to be alone in a little white room without having to fall seriously ill to get there. To hear no longer the sighs of twenty women around you and the rustle of their straw sacks as they turned and tossed in the heat, to bathe alone in the dark dawns without having to line

197

up in the community washroom, to be able to pray and to think alone . . . she knew as she knelt before her Superior what a relief this was going to be.

"Pray with me," said Mother Mathilde, "that before this year ends, our Reverend Mother Emmanuel will be able to send us a nun accredited in tropical medicine. Ah, if I could only have got one before they opened up that new house in Ceylon . . ."

Sister Luke had nodded in promise to pray with her Superior, but she was not sure that her prayers would come from the heart as long as she had strength to carry on the two jobs that now earned her a room of her own.

In roundabout discreet ways, as if talking of cloisters in general and all sisters and brothers in the vowed life, Sister Luke discussed her pinpricks and perplexities with Father Vermeuhlen. His comment, simple and consoling, was always the same. "We are His children, vowed or otherwise," he would say. "He lets happen to us what must happen for our own good . . ."

Three times at half-year intervals, she filed away the Father's clinical record with all tests marked negative. Though nuns were not permitted to keep diaries, the clinical record was a diary of sorts. When she looked at the dates written in her own space-saving script, she remembered the principal subjects she had saved up each time to discuss with him. Reading back, she could persuade herself that now at last the happy years were beginning for her, the time of perfect adjustment which enabled her to live her nun's life as it should be — without past or future gnawing at the thought.

Her first entry, made in September of '33, reminded her of her dispensation from sleeping in the community. She had

198

told Father Vermeuhlen about her Jesuit uncle who once had remarked: "The community life is the *real* penance in any order . . . it is a martyrdom of pinpricks!" and she remembered how they had laughed together over the truism, like two conspirators momentarily blessed with personal privacy.

In March '34, she had talked with the Father mainly about apes. She was then making occasional inspection trips that passed through the ape country where even *évolués* like Emil shook with fright if you looked at or mentioned aloud the apes sitting among the tree branches. She told Father Vermeuhlen about old Sister Eucharistia whom she sometimes had to take with her as companion, who always made the driver lift his cap to the apes and say, "*Yambo* — good day!" because the old nun believed her unique apostolic mission was to educate the natives away from superstition. And the black boys always fell ill after greeting the apes — peculiar maladies with fevers and coughs and sometimes pus in the sputum. "But of course," Father Vermeuhlen had said then.

On his last trip, in September of '34, she had talked about his lepers, calling many of them by name. She had made a survey trip to the colony with three nuns from other congregations and Father Vermeuhlen had introduced her with unconcealed pride to the "sons" he had trained to assist him. Since then, whenever she looked down a miscroscope tube at the rod-shaped *Mycobacterium*, she saw first the strong brown hands of Father Vermeuhlen, bathing and bandaging his mutilated Blacks and spoon-feeding the faces of the fingerless ones.

And now in March '35, the Father was due again. She watched the rains and prayed for his safety while on the river. He arrived with the last downpours of the summer rains which had swept up from Capetown in great black curtains that pulled away from the tip of the continent toward the Equator and left winter and dryness where they had passed, brought summer and blossoms to the places passed over and finally, out of sight from her eyes but not from her longing imagination, folded up in the evergreen twilight of the rainbelt forests where Emil had told her all seasons became one.

"Father André is back," she said in greeting. "He made a trip to Kenya and caught yaws. We've got him in for the bismuth and arsenic treatment and those hot demulcent drinks which now he'll probably accept because you're here to play checkers with him."

"What have I always told you, Sister?" Father Vermeuhlen's smile lifted his beard at the corners. He spread his hands palms up and she looked down as if she must answer to them directly. There were no lesions, no scaliness, no little gray patches of changing pigmentation. She looked up happily. "He lets happen to us," Father Vermeuhlen intoned, "what must happen . . . in this case, for *my* own good!" His beard waggled with his muscular laughter. "My old checker partner back again. May God forgive me for my gratitude."

With the nauseous bland acacia drink ready in her hand, she was watching them play that afternoon. They played checkers like the Arabs in the market place, crouched and cowled, seething with rivalry that made the air crackle between them as outside it crackled between each lightning flash until the thunder came.

Father André jumped three and landed in Father Vermeuhlen's king row. Emil appeared with bulging eyes on a burst of thunder.

"Mama Luke! Ambulance call. Three men drowning in a flash flood . . ."

With the same hand that had moved him into the king's

row, Father André swept the checkers off the board onto his bed. "You'll probably want a priest, Sister. Emil, call my convent. Ask for Father José."

"We did. He's not there."

"Then you go." Father André looked up at his checker partner, who was already on his feet. "I'll send a lay brother after you with the Viaticum, just in case."

Down, press, release, *up* . . . she rehearsed the tempo of artificial respiration as she swept past the desk. "Tell Mother Mathilde, please," she said to Sister Aurélie. She misread her sister's warning glance. It seemed to be saying, *Be careful.* Be careful when there were lives to be saved if you got there quickly enough? The metronomic timing of resuscitation clicked above her inner comment.

The ambulance rocked her from wall to wall. She decided on the Shafer method with the patient prone, face down, herself straddling with knees on either side of his hips, forcible pressure with hands over the back of the lower ribs . . . down, press, release, up . . . every five seconds. Father Vermeuhlen sat firm as a mountain. He moved the ribbon markers of his missal to the section of the sacraments.

Emil stuttered what news the police chief had given. Three young Italians from the mines had gone duck-hunting. The flash flood coming unseen through the reeds was a wall of water that upturned their raft, swept it away and left them wading to the sand bar midstream in heavy rubber hip boots which kept sinking, sinking, because all those sand bars were quicksand. By the time a native boy had got back to town . . . Emil moved his hands from knobby knees to his beltband and Father Vermeuhlen, without looking up, moved his markers back a few pages to where she knew were the prayers for souls in agony who had only a few moments left.

The duck-hunters looked at first like busts built upon sands. Two who had been reaching down to try to loosen the hip boots had their arms coated with ooze and all had their mouths open screaming as they clawed toward the stunted tree boughs the people on shore had tossed out. Father Vermeuhlen started to walk through the mud at the river's edge and the police chief pulled him back, crying above the storm that they had tested every approach and had found no safe footing.

The trapped Italians faced shoreward. They were near enough so you could see their faces already purpling with the pressures of the quicksand. The wind swept around and brought their howls clearly to the shore, then a clap of thunder blotted out the awful sound and you saw only their movements of panic as they tore at the reeds around them, uprooted them and threw them with despair toward the people trying in vain to reach them with ropes that blew away.

They were going mad before her eyes, forcing themselves deeper with each frenzied struggle. Suddenly they saw Father Vermeuhlen make the sign of the cross over the separating waters. For an instant their slow-motion twistings ceased. Their bulging eyes fastened on the priest already lost in the prayers of general absolution. The veering wind carried shoreward a cry no longer human, then a sheet of rain cut it off.

The mud was above the hunters' shoulders when Father Vermeuhlen lifted his great voice like a bronze gong above the storm. *Leave this world, Christian souls, in the name of the all-powerful Father who created you* . . . She had seen faces like that once before, sticking out of the hatch-holes in the tubs of the insane asylum. *In the name of the Angels and Archangels, in the name of the Thrones and the Dominions* . . .

The hunters' eyes started from their sockets as the mud pushed up against their chins. She shut her eyes before it began to slide into their open mouths. The gonglike voice tolled steadily on through the Cherubim and the Seraphim, the Patriarchs and the Prophets, on and on through the prayers for mercy to the last great pleadings . . . *Have pity on their tremblings, have pity on their tears . . . Refuse not to admit them to the mystery of the reconciliation . . .*

A whistling intake of breath around her told her that the heads had vanished. She opened her eyes. The sand bar was as smooth as water-marked silk.

Emil was crouching beside her. "Stay with the police until the bodies surface," she whispered. "Four or five hours, they say. I'll send the ambulance right back." Then she and Father Vermeuhlen climbed into it and rode back to the convent without speaking.

Afterwards, she remembered the three faces of living death washed by the torrential rain and the whine of the wind in the reeds, but she could never see what she herself had been doing. She could pick up her own activities only after she returned to the convent.

She went at once to her Superior to receive the benediction of return and to give her report. She made a rough draft of her thoughts as she crossed the cloister garden, thankful that Mother Mathilde had seen Congo deaths in all their horrifying forms and would ask few details.

Mother Mathilde received her with a coolness she took at first to be meant for support. No sympathetic comment on her soaking habit, no smile of relief that she was back. She got as far in her report as the announcement that three bodies might be expected to arrive in the hospital morgue sometime that evening and the Superior raised her hand.

"I know the story, Sister Luke," she said in a voice oddly constrained. "I've been on the telephone for the past hour with the police, the Italian consul, even the newspaper." Her unsmiling face dismissed the tragedy that was finished. "What I should like you to explain now is why you left the convent without my permission."

"But *ma Mère!* I delegated Sister Aurélie to tell you!"

The moment she said *I delegated* she knew what she had done. She had presumed permission to leave, had hurried off without waiting for official sanction, which was the same as leaving without permission. You had no alibi for this. A nun simply never left the convent without her Superior's permission. The city around you could blow up and burn down. Bodies could be lying in the streets moaning for help. But you never stepped beyond your convent walls until your Superior gave you the benediction of departure and said, "Go . . ." *Obedience, O my God, failing at this late date . . .*

"Not only did you leave the convent without permission," said Mother Mathilde as if she had not heard her exclamation, "but . . . and this gives me the greater pain . . . you failed also in charity."

Charity! It was like a knife-thrust straight into the heart of what she thought was her one redeeming feature.

"I might have wished," said Mother Mathilde, "to assign Sister Aurélie to that emergency, or another of those devoted nuns serving under you, who have not been outside the grounds for weeks. You, Sister Luke, saw risk and excitement and pre-empted this for yourself. You never once thought of your sisters. You never once thought how *they* might long for a new experience, ah yes — even for so tragic a one as this turned out to be." Although she knew that her Superior could never have spoken such stinging words had she not cared enormously for the state of her soul, each comment was nevertheless a twist of the knife. "You never thought how a sister might later enjoy clipping a little item from the newspaper (which has already telephoned me for your name) to send home to Belgium for the family scrapbook. I can understand that in the first moment it seemed natural to you to run off to save a life, but I cannot understand why the saving grace of second thought did not restrain you."

The Superior paused. Sister Luke would not look up. She knew if she did she would be letting her tears ask mercy for her.

"Charity in action," said Mother Mathilde less coldly, "is easy to give. It has witnesses. Everyone sees it. Everyone is touched by it. Even in the world, a visible act of charity singularizes the doer, often even brings fame of a sort. But charity in thought, Sister, that silent, invisible, unremitting love that always places others first and the self last . . . that is what you lacked today."

When it was over, she went to the chapel to make herself calm so she could return to the hospital looking as if nothing had happened. There were no more tears now; just an overwhelming sense of failure that seemed to drag her down like those merciless quicksands. A tarantula, black and hairy, crouched on the altar steps. She stared at it and thought: *Jump, and I won't move.*

After a while she was able to talk to God. "Why do You humiliate me again? I thought You had finished. I thought the long time of truce was Your sign that I was pleasing You at last. Why didn't You give me the grace of second thought? Why? *Why?* You alone knew my intentions and You let me believe they were selfless when I ran off . . . and then You gave me the heartbreak of Mother Mathilde's face . . ."

The tarantula seemed to be watching her. "Why don't You make him jump at me?" she asked. "Or have You some other design for one so imperfect as I? *O my God, I am truly sorry that I have offended* . . ."

When she emerged, the afternoon sun blazed from a cloudless sky. She walked slowly toward the hospital. Sister Aurélie swung the logbook around so she could read what had happened during her absence.

She read the entries written in a script like fine printing and thought with a pang of the newspaper article. In the missions when a nun was cited, the family name was always given in addition to her name in Christ. It could have been Sister Aurélie Delatour instead of Sister Luke Van der Mal, she thought, and she imagined the Delatour family back home in Bruges bringing out the scrapbook to paste into it a few column inches from the Katanga *Clairon et Courier* which would have reassured the lonely parents that a daughter given to God did not sink out of sight completely. She caught herself going on and on with remorse and cut it short.

"On your way back to Maternity, Sister Aurélie, will you tell Illunga there's a big tarantula in the chapel? It might frighten some of our sisters." She signed on the log her return to duty. "I'll be in the lab if anyone needs me," she said.

The laboratory was dense with heat and very quiet. The doctor was gone for the day. She took the slides of Father Vermeuhlen's nasal smears and set her microscope to the high power.

Her hands worked independently of her mind, which circled back through the day looking at each step she had taken. She pondered now the lapse in obedience, trying to find the

206

blind spot that had made her ignore that basic rule when day after day, for the past three years, she had gone to Mother Mathilde and asked "May I . . . ?" for every sortie from the convent including emergency ambulance calls. Three years here and five before that, she thought.

May I, ma Mère? Her hands laid out the stains and solvents, the note pad and pencil, and snapped on the small light at the base of the microscope drawtube. May I use a fourth handkerchief this week, *ma Mère?* I couldn't make the three see me through . . . May I drink a glass of water between meals, *ma Mère?* May I accept the chilled fruit again today when I go to the native hospital? May I read this medical journal the doctor lent to me?

How many times in the name of obedience and for its sake alone had she asked the little permissions which she dared not even hint at to the doctor each time she slipped away, because she knew how completely meaningless, possibly slave-like, they would seem in the eyes of the world. How many times? So often that now it no longer irked what was left of her pride to ask.

She stained the slides. May I break my sleep tonight, *ma Mère*, and visit Monsieur Diderot, who is going to die? May I skip a meal in penance for my sins of omission? Besides, I mean, doing the penance you gave me in the culpa?

She listened to her interior monologue as if she were in the world and reading a nun's mind. It was pitiful and astonishing to note the things a nun could agonize over. You'd think their Creator had said to them, This is a way of being that must not perish from this earth and you and your sisters are the keepers of it pro tem, each one of one small part of it according to her lights and strengths.

She picked up a dry slide. Some souls like Father Ver-

207

meuhlen, she reflected, had just one colossal failure in obedience and then ever after the simple one-way road of penance, instead of the tortuous path of many small failings.

She slipped the first slide under the microscope. The coarser substances in the smear were gray clouds that parted as she probed. A spindle-shaped form glided by — only one of the olfactory cells of the mucous membrane. Nothing, nothing. Negative, she said softly as she marked the slide and racked it.

She was perceptibly calmer as she always became when working with the microscope. Before the Angelus she had time for a few more slides. She slipped the second into place and bent her head over the eyepiece.

The rod-shaped *Mycobacterium* lay like a stick of driftwood on the surface of the deep-sea film. A cry escaped her as she stared at the dark staining granules evenly spaced along the length of the leprosy bacillus. Her hand shook. She forced it to stay steady so she could turn the fine adjustment screw. I could be wrong, she thought, I've *got* to be wrong.

She turned to sharper focus and brought up the enclosing capsule like a shadow — the identifying feature of the leprosy organism. Beneath it, she found three more.

With her hand frozen to the microscope, she brought them in and out of focus, the three lying at the bottom and the one on the surface of the film. My God, she whispered, where is Your divine mercy? Is *this* Your answer to that saintly soul who called out to You today from the riverbank? *How can You justify* . . .

Then, very clearly, as if he were standing beside her in the laboratory, she heard Father Vermeuhlen saying, "He lets happen what must happen for our own good and for His greater glory." And that, she knew, was exactly what he

208

would say again, with perfect faith and trust, when she would tell him the results of the test.

Tears stung her eyes. The small deadly shapes blurred on the field. Presently she heard the call to serenity of the Angelus bells.

XIII

A YEAR passed and they were in Lent again, the time of secret self-denials in the sisterhood, of nervousness and tension among the black boys. The exhaustion of the Congo summer was written on every face, clearest of all on those of the nursing nuns, who were still too few.

In the months of the worst heat, Mother Mathilde had regularly selected one of them to accompany her on her travels — in itself a sign of anxiety for their well-being. She always hinted to the teaching nuns that there was a clinic to be inspected or a school mission that had been ordered to make a mass vaccination and had called for instruction in the technique.

Twice during the year Sister Luke traveled with her to remote missions the Order was pioneering. She saw the Africa of her dreams on those trips. Both times they went partway by pirogues down misty rivers banked by dense forests looped with lianas. The black boys who poled them along sang ballads with a strange repetitive rhythm and Mother Mathilde stood often at the prow, gazing raptly forward as if she must possess ahead of the others, and before ever an oar disturbed it, each ravishing Eden the winding river disclosed. She sighed like a child when they tied up at their destinations, and once she said endearingly, "I can never bear to have it end."

Sister Luke relived her outings for weeks after. She nursed a secret hope that when her assignment in the European hospital would end, she would be transferred to one of those pioneering missions which served the natives exclusively. In a few more years she would be due for the automatic transfer which kept every nun from attaching too strongly to one community, one job and one place. The only loss would be that of Mother Mathilde, she reflected, but Superiors also had to take over a new community at specified times and there was always the chance of reunion in their small world.

She was at last a choir nun. On arrival in the colony her voice had been tested by Sister Serviens, the Cantatrice of the community and music teacher in the school; but Mother Mathilde had postponed, because of double duties, her participation in the plain chants which taxed the strength of the singing nuns even in the cool home country.

She had been singing now for almost a year. She could date her admission to the choir by Father Vermeuhlen's last visit, when she had had to tell him the results of the tests. He himself had given her the fortitude she prayed for when he said before she could speak, "Not yet, Sister? My soul is leprous, why should not my body be also?" She remembered she had wept when she told Mother Mathilde about it and she sometimes wondered if her admission to the choir shortly after related, in some way, to the despair she confessed to feeling when God's justice took such incomprehensible form.

This would be the first Easter service she would sing. The Ordinary of the Mass for the Paschal season was one of the most beautiful of the Vatican Kyriale. She practiced breath control for it under the purple skies of the Congo Lent while the rains poured down with press-button timing, from ten to eleven every morning and from three to five every afternoon.

"The *Kyrie*," explained Sister Serviens at practice, "begins as you all know in the third mode, then changes to the eighth. The third mode has E as *finalis* and the eighth has G . . ." and while Sister Serviens was striking the notes on the organ, Sister Luke saw herself with a small band of black boys in the bush, listening to her high humming and reproducing it perfectly right after her.

Sometimes when she sang with the choir she felt an impatience with the Cantatrice for not lifting with more force from the E to the G mode and urging the nuns to give their all to the final *Christ is risen.* Then she would think, I know nothing at all about this ancient music; why then do I feel so judgmental?

She had the impression that her whole psychology had changed. Her emotions flared for small things. When a sister proclaimed her in culpa, she found it less easy to smile and look thankful for having been reminded of an imperfection. Her dream life was wild and troubling. Often when the night duty nurse plucked her sheet and whispered sorrowfully, "Praised be Jesus Christ. It is four o'clock, Sister Luke," she had to wait until her dreams dissipated before she could recognize the faithful sister who bent over her bed.

Had it ever occurred to her that anything in her iron constitution could break down, she would have known at once the cause of her psychological change. Afterwards, it was so easy to chart the steps of her malady that she wondered how, at the time, she had missed every warning signal until the frightful death of one of her dressing boys somehow brought everything into focus.

It happened on a day when everything went wrong in the hospital. The doctor lost a life on the operating table at five in the morning — a defeat for both herself and him although every prognosis had been unfavorable from the start. Then Emil reported that one of the boys had come to work too drunk to stand. She telephoned to Monsieur Marcel, chief of the *Force Publique*, who always pulled her out of dilemmas with her boys. The town jail, he told her, was filled to the last cell.

"Put him away somewhere to cool off," said Marcel. "If your own prisoner pavilion is full, get Emil to find a corner on the grounds. The boy will sleep it off in twenty-four hours, Sister."

She told Emil to find a place. "Anywhere just so long as he is out of sight. Which one this time, Emil?"

"Banza," said Emil. "I shall order a flogging when he is sober."

"You'll find out the reasons first, then decide punishment."

"No good reason, Mama Luke. Only woman business. A man from his village told that his wife ran away with a hunter. But Banza has another wife, younger, full of children still . . ."

She forgot about Banza as soon as Emil went off to take care of him. She had three pregnancies coming to term in Maternity, and the same number of husbands to console in a waiting room that registered 112 degrees, with a humidity almost at saturation point. There were two typhoid cases in Contagious and the general ward was filled to the last bed with skin grafts, snake bites, and enough malaria cases to shake the walls when the chills came on.

She thanked God that Sister Aurélie was off on a trip with Mother Mathilde that day, up in the cool highlands of the Kivu.

Once or twice Emil went to look at Banza and came back to report that he snored in stupor like an animal and perhaps

213

ought to have no less than twenty lashes to make him remember that he was a man. His black face, lacquered shiny with sweat, suffered visibly for Banza's defection as if the whole Bantu tribe had been betrayed by it.

"Wait until morning, Emil."

The next morning Emil waited for her outside the chapel. The rains of the night were rising back to heaven in a white mist through which sunrise was beating its way in spokes of yellow light. It was like the dawn of creation, like the Little Chapter in Prime she had just been chanting . . . *Who is she that cometh forth as the morning rising . . .*

"Go and release him," she said patiently. "Bring him to me. Let me talk with him in your presence. We must be just, Emil."

Emil was unrecognizable when he returned to her desk. His face was ash-gray, his eyes protruded, his voice a gasp.

"Mama, come see . . ." He choked, unable to go on. Hurrying with him through hospital corridors and across the garden, she tried to find out what had happened.

"Mama see . . . Mama see . . ." He chattered in the fluty voice of fear, first in French, then in Kiswahili. "*Mama ia kutala . . .*" He led the way to a galvanized iron shed behind the hospital where garden tools were kept, flung open the door and pointed.

There on the dirt floor was a man-shaped mound of white ants that had eaten Banza clean to the skeleton. Not even a tuft of hair was left on the skull. Frozen with horror, she stared at the bloated white bodies of the carnivorous driver ants covering the skeleton like a living shroud. She never knew how she got back to the hospital.

The police chief asked twice who was speaking. Then he wanted some indication of the trouble. Should he bring the

214

paddy wagon and a squad of guards? She waited until her teeth stopped chattering, then said, "I can't tell you over the phone, Marcel," pleadingly, so he would remember that colony telephones were connected with the talking drums and that every message of importance passed directly to the bush from the native switchboard. "You come alone," she begged.

In ten minutes he was there at her desk, solid, businesslike, smiling until he saw her face. She motioned Emil to take him to the tool shed and saw both of them hesitate.

"I can't go back there again," she whispered.

Her forced calm was like a trance as she waited for Marcel to return. The after-image of the man-shaped mound in terrible crawling motion played back on the charts she seemed to study. She pretended to herself that the tumult she heard was not her conscience crying out, but the thrumming of insects that emerged from their burrows when the rainy season was ending.

Marcel reappeared smelling faintly of kerosene. He spoke for several moments before she realized he was talking Flemish with the salty accent of Antwerp — familiar, homelike and curiously consoling.

"I had Emil put a torch to the beasts," he said. "Sent my driver back to town for a coffin. That's all the natives will see coming out of that shed, Sister. A customary coffin for Christian burial. Banza was a convert, wasn't he?"

"One of mine," she said desolately.

"What the drums will tell no one knows, but the certificate will have to state death from unknown cause." As if she had spoken in disagreement, Marcel began to argue. "How could anyone say eaten by ants when we know he was blind drunk when shut up? Only last week I went out to a village to interrogate the family of a Bantu who'd died from an un-

215

known cause — unknown, that is, until I learned he'd been drinking *simba* beer most of the afternoon. Obviously, Sister, a death by poison. It happens often when the beer's not properly prepared."

He watched her while he talked of the two kinds of cassava — the sweet and the bitter manioc roots — and of the hydrocyanic acid in the bitter root in sufficient quantity to cause death if not boiled out thoroughly over high heat.

"It's very likely," he said in a professional tone, "that your boy was dead from poison before ever the ants got to him. That's what I told Emil to make him stop beating his breast and blaming himself. That Emil . . . you know what, Sister? He's been away from the bush too long. Completely forgot that some *simba* is as effective as black mamba venom."

She fought back tears as she stared at his bluff homespun face. Was he telling her that to help her clear her own conscience as well? She would never know. No one would ever know except God and the man standing before her, pretending not to see her emotion.

"Thank you, Marcel." She managed a frayed smile to which he responded with a smart salute.

She asked for an interview with Mother Mathilde as soon as her Superior returned from her trip. She took all the blame upon herself as she reported the incident in full detail.

"I should have *made* the time to go with Emil, *ma Mère.* I'm sure I'd have thought to keep Banza off the ground . . ." She coughed and covered her face with her bandanna.

Mother Mathilde looked at her as she picked up the police report. "Unknown cause," she read aloud. "I agree with this," she said firmly. "Like Marcel, I've seen too many poisonings from *simba* in my time not to include it always as the most likely cause. You must do likewise, Sister. I understand how

216

in the first shock of discovery you took it totally upon yourself. Any one of us would have done the same, constituted as we are." She smiled gently and stiffened her tone. "But now, you must put from you the temptation to excessive self-reproach. You must not go on blaming yourself. You are much too intelligent to give way to that form of self-indulgence."

The matter should have ended there. Her Superior had named it self-indulgence. But she could not rid herself of the feeling of blame. Was it, she wondered, because of her peculiar psychological change that she was unable to throw off Banza's death?

In the ensuing weeks she seemed to be continuously fighting back tears. When the doctor went out of his way to make a task easier for her, some new thing in her responded with such sentimentality that she hardly recognized herself. Then one morning in the laboratory she was examining slides.

She turned her face away from the microscope to cough. A sudden impulse came over her to look at her sputum.

"It's ridiculous," she told herself. "Like all the other impulses that come over me these days." But her hands were already preparing a slide. She coughed again deliberately and got a sputum sample. She made a stain of it and looked at it with the high-power lens. The rodlike bacilli of tuberculosis trembled red-violet in the field.

Her first reaction was relief. That's all it is, she thought. That's why I'm always tired and emotional. That's why I couldn't shake off Banza's death.

That's all . . . then she remembered that all white tuberculosis patients were sent home as fast as ship or plane could get them out because the malady galloped in the tropics. Her predecessor had been repatriated. Tuberculosis always writes

217

finis to service in the Congo, Sister Augustine had said on the ship . . .

This is my ticket home. She gasped as if the walls of the homeland convents were already closing in about her. Blessed Lord, don't let this happen to me.

But it had happened. She peered at the tiny colored rods floating in the radiant field. She began to count them automatically. Then abruptly she snatched the slide from under the microscope and dropped it in the wastebasket.

For the next hour she went on with her work. She finished her microscopy, prepared medication trays for the afternoon rounds, telephoned twice to Mother Mathilde to give reports on patients she had asked about. It was easy to pretend that nothing had happened. Another self had taken charge.

You can ride this out and tell no one, said the stranger self. You know everything about TB, its phases and cycles. The afternoon flush won't show beneath your tan. You can control the coughing as so often you've told patients they can and must. With will, you can develop appetite and Emil can fetch from the market place all the extra eggs you'll need. You're already allowed to take afternoon naps when the work permits. So then . . . you can sleep and feed yourself out of this.

Her conscience let the stranger self carry on for an hour. Then Sister Aurélie came with a chart she wanted to discuss. Her brown face sunk deep in her coif turned eagerly to her.

"You have such a gift for diagnosis, Sister Luke," she said. "Doesn't this look like gastric hemorrhage to you?"

Dark brown vomitus. Tarry stools. Sister Luke read the entries and nodded. She was about to speak when her conscience took charge. It jerked her head back from the trusting face

218

waiting to catch everything, including the invisible spray from her lips.

"Tell the boys to give nothing but cracked ice," she said, off to the side, hoarsely, as though a hand were at her throat.

Sister Aurélie smiled thanks and slipped out the door. For a moment Sister Luke stared at the place where the catch-all coif had been. It seemed still to be there hanging in the air like an empty shell. Into it came the faces of her sisters one by one — first the nurses with their whispers so discreet that you had to close in upon them almost coif to coif to hear, then the choir nuns singing out the long O-oho-O's of the *Salve*, exchanging each other's breaths between beats . . .

She flew through the corridors to the surgery. The doctor was hunched over a microscope humming to himself.

"I don't know what to do, Doctor," she said to his back. "I'm so terribly tired. I think I'm sick."

"Every time people are tired they say they're sick." He snapped off the drawtube light and turned around. "What's the matter?"

"I'm TB," she said stoically.

"That's nothing to joke about!"

"I'm not joking."

He realized that she wasn't. He took her by the shoulder. The emotion in his face almost paralyzed her. "Who told you?" He shook her and raised his voice. "*Who told you?*"

"The slides . . . the microscope . . . my own sputum."

He didn't question her findings. He never did. He held her rigid for a full minute, staring at her as if she had betrayed him. Then he said brokenly, "You're the only one in the whole Congo I can work with . . . I don't think I could do without you."

He looked around the surgery as if trying to imagine what it would be like without her. He let go of her shoulder and reached for his stethoscope.

"Take off your habit," he ordered. "Open up. I'm going to listen to those lungs."

There were many garments to unfasten — scapular, cotton chemise, the stiff bodice that flattened the breasts . . . her fingers shook as she bared her thorax. Maybe she was wrong. Maybe her tired eyes had tricked her. She sat on the table, unaware until he threw it over her shoulder that she had forgotten to take off her veil. Gruffly he told her to cough, sigh and say thirty-three.

"There's certainly something . . . seems to be in the left lobe." He came around to listen from the front. She turned her face away as he bent over her chest, seeming not to breathe as he listened. "It's a summit lesion . . . a small one." His worried face broke into a smile. "We're lucky, Sister, we can catch this one fast."

Summit of the lobe where oxygen comes in first, thank God, O thank God, she thought. Then she saw herself sitting there with bared chest. The doctor caught her look of dismay and turned away. They both knew it was forbidden for a nun to be examined without another sister present. Both had forgotten this in the tension of the moment. The doctor kept his back turned while she buttoned back the parts of her habit hanging from the waist. But he went on talking.

"You can stand the gold treatment, Sister. It's rough on the kidneys but you're strong. I'll take the responsibility . . ."

"I've got to tell Mother Mathilde," she said in a low voice. And about this unwitnessed examination and running first to him . . .

"Why?" He spun around. He wanted to keep it just between them. "Why?" he demanded again, angrily.

"Obedience," she said, "I must . . ."

"They'll send you home if you do."

"I know . . ." Two tears rolled down her cheeks.

The sight of them seemed to startle him, as though an unexpected symptom had suddenly revealed itself. She had the feeling that he was reading below the level of her thoughts. He studied her with narrowed eyes like a psychiatrist, probing and pondering. Then he spoke quite calmly.

"You're afraid, Sister. You wouldn't be able to stand the convent if they sent you home." She backed away speechless. He followed her, speaking with the cold precision of a scientist.

"I'm going to tell you something about yourself that perhaps you never knew. You know how well I know nuns. I've never worked with a lay nurse since first I picked up a scalpel. You're not in the mold, Sister, and you never will be. You're what is called a worldly nun — ideal for the public, ideal for the patients. But you'll never be the kind of nun your convent expects you to be. *That's* your illness. The TB is a by-product."

He watched her cover up her reactions. Her struggle for calm and silence started her coughing. He waited. Then he said in an offhand manner, "But I can cure the by-product, Sister, if you want."

"I want to stay," she said huskily.

His eyes flashed admiration, then closed down with cunning.

"You leave it all to me then," he said eagerly. "I'll tell Mother Mathilde first. I'll tell her in such a way that she cannot send you home. We're both responsible for letting

221

you work as you have, for counting on your moral strength while ignoring the physical condition." He grinned unexpectedly. "And we won't have to create precedent to keep you here for the gold-dust cure. The Reverend Mother and I have connived once before . . . a big fish in colonial affairs, too important to be spared even for a half-year furlough. A much more advanced case. She saw me pull it through. It would have been both our necks if I hadn't . . ."

She had the impression that he had pulled her out of a dark pit. The brightness in the surgery almost blinded her. Sunlight shot from the instrument cabinet to a row of beakers on a shelf, and there seemed to be a weird red light around his atabrine-yellowed face, not at all like a halo.

"We've got the weather with us, the dry cool season. We'll move you out to the prisoners' pavilion where you can sleep practically in the treetops. Eggs, sardines, white muscat wine . . . I'll write your diet. In three months, maybe less . . ."

"Can I work?" said the nun in her.

"Assisting me mornings only." He looked at her sharply. "But there's one thing you must promise me, Sister. You've got to burn less energy. Remember, I'll be working only on the by-product. The main malady is for you to cure." An odd smile made his face quite gentle. "Don't try so hard to be the perfect nun, Sister. Relax . . . you've got to relax."

He pulled off his gown and put on a pongee jacket. At the door he turned and gave her his customary sardonic smile. "To ease that overgrown conscience of yours, Reverend Sister, I'm going to tell Mother Mathilde that I myself discovered your condition this morning and gave you no chance to get to her first. Anything you knew before I did, you keep under your bonnet . . . *if* you can. If your pride as a microscopist doesn't get the better of you!"

There began for her a strange interlude. It lasted for three months. Afterwards, when she looked back upon it, it was a passage picked in gold out of the black and white context of her religious life.

It was the childhood she'd never really had, lived among treetops as children dream of living, with an elegant small monkey as companion and bright green crickets for him to eat. It was the time of her most perfect purity and innocence with everything coming to her through her feelings, including her awareness of God. He was the rustle of lizards in her thatched roof, the scent of mimosa through the window screens and the slap of banana leaves when the wind blew. He gave her signs of Himself each day in grace notes and when darkness fell, He gave her the sonorous symphony of His African night in great roars and rumbles of creation and extinction which made every Old Testament prophecy come true.

Everything was unbelievable, beginning with the overwhelming realization that Mother Mathilde cherished her to the point of weeping when the doctor gave his news. The Superior spent an hour in the chapel after her conference with him, then summoned her.

"I'm going to give you a special rule," she said. "With God's help, I've decided to let you stay and take the risk. It's kill or cure, as we both know." She blew her nose, looking at Sister Luke with red eyes full of anxiety and love. Then she cleared her throat and spoke in her usual steady voice.

The special rule permitted work only in the mornings, she said, assisting the doctor in surgery and preparing the day's nursing schedule, which Sister Aurélie would carry out, under her indirect supervision. She would take all her meals in her room, not to contaminate refectory utensils, and was dispensed from community devotions though not from performing these each day privately. She could attend Mass but might no longer sing with the choir. She would live in the upstairs room of the prisoners' pavilion . . .

"Like a bird on the branch," said Mother Mathilde, bringing back her captivating smile with the words. Sister Luke had to fight her impulse to rise up and embrace her.

The prisoners' pavilion was a replica of the bush station she used to dream about on the ship coming out. It was a two-storied annex at the rear of the hospital, facing out toward the bush, built in native style with a thatched roof. On the lower floor were housed the occasional prisoners from the town jail who needed hospitalization, and Hindus who, for religious and dietary reasons, could not be treated in the main hospital. Her circular room under the thatch was walled with fine-meshed screen which became visible only when lights were on. Then it was a curtain of night moths beating softly from the outside with huge brown velvet wings.

The doctor ordered her meals from the refectory, putting her on his original supplementary diet for tubercular patients which he called "oysters on the prairie." He came himself the first day to show her how his "oysters" must be consumed. He had procured from Mother Mathilde a pair of finest crystal wine glasses and in each was a raw egg yolk sprinkled with chopped parsley and lemon juice. He saw her staring at the wine glasses used only for visits of high personages.

"Presentation is everything to a TB, Sister," he said smiling. "You should know that." He put a glass in each hand and told her to swallow the yolks as if they were oysters. "In addition to this twice daily and your regular meals, you'll be awakened each night at ten to consume sandwiches of mashed sardines and two glasses of white muscat wine."

He inspected the room, examined the type of mattress, sheets and pillow case, and checked the bottles of beer standing in a bucket of ice, all exactly as he had ordered.

"Good," he said. "Drink as much as you can. No Lenten abstinence, Sister, unless you want to come out of this gold cure with wrecked kidneys." He discovered her microscope hidden under the washbasin stand, picked it up and went out the door with it, humming an air from Tosca.

And so it began — a three months of spoiling which even in the world, in places where money flowed freely, could never have been duplicated. The community spun a cocoon of loving-kindness about her. The sisters offered a Mass for her safe recovery and if some of them asked themselves, "Is this the result of real abnegation from overwork or of some soul struggle which she cannot resolve?" nothing showed on their civilized faces as they put their hearts into prayers for her.

Sister Eucharistia made the first visit, then the others came in turn. The old nun carried a baby monkey she had confiscated from a boy in the boarding school, for which she had promised to find a home, and when Sister Luke took the nervous long-tailed body on her two palms and asked, "Will Mother Mathilde permit?" Sister Eucharistia smiled and said without envy or malice, "Beelzebub told her that the cure depended on your having what you want and doing what you want," and looked happy because this wonderful unheard-of liberty had happened to one of them.

The news filtered out inevitably. Wines and champagnes began appearing in Mother Mathilde's office with cards from colonial patients who remembered the nun praying beside their beds at odd hours in the nights of their crises. Wives of the dressing boys brought eggs and chickens and occasionally a rabbit-shaped body minus the head which would have identified it as a cat. The talking drums carried the news to the bush and Father Vermeuhlen sent a letter reminding her that God lets happen what must happen for her own good . . . and telling her that his black boys were carving an ivory tusk which she would receive in due time from a runner.

By the end of her first month in the tree-house, she had Felix the monkey trained like a nun. He sat beside her at her solitary dining table, tied his napkin around his neck and ate delicately from a plate. Afternoons, when she napped, he foraged for crickets in the thatch and plucked at her covers with his tiny black hands when he knew it was time to get up and read the Office. When she knelt for evening prayers, he sat on the high hospital bed holding both feet in his hands and staring at her with his queer little golden eyes until she crossed herself; then he flung himself at her in a single leap and wrapped his long wiry arms about her neck, hugging her fiercely.

She never talked to him after the grand silence, but sometimes she laughed softly as she carried him about the room to look at the moths festooning the screens. A snap of the light switch plunged them both into the heart of the tree-tops. The thousand forms of nocturnal life that sang, whistled and moaned in the bush seemed to come in closer. The incessant drums were fever-quick like Felix's heart when the moon rose and reflected from the feathery mimosas phosphorescent eyes that never blinked.

In two months she gained ten pounds. She supervised herself with scrupulous care and understanding. The euphoria of the tubercular that filled her with love, intense, personal and passionate, and made it difficult to speak calmly with anyone she had even remotely admired before the onset of her malady, was something she could cope with because she anticipated that phase. Her optimism flew high, not only for her eventual cure of which she was sure, but for everything that would happen to her henceforth. That too, she knew, was a characteristic of the tubercular — the very quality, in fact, which made them such interesting patients. Yet somehow she felt that her own high hopes would not vanish with her malady.

She brushed away the doctor's preposterous remark about her main malady. She was obeying his orders to relax, to live from day to day and to keep her thoughts within the brackets of each sunrise and sunset. It astonished her to learn how simple life could be and how much inner happiness resulted when you took each day like a gift from God with no strings attached.

One afternoon after her nap, she was standing by the screen windows reciting the Office of Lauds. She came to her favorite passages in the Canticle of the Three Children from Daniel. Her heart leaped with happiness as she called upon the light and darkness to bless the Lord, on the mountains and the hills, the seas and the rivers and all that move in the waters. *Benedicite, O all beasts and cattle, bless the Lord* . . .

This is how a nun should be! she thought suddenly. This is what is meant by being a child of God.

She stared out at the mimosa trees. The faces of the many happy nuns she knew, who used to mystify her, who had sometimes seemed quite childish in their unquestioning acceptance of everything that happened to them, seemed to smile back at her.

Now you know, they seemed to say. *Live from day to day. There are always the graces to help us over the rough spots.*

"I had to fall ill to learn this," she said to her monkey. She shook her thermometer excitedly and walked about the room with Felix clinging to her skirts as she took her temperature. It was down to normal for the first time at that special hour when the fevers showed.

Next morning after operations the doctor caught her examining her sputum under the microscope.

"Don't rush things, Sister," he said good-naturedly. "It's not going to be easy to return to the community, even . . ." he gave her a smile only faintly tinged with malice ". . . even to this very select little gathering here in the Congo."

A week later all her slides showed negative. Back in the community she felt at first like a traveler returned from some beautiful land of silence and solitude. There was much more sound in a convent than she had remembered. The varying vibrations from a score of women made a sort of thin high humming like the singing of telephone wires strung across space.

XIV

THE monastic life had plateau periods without signpost or roadblock. The next two years were for Sister Luke one of these. Her inner peace was rich and profound. She worked prodigiously. The drama of the expanding Congo touched off a patriotic pride she never knew she had, but accepted tranquilly now as one of those atavisms which every nun brought to the convent from her former life and never quite outgrew.

She listened to her male patients talking about cobalt and uranium and the export of a cotton crop that would come close to thirty thousand tons in 1938. Railroads had thrust deeper into the interior, like bustling capillaries spreading out from the main arteries of the Congo River. "Colonization is transportation," said the colonials, boasting of track mileages to the nuns counting converts in silence.

There was a new vocabulary, compact, a little harsh. Flowing phrases like *Office d'Exploitation des Transports Coloniaux* had contracted to *Otraco*. *Utexléo* meant the great textile mills of Léopoldville. *Inéac* stood for the *Institut National pour l'Etude Agronomique*. Sister Luke felt a sweet possessiveness for A.M.I. — *Assistants Médicaux Indigènes* — which the government had created in 1935, a year after she had trained her first team of dressing boys, not with any such imposing medical program in view, she reminded herself humbly, but mainly because their big black eyes had begged her to teach them more. Nevertheless, she had put her grain of sand into a foundation. She could look at the top structure now in 1938 and remember a prayer made on a ship nearly six years ago when she had seen the first missionary sisters through a sea captain's eyes and had whispered fervently, "O God, let me do some good."

Meanwhile in Europe strange events had been happening, incomprehensible when you got only headlines. In the past four years the recreation talk had turned often to world affairs, especially when there were souls to pray for like those of the Jews persecuted by the Nazis or of the Spaniards dying in a civil war. Kings and countries seemed to be vanishing. Yugoslavia's Alexander assassinated, England's Edward abdicated, Austria absorbed into Germany and now in September of '38 a slice of Czechoslovakia claimed by Hitler and actually handed over to him by terms of a peculiar document signed in Munich and called a peace treaty.

"Do you think you'll recognize Europe when you go back?" the nuns asked Mother Mathilde.

The Superior was making ready to go back to Belgium for the election of a new Superior General, which took place every six years. For a time there had been an international crisis which had started the old nuns like Sister Eucharistia reminiscing about the days of '14-'18; but that had blown over after the Munich pact. Now the only battle Mother Mathilde had to worry about would be that of her thin blood against the wintry winds of the homeland.

The nuns made a big to-do over her departure. The teachers knitted shawls and mittens for her, aired and pressed her woolen gown and scapular. The nurses prepared the medical kit with plenty of caffeine to stimulate her circulation when

230

the ship would come into the cold currents of the Atlantic. Sister Luke was thankful that she had not been selected to accompany Mother Mathilde. She had the Congo so deeply in her blood she could not imagine even a furlough in the homeland. Belgium would look no bigger than her bandanna.

She thought of the nuns of her congregation — in India, Ceylon, China and in all the other missions of Africa — doing the same things for their Superiors as they were doing for Mother Mathilde, each community wanting its chief to look the most loved and cared for. She imagined the processions of all those elderly wise women whose hair would be gray if visible, coming into the mother house with the auras of their remote stations about them. The brown triangular masks of the Superiors from the tropics would perhaps startle the pale nuns from England and the Continent, and the novices in the mother house would go about on tiptoe in the presence of so many august matriarchs and perhaps dream longingly of one day qualifying for the missions, as she herself had dreamed. Eleven years ago! she told herself amazed.

Mother Mathilde allocated her authority meticulously for she was to be absent three months. She named her secretary, Sister Marie-Rose, the Acting Superior of the community. Sister Monique was given total responsibility for the schools, Sister Eucharistia for the nursery and Sister Luke for the hospital. To each of her deputies she gave in private a parting counsel.

"For you," she said to Sister Luke, "I urge above all moderation. Remember, since your TB attack you have had no respite from a surcharged program. But you will have it when I return." She smiled and patted a letter on her desk. "I shall be bringing back a qualified nurse to take over the surgery. Meanwhile, I pray you will have no special problems. But if you do, Sister, remember to ask God's guidance always before you act."

"There will be no problems, *ma Mère*." Sister Luke looked with devotion at the sturdy little matriarch who had seen her through so many trials in the early days. "I believe every untoward event which can happen has happened. God was good to me. He gave me my tribulations en bloc in the first years out here. Affairs have rolled on wheels since then." She smiled serenely. "We're going to try to have that addition to the Maternity completed for your return, *ma Mère*."

She and Sister Aurélie took turns supervising the building of the Maternity Annex, sharing the joy of steering to completion a project long dreamed of by Mother Mathilde. The rising birth rate in the European colony had outstripped the capacity of the original maternity pavilion. Plans for an annex had been going back and forth for months between offices of the government, of the Vicar Apostolic and of Mother Mathilde, who alone knew what a Maternity must have and patiently amended the blueprints. Progress on her notes were what the nuns went daily to check.

The edifice, cradled in its network of bamboo scaffolding, rose visibly during the months of October and November. The Italian contractor had hired boys from the bush to augment his own gang of skilled masons and carpenters, since he too was caught in the driving desire to complete the job for the return of Mother Mathilde, whom he called a saint pure and simple.

The bush boys scurried like monkeys through the meshwork of scaffolding, singing incessantly as they worked, and when their wives came once a week to the construction site to carry away the first white man's food and yard goods their husbands had ever earned, it was almost like being in the jungle. Drums were brought out and there was singing and dancing in the temporary compound that housed the bush boys.

"It whets my thirst for souls just to look at them," Sister Aurélie confided wistfully. "What an opportunity to evangelize, if one only had the time." When it was her turn to supervise, she always took a first-aid kit. "I bait my hook with this," she said to Sister Luke. Occasionally one of the bush boys came shyly to her with a bleeding finger to be bandaged or a great rolling black eye to be cleansed of a fleck of mortar. Then, speaking fluent Kiswahili and smiling disarmingly all the while, she learned his name, his clan and village, the number of wives he possessed and how many children the Supreme Being had enriched him with . . . "That Great One," she would say, "who is the same as my God . . . yes, yes, the very same."

Sister Luke shared her companion's eagerness for converts but her way, she confided, would have been through teaching had there been time. When she looked at the bush boys she saw first of all the charms and fetiches they wore — each bit of bone, bird-claw and tuft of wild beast's hair welding them in fear to the sorcerers and witch doctors who ruled their lives from birth to death.

"Teach just one of those monkeys to lance an abscess and see that pus is pus and not an evil demon," she said to Sister Aurélie, "and you'll have him started on his way out of darkness."

If she could have known with what stupefying suddenness their wishes were to be granted — hers for getting some of those repulsive charms off a bush boy's neck and Sister Aurélie's for making converts quickly — Sister Luke would have

233

torn from her thoughts such venturesome wishing every time she gazed at the bush boys.

All through November she and Sister Aurélie cultivated them and made secret plans to lure them to the Christmas Eve service in the chapel. And all through November, as Sister Luke was to learn later, a sorcerer out in the bush was telling one of those boys that if he could kill a woman, preferably a white, then he would be freed forever from the spirit of a dead wife who haunted him.

In the fortnight before Christmas, Sister Aurélie had the night watch in Maternity when the bush boy came. He had made a cut on his thumb and he held it up bleeding as he peered through the glass of the postnatal ward, where she had just brought the newborn babies to their mothers for breast-feeding.

"If Mesdames will excuse me for just a moment," she said. "It's one of our building boys come to me for first aid." She went to the door with a happy smile and opened it.

Six women saw the first act. The boy thrust himself into the ward with a club of wood held behind his back. He looked about wildly as if unable to choose which white woman — those in the beds or the tall familiar one whose clothes as well as her face were white. Suddenly he lifted his club and crashed it down on Sister Aurélie's skull.

The skull was split open at the first blow but somehow she stayed on her feet. The one nursing mother who had not fainted saw her walk slowly, very steadily toward the bush boy, backing him step by step from the ward. The mother began to scream from her bed as she saw him deliver in the corridor two more blows which drove Sister Aurélie down to the floor and out of her sight.

She screamed when Emil came and wrestled the crazed na-

234

tive into submission and continued screaming as Sister Luke came flying down the corridor, unable at first to take in anything beyond the fact that a patient needed care, though she saw as in a nightmare the two panting black forms with Emil on top and the blood on the headbands of Sister Aurélie as she stepped over the still white shape.

Her hand was absolutely steady as she shot sedative into her screaming patient, drowning away the voice of hysteria . . . "She was dead, Sister, when she walked toward him . . . dead and smiling and she walked . . ."

"Sister Aurélie is not dead, Madame . . . not dead . . . Sleep now, she is not dead . . ."

She telephoned the Acting Superior before she left the ward, suggesting politely that the *Force Publique* be summoned at once. Then she opened the glass door and stepped quietly into the corridor.

Emil's night-duty boys were with him now. They had the maniac bound securely and were sitting on him. Their eyes, feral with fright, rolled toward the body of Sister Aurélie. She knelt and for the second time in her religious life put her fingers on a sister's warm wrist that had no pulse.

"Emil," she whispered, "help me lift her." But before Emil could or would move, the other three deputies of Mother Mathilde were there, Sisters Marie-Rose, Monique and Eucharistia. The four of them carried Sister Aurélie to the treatment room and laid her on the table. Sister Luke nodded to the Acting Superior, who went away at once to call a priest.

They made the first funeral *toilette* without breaking the grand silence, each one performing the tasks for which her specialty best fitted her — Sister Monique of the arts arranging the skirts and bending back into shell shape the crushed coif, Sister Eucharistia of the nursery folding the dead hands

235

in a pose of childlike trust over the pectoral cross, Sister Luke sponging away the only trickle of blood that showed on Sister Aurélie's face and noting, with a professional coldness that horrified her afterwards, that only the headbands had held the brains in place.

Father Stephen came with the oils for extreme unction and Sister Marie-Rose with the little paper promising obedience to God until death, which she placed between the folded hands. There was a stupefaction in all their voices as they made the responses and their gestures seemed dreamy and thoughtless, like those of somnambulists hesitating on the edge of an abyss.

Sister Luke remained on vigil with Sister Marie-Rose. Kneeling on her chair, she gazed stunned at the calm profile that showed no distortions from a death by violence. After a long while, the Acting Superior broke the silence as was her prerogative.

"How did it happen, Sister Luke?" she whispered.

"I don't know exactly. I heard the boys chattering something about a sorcerer. Emil will have the whole story. I had to attend to the patient first, of course." She stopped and caught her breath. Was it possible she had done that first? The tomtoms beat the story out to the bush without pause. "All I know, Sister, is that she backed the killer out of the ward after she was struck . . ."

All I know, she said silently to Sister Aurélie, is that you smiled as you walked toward that door because you thought you had a convert on the hook. Our thirst for souls, my little sister. You baited your hooks with bandages . . . I with lancets. We were like two misers gazing covetously at that great treasure of unclaimed souls, do you remember? And how we plotted to bring them to chapel at Christmastime with our

236

Christian boys? *That* will fetch them, we said with our eyes . . .

Sister Aurélie's lips still had the rosy hue of life and were upcurved in her shy sweet smile. They seemed to move as she stared at them, as though breath beat behind them to form again the yearning words, It whets my thirst for souls just to look at them.

You'll never look again. Your eyes are closed forever, with a club. Christ wasn't satisfied with our little hooks. He wanted the whole net thrown . . .

She couldn't realize anything, least of all the fact that she was looking at the whole net thrown, as her bitter inner voice cried out against the senseless slaughter.

If she watched each step, she might find something concrete to put into the report she must write for the mother house, something to take the place of those phrases of sweetness and light which she had never been able to force from her pen. The report would be published in the convent magazine. She recalled the only one she had ever read, which began, *I dip my pen in the blood of a little martyr* . . . Watch each step. Gather the facts. Facts you can write about without squirming . . .

The Acting Superior met the nuns outside the dormitory next morning and told them that the Mass would be a Requiem for Sister Aurélie, who had been accidentally killed in the night. After the Mass, before they entered the refectory, she would give them details to prepare them to meet their publics. The burial would take place before noon. *Everything must be quick in the tropics, but you cannot write that.*

Nor can I write that it could have been I, instead of Sister Aurélie, had I been just a few minutes earlier on my night rounds, had I not lingered in the surgery ward. No, she told herself, you cannot write that because your readers know that it could have been none other than she whom God chose. There is no hazard in His plan. *She was ripe for heaven,* the nuns will say afterwards and explain away with that familiar phrase every aspect of brutal chance in that needless death.

Outside the refectory, the Acting Superior stopped the little community that had just sung a Requiem for a death not yet understood.

"Sister Aurélie died in an act of charity," she said quietly. "A crazed Black, who is now safely in the hands of the law, came to the Maternity last night and struck her down. We know that she pardoned him before she died and that her last cry to Christ was, *Don't count this sin.*"

Sister Luke watched the nuns stiffen with shock. There were little gasps and then that silence of stupefaction that had hung over the treatment room the night before. Sister Marie-Rose continued.

"We know that our beloved sister is counting on us not to avenge her even in thought, but to continue with the natives the apostolate that was so dear to her heart. Presently you will be with your boys. They are fearful of our reaction, expecting vengeance, of course. Show them that the Christian does not revenge himself, that Christ has taught us to love our enemies. This is the mission our martyred sister has left for us to complete."

That I can write. *Died in an act of charity.* But can I myself believe it? Sister Luke asked herself despairingly.

The confidence of every Black had to be won again and that made, in the end, the story of the continuing mission

238

which shot the light of faith into the report Sister Luke had despaired of being able to write.

She knew that some of her sisters had fear when, after the funeral, they returned to their posts and met their boys. Some were so revolted they appeared to be physically ill. The boys outnumbered the sisters twenty to one in every department and their black faces, suddenly ugly and estranged with shame, recalled to all the nuns the impressions of their first days in the Congo, that they were adrift, very white and visible, on a sea of dark countenances, fathomless, impenetrable and unknowable.

Her own efforts with Emil — a convert, familiar with whites for years — recapitulated in a sense the experiences of the whole sisterhood in those first hours. Emil refused to look at her when she entered the hospital. As she approached the desk, he turned quickly and started down the corridor, hunched forward as though a lash curled over his back.

"If you're on your way to the Contagious, Emil," she called out after him, "would you please take these papers to Sister Margarita?" Gray and shrunken, he turned to look at her, unable to comprehend the friendly tone. She pulled him back to her with a smile.

"The sisters are not angry with us?" he asked in Kiswahili, as if his race had lost the right to speak in the tongue of the murdered one.

"Emil, you are a Christian like us. You know our hearts have no place for rancor. No, Emil," she said gently, "we are not angry."

"But with that one then, Mama Luke . . . that shame of shames we gave over to Monsieur Marcel last night?"

"Not even with him, Emil."

"I don't understand." He stared at her, his brow wrinkled

239

in thought. Slowly a wonder overcame the fear in his eyes. He shook his head. She watched the familiar stern look of protectiveness come over his face. "If such a death happened to one of ours, Mama Luke, we would stake the murderer out along the riverbank and each fisherman would cut a piece of his flesh for bait until there was nothing left but his bones."

"You *would* have, Emil, if . . ." She touched the small gold cross suspended from a thong about his neck. ". . . *if*, I say, you were not wearing that sign of Him who taught us to forgive."

A queer little smile wreathed his face as when, sometimes in the labs, she caught him in an error he knew better than to make.

"That's what you must make the boys understand, Emil. Remember, you're their Capita, my deputy."

He took the papers she handed to him and bowed. He held his small stocky Bantu body very erect as he walked away. Midway in the hall he thought of something and came back.

"Mama Luke . . ." From the pocket of his shorts he drew forth a twisted bunch of feathers and claws on a string and laid it on the desk. "One of the boys tore this off that shame of shames last night, so that in prison he'll have no protection from his evil spirits."

She looked at the fetich lying on the logbook, covering a part of the neat newsprint handwriting of Sister Aurélie. Her heart beat so fast she couldn't speak for a moment.

"Which one, Emil?"

"Illunga, Mama Luke . . ."

Illunga . . . the last of their unbaptized black boys. Her hand closed over the charm so tightly that its claws pricked her palm. The small precise writing beneath her fist blurred

240

as she stared at it. Illunga, she whispered to Sister Aurélie
. . . it was his grief for your body on the floor that gave him
courage to touch this witch thing. You have one on the hook,
my little sister, you have one on the hook . . .

Presently she opened her hand and held out the fetich to
Emil. "You must send it back to the boy in jail," she said.
"We cannot leave him defenseless there, Emil. He must have
this to protect him against the law."

"But it will not, Mama Luke!" Emil's startled eyes rolled
from the fetich to her face.

"That's just what we must let him find out for himself,
Emil," she said very softly. She took him into the conspiracy
with a smile that brought his own back again. He went off
like a runner burdened with news for his boys.

In the days that followed, the nuns spoke often in the
recreation of Sister Aurélie, but never with any grief in their
low thoughtful voices. There was, on the contrary, a faint
suggestion of envy. *If only I had been chosen* . . .

Sister Luke felt the envy curl and twist in her own heart
one night when Sister Monique, with matchless rhetoric,
spoke of the supreme grace God had given to Sister Aurélie,
the grace of dying for Him.

There was a time, Sister Luke reflected, when such a longing to die for Christ would have seemed exaggerated, even
possibly psychopathic. But now no longer. She tried to analyze the change that had come over her in the past two years,
ever since she had had that vision in the tree-house of what it
was to be a real nun. It seemed almost as if she had been one,
since then. A true nun worked until she dropped, prayed until
she was hollow and hoped humbly and continuously that one
day the Blessed Lord would take her up to heaven through a

little martyrdom that would cause her unfinished business on earth to go on, as Sister Aurélie's was continuing.

Three more of the sisters had received, without asking, the fetiches their boys wore. They had given them back to the boys exactly as she had done, to be tried and found wanting by themselves, although she had never told them about that particular exchange between herself and Emil. She looked around the recreation circle at the faces of her sisters turning grief into a glory as they talked about Sister Aurélie's blood falling fruitfully on the black race that had struck her down. The talk did not sound sweet or childish. What caught her attention was the fact they they had all replied in the same way when presented with the fetiches. As if a single intelligence inspired all our separate brains, she thought. Then she recalled one exception and spoke it aloud.

"In the first shock, I called it senseless slaughter," she said. "I even cried out against Christ for the injustice . . ."

"I think we all did that, Sister Luke," said the Acting Superior. "It is no cause for self-reproach. If we saw and understood on the instant every one of God's mysterious moves, we would no longer be here, would we?"

The nuns nodded appreciatively, since she had spoken to them all. And from them all, as from me, Sister Luke thought, she has lifted that last shadow of remorse for those bitter hours when we prayed mechanically and cried *Why? Why?* as we followed the body to its hasty grave.

The thrumming night beat in against their small circle of light under the kiosk. The temperature of the December midsummer was stifling; the parched earth gave back after sundown all the blazing heat it had sucked in during the day. Only crickets and bats had the will to move in the torrid dark, she thought . . . and nuns. She listened to the click

of their knitting needles making a busy local obbligato to t
bat squeaks and insect shrilling.

There is no heroism in the convent. She smiled as she ɪ
called the familiar maxim of the cloister.

X V

MIDNIGHT MASS on Ch .stmas Eve in the Congo was always a moving event. Sister Luke had sung five of them, but this year she was on call and dispensed from participation. She sat in the pews, a spectator staring like all the others at the little stable the nuns had built of bamboo and palm fronds. She sensed the emotions of the lonely young *commerçants* in the pews around her, remembering Christmases when they had first seen the Infant placed in the crib, and of the rum-soaked colonials who had quit their parties and come to the convent chapel, bleary-eyed with nostalgia for the home country. Above all, she felt the electric excitement from the section where the black boys of the convent staff sat transfixed by this appealing aspect of their newfound faith. Sandwiched in between them and wearing cotton shorts and shirts borrowed from them were the wild little bush boys they had brought with them to see the show.

She could not imagine what the bush boys were thinking, but she knew their acute senses picked up the yearning and the expectancy as the midnight bells began to chime. In the hush that followed, she heard the tinkle of their bracelets as they reached out suddenly to hold hands with their guardian brothers.

The splendid processional of her sisters, clad in choir capes freshly whitened with chalk, came through the portals from the cloister. The organ gave the first chords of *O Minuit Chrétien,* lifting their voices with it in purest sweetness. Single file, pacing slowly, the line of nuns lengthened until the Acting Superior appeared with the figure of the Christ Child in her arms.

The nuns circled the altar with candlelight on their faces, their hands folded out of sight in the long sleeves that dropped winglike down their sides. They looked like angels moving toward the Manger. The chapel bells rang in and out of their singing, then their voices soared with the organ as the Superior laid on its bed of straw a porcelain figure with dimpled knees and curling fists that looked like a doll. *And Christ is born again . . . And Christ is born again!* sang her sisters as the pealing bells came in from on high.

They're sitting there just like little ebony statues, Sister Aurélie. They've got their feathers and fangs still about their necks. But they're *here,* my little sister, they're looking at *our* magic now. There's not a breath out of one of them . . . not a breath.

After the three Masses, most of the nuns took advantage of the annual indulgence to go to the refectory for fruits and a glass of wine, or chilled cocoa for the few who did not care for wine. They had to continue in the grand silence, but they could smile and talk with their eyes, and the wine, which came only four times yearly on the big feasts of Easter, Assumption, All Saints and Christmas (and then no more than two goblets each) put a sparkle in their talking eyes.

"Sister Aurélie must have seen those little savages in chapel . . . of course it is presumption even to mention the possi-

245

bility, but one must say it's quite strange they came without any urging from us."

"I missed her grievously in the processional . . . she always preceded me, sometimes covered up for me when I couldn't reach the high notes."

"Mother Mathilde is thinking of us tonight . . . Christmas in the mother house, do you remember the perfection?"

Sister Luke drank her two authorized goblets and heard her father say disparagingly, "An unlabeled Médoc . . ." Even so, she looked with concealed pity on the sisters who chose chilled cocoa. The wine lightened the spirit and gave to their bereaved group a little feeling of the joy that wrapped around the earth that night. The pageant in the mother house had a splendor, of course. But she wouldn't trade for it a single moment of her own small community's celebration, with drums and crickets in the background and a heat so dense it put a shine on every face.

She smiled as she sipped her wine. The mother house seemed to be much more than eight thousand kilometers away. It was light years distant from this refectory in the Congo where a gallant little community of sisters, each known to the other as intimately as they knew the lines in their separate palms, tied towels over their starched bibs and ate mangos after midnight.

Most of them, she saw, were eating their mangos as Sister Aurélie had urged and teased them to do — without benefit of knives and forks, which were, as she used to say, a desecration of this superlative bounty of God. They stripped off the skin of their fruits and thrust their fingers straight into the golden flesh to catch the flat ends of the pits.

Sister Monique, who had never before been seen to eat a fruit with her fingers, held up the flat oval pit with a fringe of

246

hairlike fibers around its edges from which her teeth had pulled the luscious pulp. Like an artist she might have been studying its form and identifying its botanical origin. *"Mangifera indica,"* she seemed to be saying, "believed to have been cultivated for about six thousand years . . . glossy lanceolate leaves, small reddish flowers followed by this fruit, a fleshy drupe . . ."

But Sister Luke knew she was saying nothing of the sort. She was saying to the unseen presence that was still very close to all their hearts, "You're absolutely right, my little sister, this is the only way to eat a mango." Her eyes caught Sister Luke's and smiled as she laid down the fiber-fringed pit.

Mother Mathilde returned a fortnight after New Year's Day in that fateful year of 1939. She arrived by plane in the late afternoon and there had been, as usual, the bustle of choosing which nuns would accompany the Acting Superior to the airport, and — as usual — the two humblest sisters had been selected, the supervisors of kitchens and laundry. Sister Luke heard the plane go over the hospital as she made her rounds. She said a little prayer for its moment of landing.

For the homecoming, there was to be a special dispensation of wine with the evening meal and permission had been given to say Matins and Laud privately in the chapel just before the *Salve,* so that the first recreation with Mother Mathilde might be extended. She would have much to tell her nuns of the big doings in the mother house, of the re-election by unanimous voice-vote of the Reverend Mother Emmanuel which she had already written about briefly, of the messages from the Superior General and from their families and friends who had visited her.

Sister Luke ran ahead in her thoughts to the time next morning when she would have her private interview with Mother Mathilde. She was eager to tell about her spiritual life, which would be the first subject the Superior would query her on. All the rest would come later — news of the finished Maternity, the patients already installed in it, the health of her nursing nuns who had closed up the ranks after Sister Aurélie's death and accomplished her work by doubling their overtime in that stifling season . . .

"My spiritual health, *ma Mère*," she would say. "There has been a crystallization. Our tragic event taught me many things I did not know. There's no more flux of uncertainty. No more self-indulgence with regret for the lesser faults, which are still very plentiful, ah yes. God shed His graces, more than I merit. Strong," she would say. "An inner strength . . ."

"You look like the cat that swallowed the canary," said the doctor, who had been standing before her desk watching her talk to herself. He put out his hand and grinned. "May I have the Englebert chart? I'm on my way to greet Mother Mathilde. Too bad I've got to mix pleasure with business and tell her about our psychiatric case."

He leafed through the file she handed him. "I see you were up with him again last night. What was it this time? Suicide threat?"

"It was nothing, Doctor. Just loneliness really. The night boy could have taken care of him." She smiled. "All I did was talk with him a little while. He quieted down like a lamb."

"Don't hide your light under a bushel of modesty. You're the only one who can handle him and you know it. I ought to be grateful, but I'm not when I look at you. I sometimes wonder, Sister, when, if ever, you get any sleep."

248

He studied her for several moments, then he began to hum. The plan he formulated to the tune of Tosca put a glint in his narrowed eyes. Afterwards, she remembered with what simple faith in her own mind-reading she had read that peculiar glint. He's going to prescribe mild sedatives for Monsieur Englebert from now on, she thought, so I can get some sleep.

She watched him walk away humming, using the file as a fan.

The file lay off to the side of Mother Mathilde's desk, stacked on top of the hospital reports, statistics of admissions and releases — all the unimportant matter to be spoken of later.

Mother Mathilde blessed her, embraced her, then held her by the shoulders as she said, "How I thought about you, my child, especially after that cable. I knew how close you were to Sister Aurélie, how difficult it must have been for you to accept God's will." She let go of the shoulders and returned to her chair.

"And now I know," Mother Mathilde continued, "precisely how difficult it was for you. I hardly recognized you when first I saw you in the refectory, you've lost so much weight." The Superior paused. A clinical glint shone in her worried eyes. "Tell me, Sister, have you made a sputum test since I've been away?"

"No, ma Mère. There was always so much else to do. But mainly, I didn't think it necessary." She smiled reassuringly. "I feel so strong, ma Mère. I don't even feel the need for that assistant you told us was coming by ship. It is an *inner* strength," she said firmly, as if to remind the worried keeper of her soul of the maxim she herself so often employed when cautioning sisters to go easy. *A healthy soul requires a healthy body to house it.* Mother Mathilde nodded for her to continue.

She had rehearsed this and did not have to hunt for words. They poured from her eagerly, almost with abandon. She knew before she was halfway through that she was vanquishing the concern she could not bear to see on her Superior's face. A smile played around Mother Mathilde's lips and her eyebrows lifted in her characteristic expression of pleased surprise. Sister Luke heard the exaltation in her voice but made no effort to curb it. This she was telling was no self-delusion, no abnormal sense of personal well-being. It was a lifting up of inner strength that felt solid as a second skeleton inside her. "Something like the strength after a retreat, *ma Mère* . . . I have been so eager to tell you."

Mother Mathilde continued smiling after she finished speaking. Her hand, bleached like her face by the Belgian winter, looked very white on her crucifix, but strong and purposeful as it stroked the dark wood.

"It is very wonderful what you tell me, Sister." Her low voice vibrated. "It means that the Master Himself has prepared you for what I am going to tell you. How strangely our problems work out when we lay them at His feet!"

She picked up the Englebert file.

"All the way back on the plane, I pondered this case. The family came several times to the mother house and begged me to arrange for repatriation. Then, yesterday, the doctor made the same request, even more urgently than the family." She smiled and leaned forward. "All last evening, Sister, I was pondering how to tell you that I must send you back to Belgium with this case. I know your deep attachment to the mission. But you are the only one qualified in psychiatry . . ."

From the moment she said *send you back to Belgium*, Sister Luke did not move her eyes from her Superior's. The powerful gaze penetrated to her very soul and watched it, while the low voice went on talking naturally and nurselike of a nursing problem.

". . . and the only one to whom, in good conscience, I could give this duty. Of course you know the importance of this man in the colony and how urgent it is to prevent his mental breakdown from becoming acute. All indications are that he can be cured if we get him as soon as possible to a sanatorium with proper facilities." Mother Mathilde paused.

It was her turn to speak now, to prove that her voice was as steady as the soul her Superior inspected in a continuing gaze.

"And the doctor?" she asked, with a little lift that asked, What will *he* do?

"Dr. Fortunati made it easy for me, Sister, by suggesting you. He will take his long overdue vacation when you leave. He'll bring in his assistant, Dr. Pieters, to replace him for emergency surgery, and arrange for all the big surgery to be done by the mine doctors. And I must say," Mother Mathilde went on in a lighter tone, "it will certainly make it easier for your successor to learn her way around without that slave-driving genius on her heels every moment."

Your successor. Successor . . . one who takes the place of . . .

"*Ma Mère* . . ." She hesitated.

"Yes, Sister?" The Superior smiled encouragement.

"Will I . . . will they . . . send me back, do you think?"

251

That thin voice, that tremulous wail asking Christ what next.

A flash of something very like compassion shot from Mother Mathilde's dark eyes which never let go of her own but went on boring and exploring. Her voice, however, was matter-of-fact.

"I am certain that the mother house will return you as soon as possible," she said firmly. "*I* shall certainly want you back. Of course, it will depend on how our Reverend Mother Emmanuel finds your spiritual health and the doctor your physical health. But I have little concern about either findings . . ." She smiled disarmingly. "In fact, none at all . . . after what you've told me, Sister."

Sister Luke knew that her relief for the assurance of return to the Congo was perfectly obvious. Mother Mathilde paused as if listening to her change in respiration, then she continued.

"Nor will you be detained in Belgium for the change-of-climate furlough. You are not due for that yet. Nevertheless, Sister" — she glanced down at the Englebert file — "the little change this duty brings will do you good." Her eyes, probing no more, sparkled now. "You'll have an opportunity, however brief, to renew your spiritual life in that serene atmosphere of the mother house. Ah, that oasis of silence, that pure monastic air of piety." She nodded over her own happy memories. Then presently a twinkle came in her eyes.

"But just be sure you're as generous with caffeine in your own medical kit as you were with me," she said. "Even with its aid, I shivered like a dog all the while in Belgium."

The remainder of the conference was brief. Sister Luke learned that she was to leave on the same ship that was already en route with the new sister, since plane travel might be unduly exciting for her patient. The doctor was processing papers to transmit her at government expense. The Vestiaire would be notified to prepare her woolens.

As she crossed the gardens on her way back to the hospital, she looked around at the world she loved, taking in impressions like a traveler storing food for a journey.

The impeccable canopy of the summer sky blended far off with the red earth in a shimmering horizon of fire. The bush with its gaunt primeval vegetation waited out there with thorny arms upraised for the rain. Closer in were the prim plantings around the hospital and all the neat paths bordered with whitewashed stones that picked up moonlight after dark and guided the feet cf the night-duty nuns away from the shrubs where cobras sometimes lurked after waterings.

A motionless lizard sat on a stone, looking more like the act of listening caught in a casting of copper than like a living creature of God.

"I'm coming back, you beautiful thing," she whispered. "Coming *back*, do you hear?" She watched him disappear in a flash of flame.

She went at once to the doctor as Mother Mathilde had advised. He was at his desk, filling out forms. He looked up and gave her a businesslike nod.

"Well, Sister, we've got a lot to do," he said briskly. "We must get the complete back-file on Englebert, all the skull X-rays, lab tests, consultation reports . . ."

She took out her notebook, thankful that for once he was not going to poke and probe to find out what she thought. She jotted down the instructions he gave. Mild sedatives for the three-day train ride, precautionary bindings which he was sure she would not need, two native guards from the *Force Publique* to ride as far as Lobito, then the ship's doctor to share the responsibility. He spelled out the name for her.

253

"I'm writing him a letter," he said in the same professional tone, "explaining which one is the patient."

She looked up startled and saw his sardonic smile. So he was going to poke and probe after all. She waited for it calmly.

"I was joking, Sister," he said. "Testing the reflex, as it were, of your devotion to duty."

"Considering all we must accomplish, Doctor, I suggest you keep strictly to business."

"Of course," he went on as if she had not spoken, "you really *should* be in a state warranting a bit of medical supervision, considering what lies ahead of you, Sister."

She stared at him. His narrow red eyes were scalpel-sharp.

"Don't you realize that you are about to put to the test that religious strength you're so sure of?" There was no sarcasm now in his voice or face. "The moment you walk into your mother house in Belgium, that strength, Sister, which has never had a real workout here, will meet its test . . . the strict discipline, the walls, the silence. Suppose you were detained there indefinitely. Anything can happen in a convent, as well you know. Would the strength be enough then, Sister?"

"Yes, of course," she said, as though a body lay between them on the table and he had asked, Is everything in order?

"You're sure, Sister? Sure it's not that ferocious will? Sure you've thought it straight through to the end?"

She nodded for all three questions, not to waste further words.

"Well I'm not," he said with sudden anger. His emotion caught her unprepared.

"Then why on earth did you suggest me to Mother Mathilde?" she exclaimed.

"To prove to you that you're wrong," he said slowly, grimly. "To prove to you something I've been telling you for years, even if it costs me you. To prove . . ."

She gave him no chance to say it. She turned on her heel and left the office, saying over her shoulder, "Ring for me, Doctor, when you're ready to discuss the case load."

It was all quite preposterous, but he had sowed a seed. *Was* the strength she was so sure of sufficient only for the Congo? She tried herself out by giving up bits of it as she encountered people and things close to her heart.

She saw Emil, the first great friend the Congo had given her, coming toward her now, his face aglow with devotion, and she told herself that soon she would see him for the last time. The tropic rain burst over the hospital roof and she gave up its thrilling tattoo and the sudden smell of earth — wild, tangy and unbearably sweet — that it beat up from the parched ground. Mother Mathilde called her on the telephone and she gave up the woman she loved more than any human being she had ever known, as she listened to her Superior's voice, pitched below the clatter of rain yet dominating it.

Everything she gave up hurt enormously, but she believed she could accept the pain if she had to. She could accept it, she told herself calmly, for the sake of the Almighty God if that would be His will for her. Curiously enough, as she continued her exploratory operation, she discovered that giving up the doctor would be, after Mother Mathilde, the most difficult severance.

His twisted face full of anger that looked like love (and probably would have been that had she not been exceedingly watchful over both herself and him during all the years they had worked together) hung like a yellow moon in her thoughts. His faith in her judgment, his absolute trust in it when he left her alone in the hospital, the peculiar bond that bound them breathless over a flickering life on the operating table, breathless yet daring the risk . . . *Scalpel, hemostat, catgut, Sister* . . . *Breathing light but steady, Doctor, pulse still palpable* . . . their only conversation through years and years of dark dawns . . . one by one, relentlessly, she excised them from her. His buzzer cut short the masochism. She hurried down the hall.

He was sitting at his desk, hands folded serenely on top of an immense stack of case files. He looked at her reprovingly.

"I'm surprised at you, Sister, running off duty. As if that were the first time we've disagreed on a diagnosis." He asked her forgiveness with a malicious smile. "As if you didn't know I always get mean when contradicted. I'm always fearful of that one time in a hundred when you have been right."

"One time in a hundred! . . . You monster of vanity," she said . . . and she gave that up too, their way of fighting and making up, as she fumbled for her notebook, looking down at her skirt pocket so he wouldn't see her tears.

Three weeks later she was on her way to the mother house.

Her black boys had made a bridal bower of her compartment on the boat train. Walls, ceilings and seats were solidly covered with white blossoms — orchids, azaleas and every variety of begonia. Great clusters of wistaria hung from the corners with gifts concealed among the blooms. The floor was covered with huge native baskets filled with choice mangos, chirimoyas, papayas, guavas and avocados, topped with stalks of the tiny finger-length bananas called *bitika* which her boys knew she loved.

Next to her compartment was that of Monsieur Englebert.

Two native policemen from the *Force Publique* stood guard outside his door. She gave her patient a mild sedative before the train pulled out, then returned to the overwhelming sweetness of her bower, to stand at the window and watch the most momentous years of her religious life fade from view.

Until that final moment, she had successfully dominated every emotion of leave-taking and maintained the belief that she was coming back. As calmly as though taking off for a three-day trip to the bush, she had said good-by to her sisters in the recreation, and then to the doctor in the familiar old battleground of the surgery. But, when the whistle blew and she saw Mother Mathilde and her dressing boys slipping away from her, a bolt of pain tore through her heart. The smile remained on her face staring out from its frame of white flowers. It was a smile fixed in stillness, like any one of the masks she had composed with her own fingers on so many faces of sudden and violent death.

She waited for the last view of the battered old convent Ford parked under the mimosas behind the station. Then she sat down next to the window on the only seat space her boys had left uncovered. She didn't have to look out to watch the Congo going by. She had the Congo with her in the compartment. She touched the floral upholstery and felt a lump. Then she drew forth from beneath a cushion of blooms a black statue carved in ebony.

It was a kneeling woman about fifteen inches high, with shiny black cones of breasts jutting out from under a collar of necklaces and small blunt hands carved flatly against bended knees. The face on the figure lifted with haunting beauty, its eyes half closed and the heavy black lips carved with down curves suggesting silent supplication before a god too immense to speak to or look at. She turned it around in

257

her hands. The names *Emil* and *Bakongo* were carved into the soles of the square feet on whose heels the angular little buttocks rested.

She set the ebony statue on her lap and began to cry.

Her coif cut off her anguished face from the gaze of passengers who lingered outside the glass door to look at a white sister sitting in a bridal bower and holding on her lap, as if it were something alive, one of those heathen statues one used to be able to buy for a few yards of cloth in the market places, until museums began to gather them up and label them Negro African Art.

After a while, she set the statue back on its bed of flowers. She looked down at the floor. Her papier-mâché suitcase, the most worn one the Vestiaire had been able to find because a nun returning to the mother house was given only luggage and clothing that needed replacement, sat like a poor relation among the magnificent baskets woven in the colors of the Congo summers. She leaned down and took from her suitcase her hypodermic kit and from one of the baskets a handful of finger-sized bananas.

Then she went to the next compartment to begin making friends with the gentle little man whom King Leopold had once decorated for signal service in the colony.

The guards saluted her smartly and said, "Mama Luke!"

"You may go back to your car," she said. "We shall not need you until Lobito." She saw their faces fall and switched to Kiswahili. "I must be alone to banish those devils of sunstroke. They will roam this corridor when I do. I want you both safely aside." Her smile restored their prestige. They saluted her and went away to their sleeping car with shoulders squared.

She opened the door and entered the compartment. She

258

turned her back deliberately on her patient as she pulled the door shut. "He's no more deranged than the car conductor," she whispered to God as she fussed at the lock. "Give me Your help to prove it."

She went to the window and lowered the shades to cut off the African sun that smote her heart and her patient's eyes. Then she sat down beside him and shared her bananas.

"Tomorrow, Monsieur Englebert," she said musingly, "I may invite you to my compartment next door. It is full of white flowers and baskets of fruit." She gave him a sideways glance. "Boxes of chocolates, also. You and I must eat those perishables before we come to Lobito."

"In this heat, but of course, Sister," said Monsieur Englebert. He gave her a smile of complete agreement and accepted another small banana from her outstretched hand.

X V I

THE mother house was the only place in Belgium that the Congo had not dwarfed. Its immense gray masonry and rarefied impersonalness sent a little chill through her as when she first had entered it to put on her postulant's cape.

The moment she crossed the threshold a playback of her religious life began. The nun in the porter's cubbyhole stepped forward and gave her the delicate embrace reserved for returning missionaries. Once, she had had her turn in the porter's booth and, like the young sister who received her, she had dropped her disciplined eyes immediately from the tanned face and gaunt expectant look of the homecomer and had made no comment on the worn suitcase handed over at the door, which now in her case contained something obviously weightier than the Rule allowed — the Bakongo statue which Sister Eudoxie would automatically confiscate.

Sister Luke stood still in the foyer to get used to the strangeness of having no one look at her. She recalled that the first act of a returning nun was to visit the chapel. As the bells of Vespers tolled, she slipped like a black ghost into the files of her sisters chapel-bound.

The nun pacing beside her resembled one of the Irish girls

of her novitiate days, now so perfectly molded that one would have to see the blue-eyed smile to make sure of the identity. But her companion kept her eyes bent down and her thoughts presumably on God, and so it was with every other nun whom Sister Luke glanced at, longing for just one pair of eyes to lift in a flash of recognition. Then, as always, following the chill came the beauty.

When the choirs began the Gregorian chant, she had her welcome home. After the fifteen-voiced choir of the Congo community, the hundred sopranos of the mother house nearly swept her off her feet. As long as there is this each day in this house, she thought . . . The choirs began the *Magnificat*. She shut her eyes and listened to their virgin voices singing the Virgin's song. When she opened them, she was looking far ahead. She saw the covey of short-caped postulants down in front, who were not yet permitted to sing with their sisters nor yet sure custodians of their wandering eyes as the hushed antiphon *A great mystery of inheritance* . . . told of secrets their covert glances sought to discover in the statuesque section of the Living Rules.

Sister Luke looked down at her own black scapular, the vestment of the Living Rule. Was she one? God alone could say.

The devotion ended, she went to report to the Superior General. She sat on a sort of mourner's bench in the anteroom of the Reverend Mother Emmanuel's office, in a row of nuns as secret as tombs, awaiting their turns for interview. Some nuns read the Little Office, some told their rosaries, and one — lean and brown like Sister Luke and obviously a recent arrival from a bright hot outpost of the congregation — stared at the austere furnishings of their fountainhead, bare walls, rugless floor, two Gothic oak chairs carved with the coat-of-arms of the Order and an antique desk holding a standing crucifix and small calendar which named the martyr of the day, the date and the year.

Sister Luke read the calendar. March 15, 1939. On the quay in Antwerp that morning, while she was handing over to the Englebert family her patient (who appeared more normal than the nervous psychiatrist they had brought with them to the pier), she had heard newsboys crying headlines about German troops occupying Czech Bohemia. In the black convent limousine which had swept her over the poplar-lined highways to Brussels, she had recalled the war talk among passengers on the ship. What would it be like to be in a convent if war came? she had wondered. There was something Sister Eucharistia had said about it but the words eluded her memory.

A nun emerged from the Superior General's office and another went in. Sister Luke moved up one place on the bench. This is how it will be to be in a convent if war comes, she told herself. Exactly like this with nothing changed. Each one of us secretly struggling with a problem of nature or of the soul, waiting to go in under the X-ray eyes of the Reverend Mother Emmanuel which will pierce through to the places of inner conflict where there never has been any truce, not since Christ's time began on earth . . .

"Never a truce," she whispered as she moved up another place.

She made no preparation for her talk with the Superior General. Instead, she went in spirit out through the closed door to the wide corridor where white-clad novices duty-bound past the *sanctum sanctorum* were sliding their eyes sideways to look at the Living Rules who came out smiling through tears because they had just been promoted or de-

262

moted, praised or reproved. For a while she dwelt with the novices tiptoeing past. Then her turn came.

The Reverend Mother Emmanuel stood up as she entered the office, a salute of special respect for the missionary sisters, whom she was suspected of treasuring above all others since, having been one herself, she knew their special struggles. Sister Luke looked straight into her glowing eyes as she knelt.

The Superior General stepped forward, laid both hands upon her shoulders, leaned down and embraced her cheek to cheek with a warmth that gave the impression she was being held against an understanding heart. Then she returned to her high-backed chair. The magnetic pull of the dark eyes held her own so firmly that Sister Luke did not at once see Emil's ebony statue of the Bakongo kneeling woman on the bookshelf behind the desk. It was set sideways to reveal the posture of prayer.

She waited for the voice which twelve years ago had said, "It is a life against nature," and, seven years ago, "Remember, you are only an instrument." The Reverend Mother Emmanuel smiled. "Did you have a good trip back, my child?"

"A beautiful passage, Reverend Mother. We are treated like queens when we travel." Sister Luke commanded herself not to look again at the statue.

"And how is your physical health?"

"Wonderful, Reverend Mother," she said. "And my spiritual health is likewise."

"That is fine, Sister Luke. Nevertheless, your body now undoubtedly needs some repairs. You must not forget that you have been doing overtime for many years."

Sister Luke saw the minutiae of a Superior's letters on the states of her nuns shining like so many shapely crystals in the dark eyes gazing at and through her . . . You had dysentery once, nearly fatal; then tuberculosis from which with God's help you pulled yourself. You used your own judgment perhaps too often outside your professional field, where alone a nun may use personal judgment, and there were some friendships on the human plane which you might have striven a little more to supernaturalize, but on the other hand . . .

"So, what do you think?" said the Superior General. "The routine is to keep our missionaries here for at least a month to do nothing but rest and refresh the soul in this peaceful atmosphere. Receive family and friends at all hours save those when the community does its spiritual exercises. My special thought for you would be that you get up only at six each day, follow the devotions not from the pews but from the chairs . . ." She paused, smiled. "From the chairs," she repeated, "not because you are too old or ill to stand for the services, but because I would like you to think of yourself for a while as a lamb at the feet of the Master. You were a Martha for a long time, Sister. Now, try to be a Mary."

"I shall try, Reverend Mother." Her upward glance caught the ebony statue on the shelf and the face of chiseled ivory bent toward her and she held them together for a moment in her mind. She could see no difference in the God who inspired both.

"You may chafe at first with no work to do and no errant souls in this community to bring back to the faith." The Reverend Mother's eyes sparkled. "It is amazing to everyone, Sister, how many converts you made in the colony. You must have been beloved by God and a strong intermediary between Him and the souls you encountered. I had many letters from families of colonials, from missionary Fathers, all attesting to your good work. You were liked and respected by everyone

264

out there . . ." She turned her head slightly toward the shelf where the statue was . . . "including your black boys, I see."

Now that it had been mentioned, she could look directly at Emil's ebony. Her fingers knew every curve of the smooth black wood. Her eyes caressed it for a moment. Then she looked back at the Gothic matriarch who alone had the power to send her back to the Congo.

"It is a beautiful gift, Sister," said the Reverend Mother in her most captivating tone. "And how beautifully it symbolizes the whole of that dark continent. Do you wish me to give it to your father?"

Sister Luke heard the veiled yearning in the question. The Superior General was really saying. For your soul's sake I should dearly love you to be able to give this up . . . quite totally, not even retaining the satisfaction of knowing that it remains in your family.

"Your father," she said almost coaxingly, "would consider it a handsome adornment for his desk, don't you think?"

Sister Luke smiled at her and accepted her challenge.

"I should prefer, Reverend Mother, that it be kept in the congregation to which it really belongs. When I leave here, it would make me happy to think that something from me remains in the mother house museum."

"You are generous, Sister," said the Reverend Mother Emmanuel. Sister Luke knew she would never have referred to the statue had she not had a special reason. She would have left it sitting there on the shelf where from time to time reposed the teak elephants removed from suitcases from Ceylon, the multiple-armed gods from India, the ivory Buddhas from China . . . sitting there unremarked and anonymous since never was the nun named from whose suitcase the souvenirs were taken and seldom were they referred to when the missionary knelt in that office trying not to look at the object she loved and, bravely hopeful, had brought with her into this house of total abnegation. It struck her that perhaps her deep attachment for the Congo was more visible than she had supposed.

"This will enhance our Bantu collection," the Reverend Mother went on. "Perhaps, Sister, after you are well rested, I may ask you in the recreation to tell your sisters the news of their Congo colleagues. They are always eager for firsthand news."

Sister Luke nodded obediently, but she wondered if she could talk about the Congo calmly, especially now that it had been made quite clear she was to remain in Belgium longer than Mother Mathilde had suggested.

As she left the office, she felt the magnetic eyes following her to the door. The Reverend Mother Emmanuel had invited her to come back any time she wished for another heart-to-heart talk. She would go back, she told herself, as she shut the door quietly behind her. She would go back because she was sure now that she would never weaken to the point of asking about her return to the Congo. Her first talk had proven that she had the strength not to blurt out the question closest to her heart. It had leaped from her eyes, quite possibly, but she had been able to hold her tongue.

Her father was the first visitor. "You are thin, *ma petite!*" he said, exactly as he had the first time he had seen her clad in the transforming habit. He embraced her, then stood her off from him and looked at her with combative lights in his blue eyes. "I don't believe, of course, all that rubbish about your having had TB in the Congo. It is inadmissible that anyone survive the malady in the tropics."

266

The reunion was easy then. They launched at once into one of their old professional discussions. She matched his objections point by point, but never suggested that he look at her X-rays, knowing how proudly he spurned such mechanical aid for what his own ears, pinned back with a stethoscope, would have told him more convincingly. She described Dr. Fortunati's original cure and saw the sallow face of Beelzebub as she talked and wondered how he would make out with the sister who replaced her. She saw the golden eyes of Felix peering up from the cradle of her arms as she had paced the treetop room, letting the little monkey look aloft for crickets in the thatch while she recited the Offices happily.

With memories pulling and twisting, she found she could relate no more of the Congo than the exact number and frequency of the gold-dust injections, the precise regime of sleeping and overfeeding. Her father appeared to take for granted that nothing more important than her phenomenal triumph over tuberculosis had happened to her in the Congo.

"Of course, they'll send you back after a little change-of-climate furlough," he said.

"Perhaps," she said. "But if there should be war . . ." Then she remembered what Sister Eucharistia had said about the mission in wartime. Every word flashed clear in her memory. "In 'fourteen to 'eighteen we were completely cut off from the mother house and the homeland. Our colonial troops fought the Germans out here . . . that's how, when the peace was signed, we were given the protectorate of Ruanda-Urundi. But more important to us, of course, was the first letter from our beloved Mother General after four long years of silence. And then, the sisters starting to come out again to the colony . . ."

"Are you ill, Gaby?" her father asked. "Your pupils are dilated."

"No, no . . ." She forced a smile. "I heard myself saying war conversationally, then I began to think what it would mean."

"There'll be no war," said her father. "Personally, I don't believe that psychopath in Germany will make another move." He stroked his beard as he gave her some medical facts about Hitler to explain the current boasting coming out of Germany. "Of course," he added honestly, "all this may be wishful thinking. Antoine is in the Reserve now but he wouldn't wait to be called up. The two younger are of military age of course."

"The two *gosses!*" They were lads in knickerbockers when she saw them last. In the timeless years of the convent they had never grown up in her mind. She stared at her father and shivered.

"I'd take a little caffeine until you acclimatize to our March winds," he said gently.

When her father was gone, she wanted to continue sitting in the parlor all alone to think. But she could feel the community around her, immense and watchful. It seemed to be waiting for her return to it, with its two hundred pairs of eyes cast down yet seeing all. She shivered again as she opened the door to the cloister.

I'll get used to it, she told herself, but she was not sure if she referred to the weather or to the sight of so many nuns under one roof. She took a caffeine capsule from her pocket and slipped it into her mouth as she made her way through the peopled thoroughfares of the mother house to the nuns' dormitory. It was time for the half-hour rest she had promised

Reverend Mother Emmanuel she would take for the first week.

The caffeine in capsule did not take effect as promptly as the hypos she had been given on the ship. She lay on her straw mattress that rustled as she shook and she remembered Mother Mathilde saying, "Be sure you are as generous to yourself with caffeine as you were with me . . . I shivered like a dog all the while in Belgium."

Presently she felt the action of the caffeine on her heart, which began to beat rapidly and strong. Then the action moved to her brain, stimulating every part of it. She lay wide awake, alert as an owl in the gloom. She recited word for word lines from her *Materia Medica Pharmacology* that she had not thought of in years. "As a result of caffeine, the patient's mental activities, especially reasoning and memory, are increased. Fatigue lessens. The imagination is more active. This effect is of short duration." She shut her eyes for the duration.

Presently she was riding in the convent Ford, clinging to her veil with one hand and her sack of instruments with the other. Emil was in front with the driver, turned sideways so he could speak of medical matters to impress Kalulu. They rode across town and set up for an operation in the native hospital. Dr. Fortunati came into the small bare operating room on the instant they were ready for him. He ignored the body on the table and the instrument trays and looked at her.

"I've got your successor trained up to instrument nurse," he said, "but that's as far as she'll go. She'll never replace you. She has no fight in her. She won't argue back when I'm wrong." His face was a lacquered lantern swinging in a boundless space of sun and winds. "That girl was born to be a nun, something you could never be in a thousand years, Reverend Sister . . . an overgrown child."

Emil slipped a mask over the grinning yellow lantern. The eyes above the patch of gauze became human. *Ready?* they said while the black eyebrows came together in a quizzical peak. Then she slapped the first instrument into his gloved hand. . . .

"You're not in love with him?" Mother Mathilde asked.

That was in her second Congo year just after Madame Goossens had been delivered of her fifth daughter and Beelzebub had wanted to tie off her tubes, pretending she was too old for further childbearing. In the fiercest dispute they had ever had together, she had prevented him. Mother Mathilde had seen her when she came from surgery, flushed with shame for having called a doctor a coward because he could not face a son-hungry father for a fifth time and tell him that God's will had been otherwise.

Sister Luke opened her eyes. The gray curtain of a convent cell in Brussels swayed slightly in the draught. The curtain turned into Spanish moss as she stared at it and she was on the river again with Mother Mathilde, who continued questioning her in Flemish so the paddle boys would not understand. "Because if you are in love and have not told me, my child, it would break my heart."

"Ah no, *ma Mère!*" The pirogue rolled with her sudden movement of dismay as she realized that her Superior had waited a whole week before asking, a week of worry and praying and doubtless asking herself if she had lost a soul through her own inattention. "Of course I've not fallen in love!" But isn't it wonderful, she thought, how frankly and freely we always talk together? "I only cherish him, *ma Mère*, deeply, for his skill and selflessness when there's a life to be saved. I

270

think always he is very close to God in those unearthly hours when he operates."

The prow of the pirogue curved up from the water and the forward seat was the pedestal on which Mother Mathilde stood like a figurehead. "I'm so glad you told me, Sister," she said simply. . . .

After a while the images faded. Sister Luke could look at the cell curtain and see nothing more than gray wool neatly darned in places. Her chill had subsided but there was a pain in her heart that had nothing to do with the stimulant she had taken.

On the way to Vespers she threw the remaining caffeine capsules into one of the wastebaskets that stood along the corridor. She had it rolled up discreetly in a scrap of paper such as nuns always stooped to pick up on their way to and fro through their immaculate house.

She knelt in her pew and folded her hands. "Help me to detach from those memories," she said to the Lord. "I've come halfway to help You by throwing out the caffeine which sharpens them and choosing to shiver instead. O God, how can I be a Mary if I can't get the Congo out of my blood? Help me to be like her. Help me to say *Thy will* with her perfect grace." She turned the pages of her Little Office as she prayed and moved her lips as if chanting the psalms with her sisters.

"It's still strange, Blessed Lord, not to hear crickets shrilling when we chant this Office. In the Congo, Vespers was always Your magic hour. It was late afternoon and Your creatures in the bush were already stretching and stirring, sharpening beaks and claws for the night prowls . . . when we came to the *Ave, maris stella,* the ocean of night was just below the horizon."

271

The memories persisted despite her prayers.

One day when her unaccustomed leisure weighed too heavily, she asked and received permission to visit the cancer ward of the mother house hospital.

The old incurables had not known that she was the sister recently returned from the Congo. They knew only, with a strange recognition born out of their years of suffering, that one of those saintly missionaries must just have returned, for there had appeared again on the dressing carts the bandages they cherished above all others. The last tattered shreds of the tropical habits she had brought home in her tin trunk lay upon their frightful wounds.

Sister Eudoxie had sorted the worn habits for continuing use. The parts where threads still held together had been cut into diapers for the maternity wards. The final threadbare portions, usually from the darned skirt fronts where praying knees had pressed, had been folded for one last usage before burning, into the soft dressings which the cancer patients believed brought special alleviation.

The sight of their hands patting the folds of work-worn cotton gave her an emotion. There's a whole lot more than years of prayer folded between those frayed threads, she wanted to tell them. There's struggle and heartache too. There's a sanctification of pain as well as the sanctification you imagine.

"They whimper when we remove those dressings for burning," the accompanying nun whispered. "Isn't it strange how they know what you missionaries have gone through?"

There was no place in the mother house where Sister Luke could escape the playback of memory. It gave her the disturbing feeling that she was no longer a current member of the

272

community, but rather a ghostly spectator free to come and go as she wished, with too much time on her hands.

Now and again she heard Dr. Fortunati saying, Suppose you are detained there indefinitely . . . will the strength be enough then? And she answered the sarcastic voice even more explicitly than she had done when his scalpel eyes were upon her. There is absolutely no doubt of it, Doctor; this seeming restlessness is only because I am unemployed. I need to get back to work, that's all. She haunted the bulletin board that listed transfers and reassignments.

Toward the end of her first month in the mother house, Tante Colette visited her, bringing the brothers. They talked about war, which seemed to have come closer since her father's visit.

"I simply can't believe it," Sister Luke said.

"That's understandable in a place like this," Tante Colette replied tartly. "No radios, no newspapers, no talk . . . but on the outside, Gaby, it's just like in 'fourteen-'eighteen. You'd be surprised how many people already have visas for Spain tucked away in their passports." Tante Colette smiled wryly. "The same families that deserted in the last war."

"And for us who stay . . . it will be the same thing all over again?"

"Probably," said her aunt. "A brief fight and then occupation."

Antoine, tall and handsome, disputed her. She regarded him sadly while he described the great fortifications. Belgium could never possibly be overrun a second time, he said proudly.

Sister Luke listened to the arguments flying back and forth between her aunt and her oldest brother. If there really is to be war, she thought, then there will be suffering right here and a need for nurses. Maybe that's why God gives no sign that I'll be sent back to the Congo, but only the strength to hold my tongue and not ask . . .

"Maybe you think it's a game, Antoine," Tante Colette cried. "Tin soldiers and toy forts. You don't know. You were only an infant when we suffered the last occupation with *Boches* billeted in the house and your father hiding out with a price on his head for spying against them. Don't stare at me. Ask him!" Tante Colette blew her nose and wiped away her tears. "That's why he'd have to flee the country the instant those Germans set foot again on our soil."

"He never told me that when he was here," Sister Luke said wonderingly.

"He never tells anyone," said her aunt with angry pride.

The war talk, however unbelievable, pushed the Congo back a little in Sister Luke's mind and lessened her nagging longing to get back quickly. The realization that she would no longer have that burning wish leaping from her eyes and trembling unspoken on the tip of her tongue gave her the courage to go to the Reverend Mother Emmanuel. For weeks she had weighed the greater perfection of sitting quietly and waiting for the nod to be given against what she knew would be a show of desire for change, or restlessness, or spiritual malaise.

"I simply wish to go back to work again, Reverend Mother," she said. "Anywhere," she added emphatically. "You suspected that the leisure might chafe a bit and it does. I don't make a very good Mary. My hands get restless." She smiled pleadingly. "Could you find something for them to do?"

The Reverend Mother showed no surprise. In her long

tenure of office as Superior General of the Order that had
Pray and Work for its motto, she had seldom known a missionary able to sit out the rest she had earned.

"Are you sure you are ready so soon, my child? After such a tour of duty in the tropics, you are entitled to a longer repose."

"I've gained two kilos in the past month, Reverend Mother. I've made up the lost sleep of years. I've examined and re-examined my life and with the help of God's grace have put my spiritual house in order. But now these hands . . ." She let her longing show frankly in her eyes.

"What sort of nursing had you in mind, Sister?"

"I had thought of TB nursing, Reverend Mother. Having had the malady, I've a resistance established. I've always had a special sympathy for TB's . . . their eternal hope and courage. They always seem so close to God."

The Superior General consulted her notebook.

"It so happens," she said reluctantly, "that we do have a most important post vacant now. It is extremely difficult work. I would want the opinion of our doctor before assigning you." She looked up from her notebook. "It's for an assistant in pulmonary surgery in our hospital on the Holland border."

"Pulmonary surgery would have been my choice had I dreamed there was a vacancy. It is the most exacting nursing, Reverend Mother."

"And the hardest!" A quick smile played over the Superior General's face. Then she said in a thoughtful voice, "But there is another reason why I hesitate. The Superior there, Mother Didyma, was a born missionary, Sister, but we could never spare her administrative talents so sorely needed here. She had to give up her dream of the missions. She surmounted this disappointment bravely, but each time I send

275

her a missionary, I'm sure it revives those old longings and gives her pain. When she will see your tanned face . . ." The Reverend Mother's powerful eyes shot the warning. "You will have to have a great spirit of faith if I send you there, my child."

"With God's graces, you can count on me, Reverend Mother," said Sister Luke in the most positive voice she could summon from her constricted throat. A thwarted missionary, she thought . . . I know something about that secret pain.

"Very well, then, Sister. We shall see." The Reverend Mother Emmanuel lifted her hand for the benediction.

We shall see . . . We shall see . . . Behind the three words lay a world of reasoning far more delicate and exact than a doctor's reading of a few health charts. Sister Luke knew that the state of her soul would be weighed in the sensitive balances of the Superior General's mind, that it would be on the basis of her findings mainly that she would be released from the mother house for work again, released, moreover, to a Superior who might find her presence painful.

She spent most of the next days in the chapel. She had good sturdy pads of callus on both knees from twelve years of praying and metatarsals steel-strong from bracing against stone floors. She knelt without shift or sway hours on end, firm in the conviction that her prayers would be answered.

Five days after her interview with the Superior General, she saw her name on the bulletin board posted for transfer to the hospital on the Holland border. Next to the notice was a current events clipping dated May 22, 1939, announcing that that day Germany and Italy had signed in Berlin a ten-year military and political alliance — a bit of world news pinned up, no doubt, because the nuns construed it as confirmation of the coming of the peace for which they were constantly praying.

Sister Luke read the current events clipping dutifully and saw no connection between it and her assignment, although the connection was there as prophetically as writing upon the wall.

She was to remember it a little less than a year later, when she was to see small puffs of white dropping from the skies which would look at first like clouds and then, as they neared the earth, would turn into parachutes with Nazi storm troopers dangling from the invisible cords.

XVII

SISTER LUKE left the operating room of La Trinité at five o'clock in the morning. Sunrise was just about to break over the sandy flatlands interspersed with lupin-covered dunes that rolled off northward toward the Holland border. It was May 10, 1940, a day that she, her country and the world were never to forget.

There had been as usual the practice bombs that morning, closer in than they were accustomed to hearing. But for months now, the Belgian army had been completely mobilized, the great forts facing the line of the River Meuse had been manned and military maneuvers were so familiar that they no longer suggested threat, especially to the nuns, who knew practically nothing about the war. The preparedness of their neutral country was interpreted as a gesture of prudence, and prudence, they reminded each other with little approving nods, was a gift of the Holy Ghost.

"You did well to call me in the night for that case, Sister," said the doctor. He bent over her slightly, too tall to look directly into her coif. "You have a sure instinct for crises." He smiled his appreciation. "I hope you can get some rest now that that devilish practice is over. For a few moments there in surgery, I'd have sworn it was the real thing."

She returned his smile and said nothing as she accompa-

278

nied him to the main door, opening it for him with one of the many keys that hung from her leather belt. Though once off duty she would not break the grand silence with speech, she stepped out with him for a breath of air after the long hours over ether.

The May morning smelled fresh and sweet. Dawn turned the sky shrimp-pink and there were small puffs of white clouds drifting about in it — such innocent little nonentities of clouds, she thought, remembering with a pang the mountains of charged cumulus that floated over the Congo about this time.

The doctor looked up at the clouds with peculiar attention. Suddenly she sensed him stiffening beside her. "Those aren't clouds, Sister. They're parachutes. It's invasion, by God!" He started running toward his car, crying back to her to get in and stay in.

She stood transfixed, gripping her crucifix. The flowerlike forms dropped out of the dawn with bodies dangling far beneath on cords the sunrise picked up one at a time and made shine like the guidelines of spiders' webs. She could not realize that she was seeing the Germans come a second time.

"A second time!" she whispered aghast. "Just twenty-six years ago . . ." And she was a child again, peering through the lace curtains of her grandmother's house at the Kaiser's Death-Head Hussars riding over the cobbles on magnificent matched black horses with their capes spread over the prancing rumps and tall lances slanting up with precision from the right stirrups. She thought they were princes out of a fairy tale until she heard her grandmother sobbing and saw her mother's face. Her childhood ended in that instant, but she didn't learn to hate until the foreign soldiers moved into their house and she saw her mother and grandmother waiting on

them like frightened servants and freezing into deathly silence each time they were asked about the whereabouts of
her father . . .

Hate shook her as she watched them come, this time in a
sinister kind of beauty and in total silence now that their
bombardment had cleared the way. They were dropping only
a few kilometers distant onto the flats of the Netherlands that
had been the royal road into Belgium from Germany since
time immemorial. The hate ran like flames through her blood
and she knew that if one of those distant paratroopers were to
drop at that moment onto the pavings of her convent courtyard, she would have dashed out and tried to kill him with
her bare hands.

She heard her conscience saying *Thou shalt not kill* as she
killed them all deliberately with her thoughts. Then she
spun on her heel and went back into the convent. She shut
the door without locking it. Save the door, give them no excuse to batter it down when they come, she thought and it
did not seem strange that she knew such things automatically.

She was late for chapel. Her twenty sisters had finished
meditations and were reciting Prime. She bowed to the Superior, who never glanced her way. Then she stretched herself
flat on the floor in penance for being late, leaning on her
elbows with her face buried in her hands.

She listened to her sisters chanting antique Latin while
Germans were dropping among the dunes no more than a
healthy bicycle ride distant from the hospital. You had to
squint your eyes, she remembered angrily, to see that the
bulky forms were helmeted and carried assault arms. Months
earlier it had been rumored that Nazi spies were parachuting
in dressed as nuns — the advance reconnaissance in a pre-

dominantly Catholic country, it was said. After that, nuns who wished to were allowed to grow their hair without special permission, in case the police picked them up when duty took them to town, mistaking them for Germans in disguise.

"But I would know a *Boche*, dear God, even if he came dressed as the Blessed Virgin. I would know him by the hate that rises from my very soul. I never knew I had that hate until this morning. Was that why You let me see them come again? Or does it mean that You have use for a nun who can never be neutral . . . a nun, O my God, who wanted to kill Germans as they'll kill my brother Antoine sitting at a peephole in the fortress of Namur, as they'll kill every patient in this hospital if food gets scarce enough and they see all these members of Your Mystical Body as no more than so many useless mouths to feed . . ."

A sister plucked at her sleeve. She arose and went to her pew. She offered up her Mass for the salvation of her countrymen. The souls in Purgatory for whom she most often gave her prayers seemed to be by comparison in a much safer place. Her conscience forbade her to go to the communion rail with such a burden of hate in her heart.

Her memory put that morning's breakfast under a bell jar to be kept forever as a singular specimen. Mother Didyma, who she knew had most certainly received a telephone call long distance from the mother house, probably even before she herself had seen the parachutes, started the bread basket down the table with a cool nod and then cut her own slice into the four small *tartines* she always made, laying them out in a row on her wooden plank. She buttered them sparingly, as usual. As usual she took two level teaspoons of sugar in her coffee and then covertly watched the sugar bowl pass from hand to hand to see which sisters practiced self-denial that day by abstaining from sugar — a spiritual check-up, as it were, on the soul states of her small community.

Sister Luke watched the Superior's collected face while her ears strained through the silence for an untoward sound. At that moment the Germans were crossing the Belgian frontier at four points, their planes were bombing the Brussels airport and the antiaircraft batteries in the nearest town of Hasselt were opening up on the second wave of paratroopers dropping over their eastern end of Belgium. Just as a faint ack-ack clattered from the direction of Hasselt, Mother Didyma plucked her coarse napkin from under her chin, laid it forward on the table and went to the pulpit.

"*Benedicite*," she said to her nuns.

"*Dominus*," they replied, a little muted with surprise that something different was happening in the refectory this morning.

"A man forewarned is worth two," said the Superior, reading from a paper she had prepared. "Early this morning I had a telephone call from our Reverend Mother Emmanuel. At three A.M. Rotterdam was bombarded and many thousands killed. Belgium was bombarded at five o'clock. The country's system of sluices has been put into operation and certain main roads are already blown up to prevent the German advance." Her voice was dry, without inflection. She might have been saying, This is your assignment for today. She read on.

Sister Luke was the only one not staring at the Superior. She looked at the nuns one by one — at Sister Ignatius, whose brother was with hers in Namur, at Sister Tarcisius, whose family in Maastricht was probably already in German hands, at Sister Beatrice, whose father commanded the fortress of Liège. As she looked at them, her memory put them also under the bell jar as exquisite details in the singular specimen of

282

a life that was not of this world. Not a flicker of fear or anguish showed on any face.

"I tell you this only that you will be prepared," said Mother Didyma. "There will be panic in the hospital. Our lay student nurses of course will have been listening to their radios. They will doubtless all want to run off to rejoin their families. Your sole preoccupation must be to keep them here and the patients calm. Our work must go on as if nothing has happened . . ."

Three bursts of artillery from the south broke into her speech. She paused as for an ill-bred interruption. Then she went on. "It is your responsibility to set the example of courage and calm and draw the others after you like little sheep. Remember, God loves us and will take care of us." She folded her paper. "All further developments will be posted on the bulletin board," she said, looking at them sharply to make sure that all understood there was to be no war talk in her community.

For the first time since she had joined the community, Sister Luke felt a flash of admiration for her chilly inscrutable Superior.

The next eighteen days ran together like a prolonged nightmare in which afterwards there was no memory of emotions but only of endless sequences of actions, quick, cool and unprecedented. Refugees poured into the convent hospital, first from Holland, then from all the eastern provinces of Belgium, and the nuns tightened their belts as their own slender reserves of food were shared with the frantic multitude. Every corridor and foyer was filled with cots and wheel chairs, and when these gave out, the nuns threw mattresses down.

The refugees elaborated with their wild reports the brief notices that appeared on the bulletin board. The Albert Canal breached by the enemy on May 17. The fall of Brussels on May 19, Malines and Louvain occupied and half of Belgium already overrun.

More believable were the letters from the Reverend Mother Emmanuel which were thumbtacked beneath a neatly chalked caption — *Some Recommendations from the Mother House*. The Superior General exhorted the sisters to be discreet with strangers, to make no search for their families without permission, to take no part in patriotic affairs and to consider the privations in food as penance and abstinence enough without adding any extra self-denials of their own accord. *The national food shortage, of which we are already warned*, she wrote, *will be enough penance to satisfy even the most scrupulous conscience.*

On May 26 the bulletin board announced that the remnants of the Belgian Army, parts of the British Expeditionary Force and of the Ninth French Army were fighting with their backs to the sea at Dunkirk. On May 28 it carried in a single bleak sentence the news that King Leopold had signed a surrender. *The sisters*, wrote the Superior General, *are urged not to accept or read any of the clandestine newspapers of the underground which have already begun to appear in the provinces under German occupation.*

In the fury of those eighteen days that ended with the shocking surrender of her king and country, Sister Luke, without being aware of it, did her first job for the Belgian underground. On the evening of the day Brussels fell, a middle-aged man dressed like a farmer and carrying a small canvas zipper bag came in with a cartload of refugees. But he was a patient. He bore a slip referring him to Sister Luke, specifically to a private room in her tuberculosis wing which was momentarily vacant. The slip was signed by a doctor who had not visited the hospital since the start of the blitz. She wondered how that doctor had known about the vacant room as she led the man through the crowded corridors and up two flights of stairs.

At the door of the room the patient asked her not to let any nurse visit him in the night. He had to have sleep, he said, absolutely undisturbed. Then he asked her to make one more exception to hospital practice and to come to him at four next morning. "Just you alone, Sister," he said in a low voice.

Even in a war, nuns did not arise at four to visit strange men in private rooms without first asking the Superior's permission. Sister Luke knew that if she asked, her request would be denied since she could give no reason to support it. She debated uneasily with her conscience, weighing a deliberated disobedience against something she had seen in the man's eyes — a shadow of urgency that implored her to keep his peculiar request to herself.

It was dark next morning when she tapped on his door. He opened immediately. He was fully dressed and waiting for her. He shut the door soundlessly, then turned and said, "Will you assist me in serving the Mass, Sister?"

With the practiced control now second nature, she concealed her surprise and nodded. Swiftly he opened his zipper bag and handed her a small altar stone, a missal, a standing crucifix and candles. He had already spread a linen over the bed table. She set up his altar while he shook out vestments of thinnest silk. The traveling Fathers of the Congo used to carry such compact vessels and vestments when they took the Church into the churchless bush.

A thrill went through her as she realized she was assisting

one of those priests who was going to try to get out of Belgium to Spain, and thence perhaps to England or the United States, before the Nazis would have time to round him up and give orders on what was to be preached. He had to be someone in a high position to have received permission to say his Mass outside the sanctified enclosure of a church. She listened to him murmuring the vesting prayers as he dropped the silk garments over his farmer clothes.

Presently he stepped back from the bed table as though there were three altar steps between him and it and she knelt behind him with fast-beating heart. She watched his beautiful shapely hands that had never touched a plow. They would betray him unless he rubbed dirt on them. She made a mental note to suggest this after the Mass. Then she heard his priest's voice low and reverent, *"In nomine Patris . . ."* The familiar functional hospital room became for the next twenty-one minutes a house of God.

When the prayers ended, the priest packed his vessels and linens, then turned to her with a smile. "God bless you, Sister," he said. "Now . . . if you could just get me a cup of coffee."

She used the service stairs to the kitchens so no one would see her. When she returned to the room the priest was gone. The lamp on the bed table was left lit, to draw her eyes to a note propped against it. *Pray for me* was written on the scrap of paper in the clear slant script of the Jesuit-schooled.

She carried the note beneath her scapular just above her heart for as many days as she thought it would take a man to tramp the treacherous roads southwest toward France. It gave her a lively sense of participation, as though something of herself were out there in the dangerous world, dodging Germans, seeking hideouts in hedgerows and barns when their

286

tanks thrust over the horizon. Her latent patriotism which had seemed like a harmless atavism came alive and began to beat within her like a strong and steady pulse.

She listened deliberately now to the talk of her student nurses, who, being in the lay world, had many connections with the outside. She heard that the Ardennes, through which her priest would undoubtedly travel, were entirely in German hands. She prayed to the Blessed Virgin to show him the trails she had used in her mountain-climbing days, far from the main highways which were said to be living streams of fleeing humanity over which Nazi planes swooped with machine guns blazing.

She could not know as she prayed for the safety of an unknown priest that her own father was also traveling those risky roads toward France. She had forbidden herself to ask permission to trace her family, as had most of the nuns. The suffering of not knowing where the loved ones were was an extra little cross you could carry in His name. Sister Luke wished only that in her last letter to her father at Easter, she had asked him if what Tante Colette had said was true — that he would have to leave the country should the Germans ever come again. But the thought of such personal matter passing under the eyes of Mother Didyma, and provoking in the next recreation a comment about the heroic imagination of a certain sister, had restrained her.

Food became scarcer and the nuns became hungrier. No one inside the convent had yet seen a German. Ambulances appeared regularly outside the hospital loaded with casualties picked up from the strafed highways. Priests were often in charge. Sister Luke photographed them with Red Cross armbands pinned over the sleeves of their black soutanes and the ambulances with bullet holes punctured cleanly along the horizontal arms of the crimson cross painted on their sides. She had no idea for whom she was making this documentary of inhumanity.

Meanwhile the clandestine newspapers which the nuns were requested not to read were beginning to circulate. A fleeing priest had said "God bless you" for her first deliberate defection from the rule of obedience. It encouraged her to make another. She stimulated her student nurses to read and report on the brave little news-sheets, of which one copy, it was said, was laid every day on the desk of the Lieutenant General Baron Alexander von Falkenhausen, who was now the Nazi military commander of all Belgium. No one ever knew who put the annoying sheets daily on his desk.

The underground news-sheets published the names of Belgian collaborators who had accepted appointments from the Germans as burgomasters of their captured towns, and the information that Belgian bishops had been instructed by the Cardinal to refuse Holy Communion to those who consorted with the enemy. The Belgian collaborators were called Quislings, a word Sister Luke pondered and could not solve because she had never heard that just before the blitz which captured her own country in eighteen days there had been a preparatory blitz that had subdued Norway. One of her students told her who Quisling of Norway was and how the hated name had come into their own language as a proper noun everybody understood.

"Everybody except us," said Sister Luke, smiling at the student, who she suspected was involved in the underground.

Because everything in the hospital went on as if normal, she took the telephone calls that came for her students. She would say, "I regret, Monsieur, that Mademoiselle cannot accept telephone calls while on duty," and would listen to

288

the voice that tried to sound like a priest's saying, "I am Father John, Sister . . . this is urgent." She would call the girl then and look at her face afterwards, shrouded in secrecy but not enough to conceal the flush of excitement. Then the student would ask permission to go into the town for an hour.

One night Sister Luke climbed the stairs to the dormitory of the students above the wing where the nuns slept. The girls were clustered about their radio listening to a voice speaking French with a thick German accent. A glowing offer of work inside Germany was being broadcast to all unemployed Belgians. Excellent working conditions and high wages were offered. Sister Luke waited a few moments, eagerly gathering news seldom published on the convent bulletin board; then she tapped the shoulder of the girl who received the most telephone calls.

Of all her students, this was the one closest to her heart. Lisa's delicate face made her think of the begonia of the Congo that bruised to the touch. Her gray eyes fringed with dark lashes held such a look of childlike innocence that the Procuratrice nun often asked permission to take her on shopping trips . . . and it made no difference then to the shopkeeper if the convent's ration books had run out of sugar or flour stamps.

"Sister Luke!" Lisa stood up at once. "Has anything happened in the wards?" First thought for the patients always . . . Sister Luke smiled at her own handiwork as she shook her head. The instilling of that flamelike dedication in Lisa had been the saving grace of the bleak year under a Superior to whom, despite all her prayers and what she thought they had in common, she had not been able to open her heart.

She drew Lisa over near the door where the beamed man-

289

sard started its downward slant. Then she said with a slight inflection of protectiveness, "Wasn't that excuse to go out again today a mere fantasy, Lisa? You've used that sick uncle twice, don't you remember?"

"Oh Sister, did I?" Lisa looked at her with confidence crystallizing in her wide gray eyes. Then she said in a hurried whisper, "We are distributing food ration stamps to our boys hiding out, Sister," making her one of them with the unexpected admission. "There are scores already right here in our own town who refuse this offer of the Germans, Sister. They've never registered for the ration book. They must have food stamps to pay the farmers who hide and feed them. The stamps are brought to us from Brussels where they're printed. We never know by whom, only that we must always go at once."

Sister Luke stopped her with a gesture.

"That's enough, Lisa," she said. "I won't ask for more." I won't because I cannot, she thought with a flare of longing that made her wish to be free like the girl standing before her. Free to fight Germans, to connive against them and deliver stolen food stamps to boys the ages of her two youngest brothers, who were probably among those hiding out in haylofts of patriotic farmers. "If ever I can be of help, Lisa," she said very low, "tell me."

She turned to leave, then thought of something helpful. "If it's possible to inform your intermediary," she whispered, "tell him not to say over the telephone that he is a priest. Any nun would know at once that he is not and never was one." She gave her student one of her rare smiles. "Those urgent worldly intonations were bred out of a priest's voice long before ordination."

The next time Sister Luke took a call for Lisa, the intermediary called her by name. "I heard of your help, Sister Luke," he said. "Thank you and God bless you."

That evening her conscience made her stand a long time before the bulletin board to read again the Reverend Mother Emmanuel's exhortation to all nuns not to engage in patriotic activities. It doesn't say forbidden, she told herself. But her conscience reminded her that the Superior's wish was accepted instantly as law in the hearts of every Rule-abiding nun. Had any of the quiet sisters around her transgressed as she had? She knew she would never know. The underground is as sealed as the confessional, she thought. What I do from now on is between me and God alone.

There were small pockets of Allied forces isolated in many parts of Belgium. The underground secreted them and tried to get them out. Sister Luke met her first German face to face the day she accepted a British flyer and put him in the private room the fleeing priest had occupied.

The familiar voice of the intermediary who no longer tried to sound like a priest had said over the telephone: "You'll receive a package of cigarettes in about an hour, Sister. British-made. Enough for one night only."

She found work to do among the stretchers that littered the foyer. One hour after the telephone call, an ambulatory case dressed in the rough clothes of the plowman, with a knit cap pulled down partway over head bandages expertly wrapped, came in the door — her "package of cigarettes." How she knew with instant certainty that the man was her British flyer was one of the mysteries of intuition which she would have called God's guidance had she stopped to think about it. She went forward at once and took him by the arm.

"Cough," she whispered in English as she led him upstairs

to the tuberculosis wing. The man coughed so all the foyer could hear. The bells for Vespers rang as she slipped him, unseen by her nurses, into the private room. "I'm going to lock you in," she whispered. "I'll bring food later."

She reached the chapel just in time to take her place near the head of the line with the younger sisters who entered first. Mother Didyma brought up the rear. During the devotion, Sister Luke planned what she would do to make the private room safe from night inspection. After feeding her flyer, she would tape up the outside of the door and stand the formaldehyde machine in front of it as though the room had been fumigated after a death. It was a customary sight in her wing. In her office she kept a supply of newspapers cut into strips for the taping and a pot of flour mixed with water which served as paste in her poverty-vowed congregation, which never bought anything that an inventive nun could make.

The nuns were chanting the final prayers when Sister Luke saw from the corner of her eye the porter nun approach the *prie-dieu* of Mother Didyma and slip a note upon it. Her heart began to pound. Even before she saw the look that came over Mother Didyma's face, she knew that the Germans were in the hospital. Only an arrogant conqueror could have persuaded the porteress to interrupt an Office. Only frantic anxiety for her patients could have made this scrupulous Superior leave the chapel before the end of a devotion. Mother Didyma's eyes caught hers as she arose precipitately. Mental telepathy, the language of nuns, flashed the warning.

A minute later Sister Luke stood up and awaited her turn to leave the chapel. Youngest in the life . . . first in and last out. She almost screamed. Then she saw the side exit through the sacristy and took it.

She snatched newspaper strips and paste pot from her office as she hurried past it. She dragged the formaldehyde machine from the closet and stuffed its feeder tube through the keyhole of the flyer's door. Then she started to paste up the strips. She counted the wards below which would be inspected first. The general surgery. The maternity. The contagious. Then up one more flight, and hers.

The flour paste had dried to a springy consistency. She had no time to fetch water to thin it. She fought it. She got the strip across the top crack of the door and down the hinged side, then she heard boots on the stairs and Mother Didyma's dry voice saying more loudly than she ever spoke, "Up here we have our TB cases."

She knows, Sister Luke thought, she must have seen me bypass the Admissions Office when I brought him up. A strip of gummy paper wrapped around her wrist. She tore it off, prepared another and was standing up and patting it down the latch side of the door when the inspection party came around the corner of the hall. "O God," she prayed, "give me the strength to carry this off . . ." and she helped God by reminding Him that He had the Germans' ready-made fear of contagion to work upon.

"And what's this?" said a guttural voice in massacred French.

She ran her hand down the strip to within a foot of the floor and turned around. She gave the two German officers a smile, nunlike, sweet and startled, as her eyes swept from their gold-braided caps to the iron crosses ribboned close about their necks beneath velvet tunic collars, then moved on obediently to her Superior to ask, with humble lift of eyebrows, if she might have permission to speak. Mother Didyma nodded.

"We are fumigating, *meine Herren Offiziere*," she said in

293

the perfect German that her father had ordered all his children to learn before taking them to Germany to show them his student haunts. "One of our most virulent cases, a spitting of blood at the end." The two officers stepped back a pace. "But a happy death, thank God," she said, looking straight into the blue eyes of the officer who had the most pips on his shoulder straps.

"*Ein heiligmaessiger Tod!*" he repeated, amused. He clacked his booted heels and saluted her. "We are happy, *Schwester*, that you keep your rooms so clean of infection. Perhaps . . ." he bowed to Mother Didyma and switched his speech to the tongue-scorching French . . . "perhaps we shall require these rooms one of these days, if the Reverend Mother will permit."

"Our roster of vacancies is at your command," said Mother Didyma with a frigid smile.

As the officer moved on, the Superior gave her an oblique look that said, Now I understand some letters from previous Superiors that are in your file, letters that suggested you might be a revolutionary in the life, that you are too enterprising, that you bring the world into the cloister though you never show it unless pushed or pressed . . .

Sister Luke bowed, then knelt to paste the final newspaper strips along the crack between threshold and floor. She took a long time to do that last easy strip. She talked to God as she patted the pasty paper into place.

"I'm no longer one of Your obedient Brides," she said. "Yet You answer me when I cry out for Your help. You enable me to gaze naïvely at men I hate and answer them in their own language which I have not thought of or practiced since childhood. Where are You taking me, Blessed Lord? And for what purpose? You gave me fourteen years of the

Holy Rule as armor for today, to save this one life. Was it for this that You would not send me back to the Congo?"

Before she closed the crack she whispered through it, "Everything is in order. I'll leave the door unlocked. You can break through these strips when you leave tomorrow before dawn. I regret I couldn't get food to you before they came. I'll leave a packet of bread tonight in my office . . . second door to the right as you go out."

Two raps answered her as she applied the last strip.

Soothsayers appeared while the Nazis were organizing their captured provinces. Sister Luke heard about them from her students in the strange hushed quiet that followed the conquest. With most main roads destroyed and most bridges demolished, communication in Belgium was reduced almost to the level of feudal times. The soothsayers arose all over the land like a ghosty revival from the Middle Ages. They traveled about with a map of France and a pointed pendulum on a string which operated like a plumb line. They held the pendulum over various cities of France and where it began to circle, there, they said, is your lost family.

Lisa, she observed, was the only one of her students who showed no interest in the soothsayers. Sister Luke wondered if it was to imitate the nuns in their attitude toward sorcery, or if it was because the girl's connections with the underground were so well established as to give her perfect assurance about the welfare and whereabouts of her family. Since their talk together under the eaves of the students' dormitory, there had been no sign from Lisa that any world, other than the suffering tuberculosis wards, existed for her.

The first soothsayer to come to the hospital to offer family-search services to the patients was a middle-aged woman of the shopkeeper type. The nuns permitted her entry and pretended not to look.

Sister Luke heard the exclamations of patients and began to look.

"Rouen! But of course," one cried. "Why didn't I think of it myself? That's where my wife's family originated." Or, "Tours! Papa is in Tours . . . there was a business connection there . . ." The little pendulum moved from city to city over the map of France and tempted her to test it.

She block-printed her father's name, profession and place of former residence on a slip of paper and gave it to one of her patients to present. "From an open case who cannot be visited," she said.

I've committed every sin now except theft and adultery, she thought as she patrolled the ward while the soothsayer worked her plumb over the map. *Appetite comes with eating* was an old French proverb. It flashed through her mind as she paced.

Presently she heard the soothsayer. "Van der Mal . . . that's a familiar name!" The flurried breathing of her patient told her the plumb was swinging. Then the soothsayer announced, "Bordeaux . . ." and her patient who had given the name cried, "Sister! See how strongly it circles . . ."

She went over to the bed to see. The delicate derisory smile about her lips belied the thudding of her heart. Of course he would have got through, she thought. With his ribboned rosette in his lapel which so closely resembled the French *Légion d'Honneur,* he would have been able to get gasoline throughout France where no one else could. He traveled light, she was sure — just his black satchel of medical instruments and the meerschaum pipe if he had had to flee in a hurry and no more than one suitcase of clothes if he had had advance warning. You can go around the world in one suitcase when it's properly packed, he used to say.

She knew what it must have cost him to leave his sanatorium and the special patients whose cases he had been studying for years. She was certain that Tante Colette was not with him. That doughty soul would have elected to remain behind, to hide the family silver and the monogrammed linens against the day when her idolized brother would come home again.

Sister Luke took another notch in her belt but felt no hunger pangs. The vision of her father safe in Bordeaux, or as safe as anyone could be in a place the Germans had not yet invaded, compensated. That he was alive after traversing those dangerous highways to the west was more than enough to thank God for. Not until she was in the chapel that evening, making her examination of conscience, did she realize that she had fallen like a simpleton into a charlatan's trap when she had pinned her faith to a bronze plumb on a string instead of putting it on the altar at which she stared.

Then one day Lisa signaled with her eyes. Sister Luke glided out of the ward to the treatment room to await her. The girl came in with a medication tray.

"I heard the Germans are coming again tonight, Sister," she whispered. "I had a package of newspapers to distribute. Sister, I didn't know what to do with it until tomorrow." She pleaded with her eyes. "And so, Sister . . ."

The packet of clandestine newspapers was in Sister Luke's desk, since Lisa knew she had the second shift that night, from eleven-thirty until eight next morning.

Sister Luke sat at her desk and pretended that the forbidden newspapers were not there in the second drawer to the left. She had slept from the *Salve* until eleven, when the night nun had plucked at her pillow. She turned over in her hand the chocolate bar the Superior had given her to eat just before midnight, to carry her through the crippling second shift in which nuns had to fast from food and water until the morning Mass. She wondered where Mother Didyma procured such luxuries for her night nurses in wartime.

To make up for her many sins of commission, she examined the chocolate bar's Swiss wrapping, read all the gold print on it, smelled it once and put it in her pocket. She would give it tomorrow to one of the laundry nuns who never had night duties and never saw chocolate bars. She knew she was doing all sorts of small things to keep herself from opening the drawer to look at the papers the Reverend Mother Emmanuel wished her nuns not to read.

Presently she opened the drawer. She glanced down at the packet of printed sheets bound with a cotton string. The lead story was dated June 23, 1940, and stated that at six-fifteen that day the French had signed peace terms with the Nazis, to go into effect six hours later. The Germans had occupied St. Nazaire and had pushed on to within eighty kilometers of Bordeaux when the capitulation was announced. Bordeaux! She pulled a paper from under the string and read the whole story.

She turned the sheet over, telling herself, "I've gone this far, I may as well finish, God help me." There was a note about the German's Siegfried Line designed by Dr. Fritz Todt, running from Holland to the Swiss border, which was already under bombardment by the Allies, and a warning to Belgians not to sign up for any work inside Germany, especially for the current mass-recruiting program called the Todt Plan.

Another article, signed by the Archbishop of Malines and Primate of Belgium, denounced the racial and religious persecutions already started in Belgium by the Nazis, and this was followed by a letter to the Cardinal from the Pope in which the Holy Father spoke of the horrors of occupation and persecution afflicting their small brave country. *Many Papal powers*, she read, *have been delegated meanwhile to the Cardinal, who will remain in the occupied country.*

"Many Papal powers . . ." she repeated the three words silently trying to think what they meant; then her eyes caught a boxed story at the bottom of the page captioned *Murder on the Meuse.*

It read at first like one of the stories the refugees told. There was a section of the Meuse below Dinant in the peninsula of France which thrust up into Belgium at that point. Somewhere on the highway between Givet and Fumay, two kilometers of the refugee stream out of Belgium had been machine-gunned by Stukas. One of Belgium's renowned doctors was in the bottleneck where traffic halted. He refused to take to the ditches until he had given first aid to the wounded scattered through the adjacent fields. Then he had recited the prayers for the dead, standing there bareheaded in the field, the article said, looking straight up at the Stukas as he prayed. Then he started toward the ditches. The next wave of Stukas caught him. "We drew his body into the ditch afterwards and removed his rosette of the Order of Leopold. If his son, Antoine Van der Mal, will get in touch with us, we will deliver the ribbon . . ."

Shock stiffened her. Tears rolled down her cheeks soundless as water over marble. Her frozen exterior contained the storm of grief, letting no sob or moan emerge. For a long time she sat there clutching the paper.

Then there were sounds on the stairs, the flurry of a nun's slippers hurrying ahead of boots. She thrust the paper into the drawer as the porteress came into the office.

"Two Germans, Sister . . . inspecting . . ."

The men of the Gestapo stood outside. They informed her they were making a blackout inspection. They examined the small dim bulb in her desk lamp and the black paper shade pulled down over the office window.

"Any other lights on this floor, Sister?"

She made a sign of three with her fingers and led them down the corridor to show the two small lights in the wards and a vigil lamp in a private room where a woman lay under an oxygen tent.

She held her clenched fists beneath her scapular as she walked beside them looking straight ahead, her coif cutting off her face so that they did not see its storm of hate.

XVIII

THE years of the German occupation ran together like the print of the clandestine newspapers when you tried to read them in the dim light of the Belgian blackout. Only headlines stood forth. Nazis in Russia, 1941. Commando raid on Dieppe, 1942. Rommel pushed back to Tunisia, 1943.

Sister Luke was never sure afterwards in just which one of those years after her father's death the three words *many Papal powers* flashed again in her memory and then slowly, compulsively, took form and meaning. Nor could she date her first visit to the confessional to say that she no longer belonged in a convent. She remembered only that the voice behind the grille had replied with so little surprise, you might have thought it an everyday occurrence to have nuns whispering distractedly of defeat and suggesting return to the world.

Her defeat had so many facets, she could not define it all at once, but only her scorching shame for being a hypocrite in the religious life, for wearing the garb of obedience while flouting the Holy Rule, and the Cross of Christ above a heart filled with hate.

"I can never learn to see Christ in a German, Father, not if I stay a hundred years in the convent. This is only one of my faults . . ."

She sat under the heel of the Nazis growing hungrier and

angrier. With her sisters she was praying that the Americans would come soon, but, on her own, asking God to forgive them for such childish hopes in a world that seemed to have gone mad and which drove her mad because she couldn't lay hands on an atlas to see where the conquest had spread which had begun, so to speak, on her own doorstep. Even in her own heart in that flame of hate she had been fighting for three long years . . .

During those years the student nurses grew thinner, like the nuns, but without the stoicism that enabled the nuns to face the trials at least with outward calm. Sister Luke discovered with shock that her students were eating remainders of food from the trays of tubercular patients, to whom the best that could be procured was given. The girls swallowed pats of butter as they walked from wards to diet kitchens and bits of meat left on plates the tubercular patients had coughed over.

"Don't touch the food on those trays," she begged them. "I know you are hungry, but you risk contamination with every mouthful taken from them."

Often in the weekly culpa she was proclaimed for having needlessly prolonged a conversation with a student. She knelt and accepted her penance, marveling meanwhile at the integrity of the sisterhood, which would keep its Holy Rule alive in the midst of chaos. Every nun knew that hers was the only floor that had not lost a student nurse to the perilous roads in search of family.

With dogged regularity she visited her confessor. And, month after month, the Father counseled her to be prudent, to pray for strength, to offer up to God her sufferings under the occupation and to meditate on Saint Peter in chains.

Her spiritual struggle was the loneliest one of her whole

convent life. Her prayers were arid. No grace came, no relief, no inspiration to guide her tormented conscience. The abyss of silence between herself and God did not frighten or dismay her now, as once it might have. She understood it perfectly in terms of her religious formation. God gave the grace to do His commands, of which a major one was to love your enemy. Each time you failed, you took something from Him. He would return, give you another chance and other graces to strengthen you. Just so many times, she reminded herself . . . then He would ask no more and no more would the grace be given. It did not mean that He had ceased to love you, only that your transgressions had made Him too sad to speak.

The chaplain spoke often with her, in the confessional and in her small office on the tuberculosis floor. But he was a frail and ailing old soul to whom the world outside the convent wall was the Apocalypse come true, with ten-horned beasts coming up over the land and all its rivers and springs turning into blood. "In the world . . ." he would whisper and shake his grizzled head while nibbling a chocolate bar which Mother Didyma occasionally presented to him to keep up his strength also. "Why don't you try to have a talk with your Superior, my child?"

She'd certainly agree with me that I don't belong in a convent, Sister Luke would think; but she always managed to hold her tongue. Just once she had tried to explain to her Superior why, in these days of so much suffering and dying, she was repeatedly late for meals and devotions when the bells caught her in the midst of a spiritual talk with a frightened patient. "It always seems like time stolen from souls, *ma Mère*, to break off abruptly and turn away . . . for food, or to read an Office."

It was as if she had torn up the Holy Rule before Mother Didyma's narrowing eyes. She had had to keep her gaze fixed firmly on the crucifix above her Superior's chair to remember that the Christ of the community was speaking to her and not a thwarted missionary talking scathingly of the spoiling the missions engendered in weak sisters sent out too young. Laxity in obedience, independent judgment, self-esteem masked as spiritual enterprise . . . She never went back again to try to open up her heart.

Her conscience compelled her to report each failure, such as yielding to the temptation to read the clandestine newspapers, giving to her students (instead of returning it to the kitchens) the food from a tray sent up for a patient who had died while the tray was in transit, and, continuously, like a repeating record that made each week's culpa sound the same, her failure in charity to the enemy, whom she could not learn to forgive.

Each appearance of the Germans inside the hospital fed the hatred for them which she had never, with all her praying and struggling, been able to transmute. After they established a *Kommandantur* in the town, they came more often, growing so strict about blackout regulations that Mother Didyma thought it prudent to appoint a "blackout nun" whose responsibility was to see that every shade in the hospital was pulled down at sunset.

The shades were of black paper which began to show wear after the first year. The nuns kept them hung together with safety pins and adhesive tape and the sight of them enraged the Gestapo. But, as long as no light penetrated to the outside, Sister Alberta was safe. One night, however, a crack of light showed through. The blackout nun was ordered to report next day to the *Kommandantur*. As punishment, she was

304

commanded to appear each morning thereafter for one month, at five o'clock, to roll up every blackout shade in the headquarters, which was in a confiscated château that had ninety windows and was a good half-hour walk from the convent.

Sister Luke raged inwardly when she heard the little nun rising at four in the morning to go forth like a janitress to make ready for the day the offices of the Nazi command. The fact that Sister Alberta uttered no complaint, but shouldered her humiliating task with a smile of utmost sweetness, only increased Sister Luke's fury and showed her again what irreconcilable differences lay between her and her outwardly seeming sisters.

Then the Nazi persecution of the Jews began and she saw fear of the Germans translated into physical form. One of her best student nurses was a Belgian Jewish girl with classical Semitic face that recalled portraits of founding fathers of the diamond banks of Antwerp. Jessie asked a leave of absence on the day the underground paper carried news of the Nazi edict that all Jews wear the Star of David armband, with the companion story of what happened in Antwerp as soon as the edict was published. Practically every Gentile of the city came forth wearing the discriminatory armband, and in several churches there were fine silken armbands embroidered with the Star of David fastened about the wooden arms of the Christ statues. The Germans had to repeal their order.

"You're not afraid of them, are you, Jessie?" Sister Luke asked. "Look . . . we've made them a laughing stock. They can't bear to be laughed at as we Belgians know how to laugh . . ." She stopped, hearing herself saying *we*. We in the world, she thought. We who put sugar in their gasoline tanks, we who burn cigarette holes in their uniforms in crowded

305

trolleys, we who collect the tassels off their sabers, snipping them skillfully from the rear when traffic halts bundle us all together on street corners, we who are taken as hostages . . .

"Yes, Sister. I'm afraid," Jessie said. "But if you could possibly give me a month's leave, I wouldn't be any more."

Jessie returned at the end of the month unrecognizable. Plastic surgery had altered her handsome profile. Peroxide had turned her raven-black hair into something resembling straw. The nuns pretended charitably not to see the desecration of the classic countenance, but Sister Luke cursed the Germans every time she looked at Jessie. Her conscience compelled her to inform her confessor that she was cursing the enemy and living for the day when God's wrath would be loosed upon them.

"You must pray, Sister . . . pray God to deliver you from revenge in the heart," the old Father said sadly.

In a sense, she was delivered of it not long after. But, as far as she could see, it was not a delivery wrought through prayer. A Prussian war nurse was brought to the hospital with a shrapnel hole in her lung. Sister Luke had heard of these Nazi nurses who roamed the front lines and sorted out their own wounded under fire. The French underground press referred to them as "the gray mice" — gray because of their gray nursing uniforms and mice, Sister Luke supposed, as a Gallic witticism to describe their tigerlike courage.

Sister Alberta accompanied the stretcher to the tuberculosis floor, her sweet face clouded with compassionate concern.

"She bleeds badly beneath that field dressing, Sister," the little nun whispered. "She'll need a transfusion at once. I offer my blood if it matches."

Sister Luke looked at her, worn to candle thinness by her recent tour of punishment duty in the Nazi headquarters.

306

Then she looked at the Prussian "gray mouse" on the stretcher. She turned up the Wehrmacht identification tag that gave name, age and blood type. "If the doctor orders transfusion, it will be *my* blood, Sister Alberta."

The eyelids of the Nazi nurse snapped open. She stared at the two nuns bending over her, her eyes as hard and shiny as the enameled swastika brooch that fastened her high collar.

"There will be no transfusion, do you hear?" she said in harsh precise French. "I would rather die than have Belgian blood in my veins." She closed her eyes as if she could no longer bear the sight of them and they carried her to a private room, next door to the room where two aged Jews were lying up for the duration as bedridden patients, paying their way with uncut diamonds.

Sister Luke watched the German fight for her life for two days. The doctor would not risk operating unless she accepted transfusion. He offered to seek a matching blood among the German officers in the town. The Nazi nurse informed him haughtily that German officers gave their blood only for the Fatherland and forbade him to try any tricks to get mongrel Belgian blood in her veins. Despite herself, Sister Luke was compelled to admire her enemy's will, forged in a hate that matched her own.

The deliberate choice of death in preference to receiving the blood of an enemy made her wonder if she would have the same courage were she ever to fall wounded into German hands.

"One cannot gainsay it, they have patriotism," she said in the recreation after some other nun had introduced the subject of the German nurse. "I wish I could be in her place," she ventured. "Be able to show my patriotism by dying as a martyr for my country."

307

Mother Didyma looked up from her mending, first at Sister Luke, then around the circle of sisters as though following the trail of her unmonastic desire.

"You can be a martyr every day," said the Superior. "And I am sure we all are . . . dying to ourselves each day, not for love of country but for love of God, without witnesses or iron crosses as rewards. We in our dying," she said firmly, "stand alone in the presence of the Master. We have His smile and His gratitude, which are of much more worth, are they not?"

The Nazi nurse died next day. Refusing opiates, she was conscious until the end. Her loss of blood made her look embalmed before she was dead. The hard blue eyes were wide open, gazing with scorn at the nuns bending over her when her breathing ceased.

That's the first German I've actually seen die, Sister Luke thought as she closed the eyelids. There was a quickened beating of her heart as though gladness had come into it with her thought.

But later, her satisfaction for an enemy's death tormented her conscience. She prayed for forgiveness but felt no corresponding relief. It was as though she addressed a friend too sad to reply.

She talked to the chaplain when he came to the ward next day.

"My whole lifework dedicated to saving lives, Father . . . and I was *glad* for that death. I rejoiced inwardly to see an enemy die. And in this habit, Father . . ." She looked down at her hands knotted whitely together on the desk. Lifesaving hands with no heart behind them, she thought bitterly. Hands that once I offered up to God as the best part of me. *And mine to you, O Lord . . .*

308

"We all sin, my child. Not one of us is perfect," said the old Father. "Don't you hear me saying every morning at the altar, *Cleanse my heart and lips, O Almighty God? Munda cor meum . . .*" he chanted softly.

"*Your* heart and *your* lips!" She looked at his delicate face with its colorless lips pinched with hunger and piety, yet curved in a smile and longing for a burning coal to be placed between them instead of the vitamin tablets she would have administered had she been able to steal some from the German nurse. "There's a big difference, Father," she said quietly. "Too big for me to cope with any longer. I'm asking you quite simply to lay my case before the Cardinal."

She picked up the list of names she had prepared of patients who wished to talk with him. "We've got open cases in the ward now, Father," she said, "since the private rooms are all full up. I'd put a mask on you but I don't approve of those reminding masks with TB's."

"Neither would Christ, Sister." The chaplain took the list and stood up. "Wait a little more, won't you?" he pleaded. "Make a novena to our Blessed Virgin. She always works miracles, haven't you noticed?"

She watched him walk away, his thin undernourished hair floating like a war-worn halo about his head. I'll wait a little, she whispered to the frail figure in flapping soutane. I'll wait because you asked it. I'll say a novena again . . . also because you asked me to. But nothing will happen . . .

A fortnight later she resumed her discussions with the chaplain where she had left off.

"Christ will not abandon me if I go out, Father. I have given too many cups of water in His name and He knows I would go on doing it, whether working for Him as a nun or as a war nurse." She besieged him when he came to her desk, she besieged him in the confessional. It was as though she were waging a private war among contestants who frequently changed sides, including herself.

"In the world, my child," sighed the Father. "It's a risky place to be now."

"I agree," she said. "But would it not be a hypocrisy to remain in the convent only through fear of the world? It must be voluntary, through love of God alone and without any grumbling and inner murmuring, Father. Otherwise, it has no merit in His eyes. My staying has no merit. He knows why I remain . . ."

Because you, His vicar on earth, are doing your duty as you are vowed to do and will not make a move unless I threaten. You care only for my soul, not for the house of mind, heart and emotions it lives in. It's my responsibility to keep that house in order and I have failed. A healthy soul needs . . .

"I believe, Father," she said, "that even the smallest gesture of charity made in the world, with joy, would be ten times more pleasing to God than all the work I do here under a Holy Rule I only pretend to obey."

It was strange to be holding theological discussions with an aged priest while British bombers were roaring overhead toward Germany. She listened to the high hum of the formations and sent prayers winging after them.

"Perhaps," said the Father. "But how do you know you'd please God more in the world than you do here?"

"Because God hates a hypocrite," she replied very firmly.

"I know," she said to the chaplain on another day, "what a lost sheep looks like. And if I were in the world, I would know where to take it when I find it."

"I have no doubt of that, Sister. But who would be the lost sheep? You, or the soul you meet along the way and lead back to God?"

Never once while she thrust and parried, growing ever more tense with the strain, did the impulse to walk out overcome her. It had been done before. God had all sorts of runaways, including runaway nuns. She wanted an official paper in her hand, her formal laicization which could stand as passport at least for her soul in its passage from a promise into the world. Like all passports, it was hard to get.

They went often to the cellars now in the beginning of '44 as the overhead fights augmented in fury in preparation for the D day landings. The bravery of the nuns under bombardment was another precious detail of the religious life Sister Luke put under the bell jar of memory. The sisters thought of nothing but the safety of the patients. They toiled down the long stairways with the stretcher cases and encouraged the ambulatory with little nods and smiles. Not one of them would have remained in the cellars during the air raids had Mother Didyma not said, "God helps those who help themselves . . . everyone to the cellars!" Then it was an order and they stayed below through obedience.

Sometimes in the cellars Sister Luke reread the few letters she had received from her brothers, sharing them with her patients as if they were all one family. Antoine, who had been captured in the fall of Namur, was in Norway, a prisoner in a Nazi concentration camp just under the Arctic Circle. The two younger were somewhere inside Belgium, unregistered, doing what they could to harass the occupation forces. Their cards and letters were written in pencil, which meant that every positive in them must be read in the negative. The patients' eyes sparkled when she read the scribbled postcards from the young brothers inside Belgium, extolling the progress of the thousand-year Reich, which meant that it was going to end soon.

Most often, as she sat in the gloomy cave, she pondered material for her next talk with the chaplain, the sole intermediary between herself and the Primate in Malines who had Papal power to free a nun from her vows. No reasons she had given him so far seemed to satisfy him. She examined herself as if she were a body laid out upon a table. There were many recent wounds but none grave or deep enough to account for her spiritual revolt against the Holy Rule and her inner refusal to continue trying to live up to it. The surface wounds, moreover, were probably common enough in the religious life in wartime — deliberate disobediences when patriotism flared, anger for the enemy each time his planes went over, longings to be free to get out and help in the fight, even gladness when you saw an enemy die before your eyes. Surely the chaplain had heard every one of them time and again from the sisters sitting with her under the low stone arches, passing their beads through their fingers while the bombs made everything tremble except the serene smiles on their faces.

There had to be something deeper to account for her total despair. Something that went down through flesh and bone into the marrow, something that went back beyond the war years. It has to do with conscience, she thought, that old pain so chronic now that it's completely diffused. It was like looking for a needle in a haystack.

Then one day in early May of 1944, Reverend Mother Emmanuel came for her annual visit. Mother Didyma put the notice on the bulletin board the night before and the list of her nuns in the order of their age in the religious life — as they would be received for their private talks. Sister Luke found her name midway on the list. She knew that this time she would not go to the Superior General.

In the recreation she chose a seat next to Sister Frances, who preceded her on the list. Casually, as if it were a matter too trivial to share with the circle, she said in an aside, "By the way, Sister Frances, after your talk with the Reverend Mother tomorrow, would you please tell her that I pass up my turn? I've really got nothing to say and why take up her time?"

Next morning she watched her nursing sisters slipping off duty one by one, their faces calm and composed. Sister Frances nodded to her when her turn came, signaling that she had not forgotten the message. The work in the ward was heavy, with three pulmonary postoperatives to attend besides all the other patients. The inner voice that mocked her as she moved from bed to bed seemed to come from somewhere outside. *Coward*, it said over and over.

After a while Sister Frances returned and beckoned her aside.

"Reverend Mother wants to see you anyhow, Sister Luke," she whispered. "She said to tell you that even if you have nothing to say, she has something she would like to ask you." Sister Frances smiled and took the temperature charts from her hands. They both knew it was an order.

Reverend Mother Emmanuel gave her the wondrous smile that disarmed completely as she made her reverence and knelt. "Only for that smile was I a coward," Sister Luke told herself tremulously.

"Why didn't you come willingly, my child?" the Superior

313

General asked. "Didn't you know that by inspiration I was aware of your struggles? Haven't you been praying and calling out for help?"

"Yes, Reverend Mother." Sister Luke looked straight into the dark eyes from which nothing could be hidden. "But it's too late for discussion. I'm at the end of my struggles."

"There is no end when one loves the Lord as you do," the Superior General said gently. "You are perhaps discouraged, Sister, though this is difficult for me to understand in view of the reports I've had about you. Your sisters love you, the doctors trust you and your students respect you enormously." She nodded, smiling. "Or perhaps you are in one of those moments of aridity when you pray and pray and nothing happens?" She told the sweet familiar story of Christ asleep in Peter's boat when the tempest arose and of His disciples' fear when He made no reply to their cries until they woke Him . . . and Sister Luke knew her Superior General was giving her time to compose her thoughts, even giving her a few helpful leads. "Sometimes, my child, when we are in the midst of our own tempests, as you undoubtedly are at this moment, Christ may be sleeping. His silence is no cause to lose faith. Did you have patience? Have you struggled long enough to be able to say so surely that you've come to the end?" The Reverend Mother folded her hands over her crucifix and waited for her to reply.

"I think, Reverend Mother, that I've been struggling for years." Sister Luke hesitated. "For years . . ."

Then quite suddenly she saw her spiritual crisis clearly as the inevitable result of something that had lain in wait for her for years. She classified that latent menace as if she had found its name in the text she might have been reading, her voice was now so calm.

"In the beginning," she said, "each struggle seemed different from the preceding. No two ever seemed for the same cause, until they began to repeat and then I saw they all had the same core. Obedience, Reverend Mother. Obedience without question, obedience without inner murmuring, obedience blind, instantaneous, perfect in its acceptance as Christ practiced it . . . as I can no longer do. My conscience asks questions, Reverend Mother. When the bell calls to chapel and I have to sacrifice what might be the psychological moment in a spiritual talk with a patient, my conscience asks which has priority — it or the Holy Rule. In my mind, I have never been able to make this clear." She paused, struck by the thought that once before she had tried to say this . . . to Mother Didyma. She caught her breath sharply.

"Continue, my child," said the Reverend Mother.

"I believe that most of my failure stems from this conflict. There are times, Reverend Mother, when my conscience decides I must do something opposite to my Superior's wishes . . . you remember that tropical medicines examination?" Sister Luke's voice rose one note above the calm reading tone. "How did I know that that suggestion did not come from you? Yet even had I known that it had, I could not have failed . . . not even for you, Reverend Mother. My conscience could not have accepted such a hideous waste of time and mental effort, nor could I ever have persuaded myself that God would have wished it. There are scores of other examples I could cite, but you know them all. You receive the reports. And when you read Mother Didyma's . . ." She smiled bleakly. "Late every day for chapel or refectory or both. That's how far this has gone, you see. I hear the bells but I can no longer cut short a talk with a patient who seems to need me. When I have night duty, I break the grand silence, because that is the time when nature relaxes, gives a little peace and sometimes makes men in trouble want to talk about their souls. And that is the time when reason begins to query the Rule most unanswerably. Why must God's helpers be struck dumb by five bells in the very hours when spirits expand and seek to communicate?" She stopped abruptly on the word *communicate*. Sick with grief, she stared at what she had communicated.

A shadow of sorrow lay over the Gothic face bent toward her. After a long silence, Reverend Mother Emmanuel cleared her throat.

"Are you going out, my child?" she asked.

"I think so, Reverend Mother. I've been talking with the chaplain."

"Before you decide definitely, would you like to come back to the mother house for a while?" There was a veiled pleading in the dark eyes.

"No, Reverend Mother. No, I prefer to remain here." It was almost impossible to go on, but she had to give the reason, the final truth as she saw it. "The mother house is, for me, such a citadel of perfection as to be almost unreal, Reverend Mother. *This* is the reality of convent life!" Her hand flew out in the only gesture she had made during her audience, flew out with palm flat up to describe in one sweep the pine desk furnished with a flannel penwiper such as nuns made from colored scraps, the stiff plain chair with a tasseled pillow on the seat to suggest the tapestried thrones of the mother house, the bare walls with the calendar of a local merchant hanging from one of them. "It is here where the reality is, Reverend Mother," she said huskily. "This is where I must fight it out."

The Reverend Mother gazed at her with an expression she

316

would have turned her eyes away from had she been able. "Then I can give you only one advice," she said. "Pray, Sister, and try to follow our Holy Rule step by step. Make one more effort for God . . . and for me as His instrument. When I go from here, I shall take you with me in my heart and keep you each day in my prayers."

She traced the sign of the cross on Sister Luke's forehead with a thumb firm as a sculptor's, flattened at the tip to make a clean and lasting mark. The film of tears in the Superior General's eyes magnified their pitch-black pupils and made them seem like two jet mirrors in which Sister Luke saw two very tiny nuns reflected whitely.

The talk with Reverend Mother Emmanuel haunted Sister Luke. Torn with desire to make one more effort, she nevertheless had the strange feeling that she had said farewell in that interview and that the all-wise loving woman who had listened to her knew this also.

The two tiny nuns Sister Luke had seen reflected in her Mother General's eyes were an accurate mirroring of her divided inner state. One part of her returned to the community, followed the Rule with scrupulous attention, obeyed the bells instantly, cared for the patients during the grand silence like a guardian angel endowed with every grace save that of speech . . . and the other part counted the bridges already burned behind her and waited for the last straw to fall on her burdened conscience — watching for it fearfully lest it fall too soon and cut short the decent waiting period she longed to render to her Mother General, whom she knew was praying and hoping for a miracle.

She added hypocrisy to hypocrisy day after day and told herself that that inevitable last straw would be one of these.

Any one of them, she thought. They're all alike in their deceptive substance.

But the last straw turned out to be food . . .

From the start of the German occupation, every patient had to bring his food ration tickets when admitted to the hospital. Frequently, toward the end of a month, a patient came in saying that he had spent all his food stamps. Until the issue for the next month was made, the nuns finagled and made combinations and fed him from the tickets of patients dying, or from those on diets who had sugar and fat coupons in surplus. Sister Luke looked with admiration on the Procuratrice, who could do with an array of sugar, fat and meat coupons for a hospitalized population of three hundred what only a female with the conscience of a nun could have achieved. The Procuratrice was always robbing Peter to pay Paul without ever having Peter feel anything except specialized care for his diet.

Occasionally the calculations failed. Then the needed extras came from the nuns' food-stamp books. Mother Didyma began to welcome German private patients sent to her through the local *Kommandantur*, since it meant that with a German of rank bedded down in her hospital, very often a whole pig or the carcass of a lamb was delivered to her office without benefit of ration stamps, a windfall for her hungry nuns. The Germans were assigned most often to the tuberculosis wing, which had more private rooms than the other floors.

Sister Luke tried not to see herself and all her labors for God translated in terms of food. Though she was perfectly aware that her Superior welcomed Germans for the sake of her overworked and underfed nuns, the meat the conquerors provided stuck in her throat. As often as she had the strength to do so, she passed the meat dish to the nun sitting next to her in the refectory without partaking of it, and filled up her plate with the customary rutabaga, carrots and potatoes instead.

The final straw was added when she had to receive the mistress of the highest-ranking German who had ever visited her floor. He was a lean fair officer with gray eyes that fixed her like polished bayonets when he told her, in daring worldly terms as though her presence placarded her understanding of them, that he was leaving the treasure of his life in her hands. The treasure was a Frenchwoman, daughter of a wealthy merchant who received special concessions from the German occupation in France in return for the petty information the girl supplied to her Gestapo lover.

From the moment Mademoiselle Jeanne was received as a patient, lamb and pork from Belgian farms, smoked salmon from Norway, butter and chocolate from Denmark and cheese from Holland began appearing on patients' trays and on the refectory table. For the first time in years, Mother Didyma looked relaxed.

The price of the unrationed windfall was service to a spoiled darling of the French upper crust who was a traitor to her country. By comparison, the German lover was less odious to Sister Luke, upon whose back fell the intimate nursing task. After the first night the Frenchwoman demanded of the Superior that a nun sleep in the room with her. Sister Luke was appointed. "This is such an obscure case," said Mother Didyma.

Sister Luke bowed obediently and moved a cot and screen into the room of the perfectly healthy Frenchwoman whose lover, she was certain, had placed her in the convent hospital for safekeeping, while his business occupied him, simply be-

319

cause he could not trust her. Mademoiselle Jeanne's face had the limpid beauty of a Fragonard, but behind her indolent violet eyes lurked the gleaming practicality of the accomplished demimondaine.

Petulant, spoiled and very bored, Mademoiselle Jeanne spent her days thinking up special services to add to the burden of the nuns, whom she obviously despised, and her nights trying to make Sister Luke talk.

"Are the sisters afraid of the Germans?" she would ask.

"This is not important for your soul or your body, Mademoiselle. I am in the grand silence. Call me if you really need me . . ."

"Then you don't reply to my question because you don't wish to admit that they are . . ."

And Sister Luke would lie awake trembling with fury for the slur against her sisters, even wishing for an air raid so she might have excuse to bundle her so-called patient into the cellars to have a look at absolute fearlessness in action.

Mademoiselle Jeanne thought of everything to torment her. Her morning gruel had to be strained to the consistency of velvet-smooth cream. If not, she sent it back down three flights of stairs to the kitchens. She complained that the suppositories were too large, and each morning, when her lover called, she moaned her complaints over the telephone.

One morning Sister Luke had had enough. She snatched the receiver from her patient and said in German, "And since when, *mein Herr,* has our occupied country been manufacturing anal suppositories custom-made to fit the patient?"

She heard him laugh then, great peals of merriment that made the earpiece vibrate. A side of beef was delivered to the convent that same afternoon, ticketed with her name. She went straight to the chaplain's office.

320

"I'm a food stamp, Father," she said. "Have you written that letter to the Cardinal?" Seeing from his expression he had not, she went on: "Because if you have not and have no intention of doing so — you must forgive me Father, but I shall leave without permission. I have come to a place . . ."

She was too exhausted to even try to tell him of the other troubles she had laid at the foot of the altar that morning at Mass. Tense and red-eyed from a sleepless night, she had first planned her day's work, the assignment of each nurse and student, the menus for special patients and the request she must make for ten ounces of cognac for one of her dying patients whose tongue was dry and black, and she had fought before the altar her coming struggle with the pantry nun, who was going to say, as always, But I must have a requisition for the cognac, Sister. You'll get no requisition. Why should that poor man pay when he hasn't had a tray of food in eight days and all his tickets used meanwhile for others? Where in the name of God is charity that we cannot afford to put a few drops of cognac in water on the tongue of a dying man? Then she heard herself fighting in front of the tabernacle. Once again that morning in the Mass, as so often of late, she denied herself communion — the only food that counted. As her sisters knelt at the rail, she had buried her face in her hands and tasted the bitter salt of her tears.

"I have come to a place," she repeated to the chaplain.

"Are you sure, Sister, that this won't be a scandal for the young nurses who followed you into the convent? There have been quite a few as I recall." He delivered his last shot wistfully.

"If any of my students entered the convent out of admiration for a nun instead of for the love of God and of Him alone, then I should be the first to tell them to leave at once. Father, I beg you to write that letter."

"Very well, Sister. I see your mind is made up. We as priests can only listen, pray and advise." He gave her a rueful smile touched with a bewilderment she understood. "But there is always an enigma, is there not? In the end, the final resolution lies between the soul and the Blessed Lord. I'll write tonight, Sister. I shall tell the Archbishop that I as your confessor see no cause why your petition should not be granted."

Afterwards, it seemed as if Providence had had a hand in her timing. The chaplain's letter to Malines was dated Trinity Sunday, June 4, 1944, the day that Rome was liberated by the Anglo-American forces, while nearer home, just across the Channel, huge Allied fleets and armies waited in England for the D day command of General Eisenhower to start forward for the liberation of France. The kind of world into which a nun emergent could fit swiftly and without embarrassing detection was being prepared. In the storm so soon to be unleashed, all swirling shapes would look alike. But at the time, inside Belgium where the quiet of a dead-end street prevailed, nothing of this could be guessed.

The German officer came to remove his mistress a week later. Sister Luke heard him speaking English with one of her British sisters on the way up to her ward — "A flawless diction," the sister said afterwards. "Had I been blindfolded, I'd have said Oxford."

He brought his mistress a coat of Russian sable and a box of candied violets from Paris. "One has to wheedle her to get her to accept an invitation to the Bavarian Alps," he said to Sister Luke as he dropped the beautiful coat over the French-woman's shoulders. "This fits, *chérie* . . . made to measure!"

He started laughing again as he had laughed over the telephone. He did not glance at Sister Luke until he picked up the Frenchwoman's bags. Her eyes widened at the sight of a German officer carrying luggage like a porter instead of summoning her to the task.

"Perhaps I'll be seeing you again, Sister," he said. He thrust a roll of currency into her hands as he went out. She counted it before turning it over to her Superior, just to see how much, besides lamb and beef carcasses, her forbearance had earned in the eyes of the conqueror. Between two bills, she found a small note. *If you ever come out, go at once to . . .* and there was a Brussels address.

All that day she tried to put two and two together. Only clairvoyance could explain how the German officer knew of her conversations with the chaplain. Not even the underground had guessed her intention. The underground, she thought . . . and then she remembered Lisa.

On the evening of her final plea to the chaplain, she had gone to the students' dormitory for a talk with Lisa, fearful that the girl might be one of those who out of admiration would follow her into the convent. She knew that in Lisa's eyes she seemed a cornerstone of monastic security and that her student had talked of taking the veil after her nursing courses were completed. It had cost her nearly all the courage that remained to her to stand before her student and say, "I'm going out, Lisa," and it had cost her her last ounce of control not to embrace her student when Lisa had assured her that it was not through admiring emulation of a sister that she wished to give her life to God.

"I've watched so many men die, Sister," she had said. "The fear when men die without faith is one of the big reasons, I think. Right now it seems to me that only in the cloister is

323

there any faith left on earth. It's God's underground in a sense . . . the call to it seems as urgent as those telephone calls that summon me to pick up food stamps, Sister, never knowing who is speaking or who delivers the life-giving stamps."

So then, she thought, Lisa must have been the conveyor of her secret to the German officer. "To the German," she told herself steadily, "who is not a German but an Englishman disguised as one for reasons of espionage and connected somehow with our underground." That was why he had picked up the Frenchwoman's bags instead of ordering a nun to do it. That was why he had laughed, instead of ordering her arrested, when she had angrily intruded on his telephone call to his mistress.

As she had prayed that her confession to Lisa would not disturb the girl's intention to enter the convent, and had had that prayer granted with wondrous fullness, so now she prayed for the safety of the gray-eyed Englishman on his way into Hitler's heartland, using a mistress, irreproachably treasonable to her country, as a stylish screen for his own counterespionage.

She kept his note beneath her scapular. I have this, she thought, and my hair . . . hair enough since that dispensation when I chose to let mine grow. She could feel the heat of her new short hair beneath the cap and coif.

Sometimes, in the shower, she ran her fingers through it and tried to imagine what it would look like in a mirror. Were there any gray streaks yet? When you were past thirty-five, with six of those years passed in the Congo where every year aged you twofold, you couldn't be sure.

XIX

THE wait for the reply from the Archbishop seemed endless. From the moment the old chaplain had agreed to write, Sister Luke had no idea of what was to happen next. It was like waiting for a D day of sorts.

She combed her memories of convent life, trying in vain to recall if she had ever heard a whisper of how secularization was accomplished. Once or twice in communities where she had been, a nun had quietly disappeared from the scene. One from the Congo had been flown home under mysterious circumstances. Their names were never mentioned thereafter in the sisterhood. Intuitively you knew that they had returned to the world, although no official announcement was ever made and all details of how such a transformation took place had to be guessed.

She was sure there must be a definite procedure, an exact set of acts to be performed. She wondered if, before she came to the moment when she must make them, she would discover what they were. Activities up to a point were easier to imagine once back in the world. She would have to exchange immediately her nun's identity card for a civilian's. She would have to learn about money and how to get around on street cars and buses without a convent chaperone to lead and pay the way. And beyond that were seventeen years of separation from books, plays, scientific discoveries, political affairs . . .

But it was that gray middle place, somewhere between the signing of the papers and the removal of the religious habit, that was a little frightening. It gave the taste of death when she thought about it, not the tender memorial deaths inside the cloister where the refectory place of the deceased was set every day for thirty days, but something sudden and absolute like a vanishing into space.

The high whine of death flying over Belgium in the form of jet-propelled rocket bombs aimed for Britain seemed to explain to her sisters, aware of her concern with the war, the look of death on Sister Luke's face as she waited. Since the Normandy landings a few days after her petition had been sent to Malines, she had hardly spoken except as duty or courtesy required. Lisa never betrayed by look or word that she was aware of what was going on. She's already a nun, Sister Luke thought, and a far more perfect one than I have ever been.

On a day in early August her uncertainty ended. She could not guess when the dormitory bells clanged that morning that her last day in the convent had dawned. But as soon as she entered the chapel and faced her Superior for the bow, she knew that her papers had been received. Mother Didyma knelt at her *prie-dieu* with hands clasped so tightly the knuckles were white. Without seeing her face that the coif cut off, Sister Luke suspected that she had been weeping and was now struggling for poise after learning she had lost a soul from her community.

A rush of sisterly sympathy, the first she had ever felt for the glacial Superior, turned her meditation into a soliloquy. "I wish I could have told you beforehand, *ma Mère*. But my

326

talk with the Mother General was the last I could endure on this painful subject. Everything since then has been said between my conscience and God. And you must know of course that I took pains to find out that in wartime you will not be humiliated for my defection. But your pride suffers because I chose the way of the confessional instead of through you . . ."

A strange peace flooded her soul, and when she looked inward at the place where anger had burned and gladness for deaths of the enemy, there was nothing but the silvery quiet of ash. She went then to the communion rail. Only one profane thought intruded as she waited for the Host to pass. She hoped that the community would remember this afterwards and realize that she had made her peace with God. I'm not leaving the Church — only you, my sisters, and our Holy Rule that I am not strong enough to conform to . . . remember this and feel no slight or sorrow. Then she prayed.

She moved with grace from the altar rail back to her pew wondering where her next Bread of Heaven was coming from. A rocket bomb whined over the chapel as she knelt to say her thanks.

Then began the last slow steps with her sisters which had never been seen or described in advance. Mother Didyma headed the procession out of the chapel. She waited in the hall until all the nuns were assembled. Then she said to the community, "After the breakfast, the sisters may convene for a few minutes in the chapter hall to say adieu to Sister Luke, who is going to Antwerp." Her cool eyes sought Sister Luke. "And you, Sister, will please come to my office immediately after."

The procession moved into the refectory bound in silence. There were the prayers, the seating and the passing of the bread. Sister Luke took the thickest slice from the basket and

327

covered it heavily with jam. The nurse had taken over the nun in her. You're going to eat, said the nurse, even if it kills you; you've got a long journey ahead.

The farewells in the chapter hall were brief, and poignant because two of the nuns with whom she had always felt a wordless bond had guessed her intention and showed anguish in their eyes as they embraced her. One whispered, "Have you thought of your black boys waiting for you in the Congo?" and the other — "Are you sure this is God's will and not your own?" Nineteen times she felt a smooth cheek laid against her own and smelled the sweetness of soap and starch. The only thing she had to leave them was her smile. She gave them it from her heart, then turned abruptly and went out the door without looking back.

The next steps were toward the Superior's office. She walked hurriedly, desiring only to get everything over now as quickly as possible. She had the odd thought as she stood outside the Superior's door that she ought to have gone upstairs to the dormitory and turned over her straw sack and made her bed. The memory of those orderly acts which she had performed every morning after breakfast for seventeen years made her hesitate for the fraction of a second before knocking.

Mother Didyma sat behind her desk looking at three papers laid out upon it. Despite her desire to show the sympathy she had felt in the chapel, Sister Luke froze under the gaze of the woman she had never understood. Confronted by a *fait accompli*, the Superior wasted no words.

"I presume, Sister, that you had the goodness to inform our Reverend Mother General on her recent visit to us?"

"I had not come to a clear decision then, *ma Mère*. I told the Reverend Mother only that I *might* go out." Sister Luke longed to add, Which is perhaps why, since she hoped ever

328

for a miracle of grace, she did not discuss my spiritual state with you, Mother Didyma; but the cold eyes asking only for facts discouraged her impulse. "I asked the chaplain to telephone her when the petition was granted," she said stiffly.

"And why, may I ask, was I not informed?"

"Because I could see no issue from further discussion, *ma Mère.*"

"Have you weighed well the enormity of this step you are taking? Your physical health, for instance, the state of the world you desire to return to?"

"Yes, *ma Mère.*" Sister Luke looked steadily into the Superior's eyes to show she was not afraid.

"Very well, Sister. I must ask you then to read this paper very carefully before signing. There are three copies — one for you, one for us and one for the Papal archives. Once you place your signature upon it, you are no longer a member of the congregation." Stonily the Superior handed her one of the papers.

It was under her eyes then, the tangible answer to all her years of trial and error. The nurse in her said, Don't let your hand shake.

The seal printed on the letterhead was a Cardinal's flat hat with stylized tassels dropping symmetrically about a shield inscribed *In nomine Patris. To Sister Luke,* she read, *in the world Gabrielle Van der Mal: Upon your request, by Apostolic authority delegated to Us* . . . The lines began to swim together . . . *special circumstances conforming to Canon 81 . . . We relieve you from the bond of your vows . . . declare you reduced to secular state . . . under the following conditions . . .*

The three conditions were set apart from the body of the letter. She must formally accept the letters of secularization.

She must quit the habit of religion and never put it on again. She must agree never to request anything from the congregation for services rendered. *In full liberty and after mature deliberation* . . . and there were the blank spaces for date, town name and signature. She looked up.

Something meanwhile had happened to Mother Didyma's face. Beneath the glacial surface there was a suggestion of movement and flowing, as though a hidden spring were trying to break through.

"Is there nothing, Sister, that we can do?" she asked.

"Nothing, *ma Mère*."

"You would not consider having one more talk with the Reverend Mother Emmanuel before signing?"

"No, *ma Mère* . . . it could bring only pain to both of us . . ." The pain showed in her face, she was sure. She had to wait a moment until her voice steadied. "Because my decision is irrevocable."

Was it that irrevocable word *irrevocable* that made Mother Didyma stiffen again? Or was it the emotion she herself had betrayed when she spoke of the great lonely woman whom she had not the courage to face? She saw the ice close over as Mother Didyma handed her a pen. Afterwards, she believed that the ice came to strengthen the Superior for what she had to do next.

"This is your copy," said Mother Didyma brusquely. "From this office you will go directly to our affiliated house in Rue Grande. There you will find everything ready for you." The Superior fumbled in her desk as she spoke. She brought forth four notes of five hundred francs each and held them out for Sister Luke to take. "And there is this in conclusion," she said.

Sister Luke stared at the notes, which added up exactly

to the token dowry her father had brought to the congregation seventeen years before. For an instant she couldn't move. She tried in vain to voice her thoughts. *Must I take it? The congregation owes me nothing, nothing. The debt is all on my side and will be forever.* Some maniac cried from within . . . *Take it . . . tear it up and throw it back . . .*

Then she put forth her hand and accepted the money. It was her last act of humility in the convent and the most total humiliation she had ever experienced. The bitter pain of having to end her life in Christ with a money transaction overrode all other feeling and thought, and she was unaware that the Superior was leading the way out — not through the cloister where she now no longer had the right to walk, but through the parlors where visitors came and thence through the public foyer to the main door of the hospital. She didn't notice that the customary embrace at the door was not given, nor did it occur to her to kneel there for a departure benediction. The blow to her pride of the next to last act of secularization carried her out of the convent as if anesthetized.

And, in a way, it prepared her for the final step.

There was a fifteen-minute walk to the affiliated house, which was a small boarding school for girls. She walked swiftly, saying over and over to herself, *And there is this in conclusion.* Once she thought to take the two thousand francs from her skirt pocket and drop them into the gutter. But there were a few early risers in the street and she was still wearing the garb of one vowed to poverty, watchful over centimes. Seventeen years of respect for the habit could not be undone by fifteen minutes of burning pain.

The old nun in the porter's lodge at the school nodded from her cubicle that was festooned with pulleys and studded with bell buttons. "Go to room twelve," she said. "Every-

331

thing is ready. Press the button when you are dressed and I will open."

The room was small and windowless and it had two doors. An unshaded electric light hung over the only furnishing — a table with clothing folded upon it. There was a navy-blue suit, two white blouses, two sets of underwear and two pairs of newly cobbled shoes that looked too large. On top of the underwear pile was the short black veil edged with white which the lay nurses of the country wore in place of hat, and the unused portion of her current book of food stamps. A worn papier-mâché suitcase such as missionaries brought home to exchange for new ones stood beside the clothes.

As she shook out the secondhand suit, she remembered how once upon a time in the Congo she had caught herself looking at the colonial ladies sipping *apéritifs* on café terraces, to see what was being worn in the world that season. *Utex-léo*, she whispered, recalling a handsome blockprint summer suit of Congolese cotton. She saw its design clearly and the woman who wore it. The trivial association overlaid, like a protective film already mercifully formed, all the deep abiding memories of the Congo, of Mother Mathilde, of Emil and her black boys, which would have tortured her had they come alive at that moment. She raised her hands and removed her veil.

Piece by piece as she took them off, she folded the nun's clothes in the traditional way. She made herself perform this final act of obedience in penance for the storm of revolt she could not otherwise subdue. She wondered if any other sister going out had been so overcome by the sudden gracelessness of the final convent hour as to yield to the impulse to throw the holy habit pell-mell upon the table.

She stripped to the skin and then stood a moment looking

at the two doors, the one through which she had entered and the one through which she would leave. There was something furtive in the transition, as if what God permits must be accomplished in shame and secrecy. You come in as a nun and you go out as a civilian. No human eye records the transformation, not even your own since there are no mirrors. You are even sent to a strange house where you are unknown, to make this painful passage out.

She shivered and began to put on the rayon underwear that had a peculiar sheen like silk. It felt so light and scant, she had the impression that something must be missing and looked through the reserve pile to see if two of anything were in it. She paused over the white blouses that were not quite identical in cut. It confused her to have choice. The blue suit felt shoddy after the fine-spun serges of the nun's habit. What young woman entering the convent had left it behind, and in what year? The sleeves of the jacket were too long.

When she had everything packed that was not on her back, she inspected once again the folded black serges on the table, with the starched coif laid atop like a white shell inside which she had coiled her leather belt and long rosary of wooden beads. Her crucifix she had put in her suitcase without any twinge of conscience. It had been a nameday present from her Jesuit uncle years ago in the Congo, and Mother Mathilde had permitted her to keep it.

She stood the stout nun's shoes a little farther away from the folded clothing and fought down a lump in her throat as she looked at the blunt leather toes misshapen from the press of praying.

If we were not practiced in daily dying, she thought, all this would be quite difficult to go through with. She picked up the short nurse's veil. There was a small safety pin in

333

the hem of it. The pin, oddly enough, was the *coup de grâce* that brought the first tears, not because it drew blood from her finger as she unfastened it . . .

We have thought of everything, it seemed to say. There is not a single item for which you need ring to summon a sister to that entrance door to see you as you are now. We keep the good sisters from a view of such as you, even as we protected you during all your years from the distressing sight of one going out.

She pulled the short veil tightly over the upstanding crop of hair whose unkempt texture she could feel but not see, and pinned it closely at the nape of her neck. And now there was just one last thing to do.

From her pocket she took the note that the Englishman disguised as a German Gestapo officer had given her. It was as though someone waited for her out there in the street, or courtyard, or cornfield, or whatever it was that the exit door opened out upon. She memorized the Brussels address, then tore the note into tiny shreds which even a nun with all her endless patience could not have put together again. She dropped the confetti into one of the shoes on the table, there being no wastebasket in the room. Then she pressed the button set into an enameled plaque that said *Pour sortir*.

She watched the wire rope that ran along under the ceiling between the entrance and exit doors. As it tightened, she murmured, "O God, You've permitted me to come this far . . . stay near me now for the rest of the way . . ." The exit door clicked and swung open. She picked up her suitcase, pulled once again at the short skirt, and walked out into the world on legs in which the bones had become suddenly as supportless as pillars of cotton.

The world was a narrow cobbled street with early morning

sun slanting across it. At the far end, the street ran into a square where a corner café was opening for the day. The nurse in her said, You could do with some of that roasted barley they're using for coffee these days, besides, it's too early to get your photographs taken. She made a conscious effort to stay away from house fronts and garden walls as she walked toward the café.

The waiter eyed her nurse's veil and brought her a cup of dark fluid promptly. His elderly face creased in a smile as he served her.

"You've probably been up all night delivering a soul into this troubled world, Mademoiselle," he said with a slight inflection of curiosity.

"But yes . . ." She returned his smile shyly. "Yes, I have."

"If Mademoiselle has the coupons, there can be a fresh-baked bun."

"Thank you. This is quite enough." She picked up the tablet of saccharine lying in the bowl of the spoon and stirred it into the brown drink. The waiter's instant acceptance of her as a nurse turned her thoughts to the lay veil the convent had given her.

They could have given me a hat in exchange for the one I wore when I went in, she thought, since everything else was such an exact return. She sipped the imitation coffee. The singular exception the convent had made in its choice of headgear, which proclaimed to the world she was a graduate nurse, was the gleam of charity she had sought behind the shocking chilly scrupulosity of the final rendering. Seeing the gleam made all the difference. When she looked up, the square was lively with motion and brightness.

After a while she began to feel like a tourist who had come in on an early train and had time to kill before the shops

335

opened. Her father, an expert on tourism, had always said, "The first thing you do in a strange town is find the central café, take a table there, and then sit for a time and watch the world pass by."

Without the protecting coif, she seemed to be looking at the world through wide-angle lenses. Off to the right she saw the waiter dusting tables, then the arc of shop fronts across the square and a street with a tram line that came in from the left. All movements in the expensive scene she could see without turning her head. A tram bustled into the square, made the loop and bustled out again. By moving only her eyes she could follow the people who got off, fumbled in their pockets for keys as they approached their places of business, opened up and went in. Presently iron shutters were rolling up, and here and there a colored awning descended like a bright eyelid over some special window where, she supposed, there were display goods too delicate for exposure to the sun.

An old farmer with a string bag of endives over his shoulder came toward the café. He looked over all the vacant tables, then chose the one next to hers. He set his endives down on the cobbles with care, glanced at her suitcase and smiled.

"We've got God's plenty of time to kill before the Brussels train departs," he said congenially. She smiled back at him but could think of nothing to say.

The habit of silence, she reflected, the years of abjuring trivial talk, was just one of the many telltale disciplines she must learn to relax, and she remembered how she had looked with compassion at the two departing companions of her novitiate days, wondering how long it would take them to unlearn only a year and a half of the nun's stylized self-effacement.

There will be help for me with my seventeen years to undo, there must be. "For every cup of water given in Your Name . . ." she whispered. She could not know, as she prayed for deliverance from convent mannerisms, that her nun's inner formation was a Gibraltar that would never be leveled — that the ingrained habits of acting with charity and justice, with selflessness and sincerity, were to stamp her always with a certain strangeness and make her seem to future nursing colleagues like some sort of enchanting revolutionary who practiced a way of life quite new and unheard of . . .

She looked up at the sky as she reminded God of the many cups of water she had given. There was a high eerie whine pitched on the single note of speed. A thin white streak cut across the blue.

"As long as you can hear it, it's not meant for you," said the farmer. "Pray God we'll never see and *not* hear them . . . they make no sound, those V–1's, when they drop to target. That one's for Britain again," he said sadly.

It gave her an emotion to see her first V–1 going over. She had heard them often in the convent but had never gone to the window to look. She did not know as she watched the streak of white that it was a herald of sorts.

Just eight weeks from that morning in August of '44, the V–1 warfare was to be loosed on her liberated country, aimed especially toward the main Allied supply line — the great port of Antwerp. She was going to be there in the uniform of an English army medical outfit, worrying then no more of how she walked or talked but only of the bodies that might still be breathing in the traps of rubble through which she crawled. The Belgian underground was recruiting nurses for that medical corps even as she sat in the little café wondering what the mysterious Brussels address was going to mean for her.

337

She looked out again over the square which was the world on a small scale with nothing yet revealed that looked like pitfall for one who had not been about in it for some time. You can learn a lot in the beginning just by studying what's in those shop windows, she thought. Then she saw two Germans in slick high officers' boots stroll in from the street to the left. They stopped a workman, looked at his papers, nodded and passed on.

"I must go now," she said to the farmer. She took time to add politely, trivially, "Good profit on the endives, Monsieur."

Then she picked up her suitcase and walked with the nun's speed, yet no outward show of hurry, to the department store she had been watching open up. That nun's identity card was one document on which no German eye would ever gaze, she told herself fiercely as she glided into the store. A salesgirl directed her to the photography booths on the mezzanine.

She sat on a revolving stool before the first mirrors she had been free to look into in nearly two decades. Turning slowly, she looked at herself first full face, then in profile. The face seemed surprisingly young beneath the bandannalike veil. One lock of hair escaped from the front and stood straight up like an exclamation point above the analytical blue eyes.

"It's not yet gray," she said to the mirrored reflection of a civilian nurse. She sat perfectly still while she put coins in the slot and pressed the button. Lights flew on and there was a click and a whirring as she stared at herself. Then the lights went off and she listened to the mechanical camera digesting with watery sounds the composition of lights and shadows it had seen for a second. She stayed in the curtained booth

338

while the photos developed, keeping her eye on the trough through which a printed sign said they would appear.

There was one more step before she would be officially a registered civilian. She thought about it a little tremulously as she waited. Just what did one say to a city hall clerk when presenting a nun's identity card to be exchanged for a civilian's? Would the clerk think she was just another of those underground workers who were always switching identities? Or would he look at her with that peculiar morbid interest you often saw in people's eyes when they talked about nuns who were no longer nuns? As if, she thought, an ex-nun were an escapee from some sort of torture chamber a little bigger than the Iron Maiden in the Nürnberg museum, big enough in fact to clasp a whole female congregation in its unyielding mold and squeeze the sex out of it along with every other normal human yearning. That's all they know of it, she whispered to the civilian nurse watching her with steady eyes in the mirror.

And suddenly she heard the nurse saying back to her the *Capitulum* of Sext . . . *And I take root in an honorable people and in the portion of my God His inheritance: and my abode is in the full assembly of saints* . . . and she knew without looking at her watch which Office her sisters were chanting at that moment. She imagined she could hear them in the curtained booth lifting up their hearts all together for the *Deo Gratias*. Then the automatic camera whirred and a strip of photos shot into the metal trough.

CPSIA information can be obtained
at www.ICGtesting.com
Printed in the USA
LVHW042113120919
630869LV00005B/162/P